Take a leap of faith—
into the arms of love.

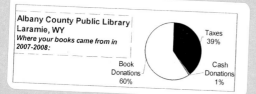

Only You

Sally Laity

Loree Lough

Debra White Smith

Kathleen Yapp

BARBOUR
PUBLISHING, INC.
Uhrichsville, OH

Published by Barbour Publishing, Inc.
P.O. Box 719
Uhrichsville, Ohio 44683
http://www.barbourbooks.com

ecpa Member of the
Evangelical Christian
Publishers Association

Printed in the United States of America.

Only You

Interrupted Melody

Sally Laity

"My, my. You do have your work cut out for you." Dorie Brooks shrugged out of her tweed coat and draped it over an elbow as she bent to unzip her boots. The Pennsylvania sunshine streaming through the stained-glass insert in the front door made a kaleidoscope of colors against her brunette waves, accenting a few silvering strands.

Josie Marshall responded to her best friend's remark with a weary smile and hung Dorie's wrap in the entry closet. She tilted her head toward the mountain of cartons cluttering her normally immaculate French provincial living room. "Somehow I never figured there'd be this much left after Mom's estate sale."

"Good thing you like to keep busy," Dorie teased, a good-natured sparkle lighting her merry blue eyes. She placed her suede boots together on the boot tray and tucked a lock of hair behind an ear.

"Right." Josie smiled. "I was just about to have some cappuccino. Want some?" At Dorie's nod, she led the way to the kitchen, indicating one of the teal-and-rose-cushioned stools at the breakfast bar. She turned on the hot beverage machine while her slender friend took a seat.

"Too bad you couldn't hang on to your mother's old

place," Dorie mused in a more serious tone. "So many memories and all."

Josie felt a twinge of sadness as she turned and leaned against the tile counter. "I probably could have. I gave some serious thought to selling this house and moving back home. But Mom's house is way too big for one person. Far more than I need—to say nothing of all the work it'll take to get it back into shape after her long illness. The more I thought about it, the less practical the idea seemed. And I sure don't want the hassle of dealing with renters, wondering if they're taking proper care of it, know what I mean?"

"Do I ever." Helping herself to a croissant from a nearby platter, Dorie spread butter and raspberry jam on it, then took a bite.

"I'd rather remember it the way it was, when my parents were both alive. Nothing can take away those memories. And I didn't put everything in the estate sale. I kept plenty of things that have special meaning to Mary Ruth and me."

"How is that daughter of yours doing?" Dorie asked, nibbling more of her croissant. "Too bad she and Craig couldn't move back from California and take over that house."

"Not much hope of that, I'm afraid. His work is there." Josie reached for a letter from the wicker mail basket beneath the wall phone and withdrew some photographs. "I just got new pictures of Mary's girls, though. What do you think of these?"

Dorie wiped her fingers on a napkin and took the

snapshots, perusing each one. "You know," she said, glancing up, "to look at you, no one would guess you're actually a grandma to girls of six and four."

"Guess it happens to the best of us." Removing a pair of bone china mugs from the cupboard, Josie filled them and took the stool beside her friend, handing her one of the hot drinks. "I see such a big change in Jessica and Susan from one visit to the next."

"Mm." Popping the last of the croissant into her mouth, Dorie switched topics. "There's an extra choir practice tonight, huh?"

Josie nodded. "The program's sounding pretty good, considering the music arrived so late. Sure hope everything goes smoothly on Sunday night. I'll be playing on my own piano, so that should help. The touch is so comfortable."

"So that's your grandmother's grand in the living room, then?"

Another nod. "The movers brought that one in, and took mine to the church. I've been looking forward to having Gram's piano for a long time. Mom never seemed able to part with it. Just having it there in the house kept the memory of Dad's playing alive. In truth, it's hardly been used in the eight years since he's been gone, and has lost some of its vibrancy. I've arranged for a technician to come and check it out this afternoon."

"Well, having the piano around should make your life perfect, right?" Dorie said, tongue in cheek. "The missing link between you and happiness."

Josie rolled her eyes. "Don't start on that again, okay?

I'm satisfied with my life the way it is. I've had about all the blind dates I can handle."

"But this new guy, Mike, he's—"

"Not for me," Josie finished firmly. "I'm not interested. Trust me. That shouldn't be too much to ask of a best friend."

Dorie stared, then appeared to accept the statement, if only for the moment. "Need help getting any of those boxes out of the way before the technician gets here?"

"Well, actually, if you wouldn't mind lugging an end of one or two, I'd sure appreciate it."

Three hours later, the sound of truck tires crunching over the gravel drive drifted to the spare room as Josie sorted through the myriad items from a stack of cartons. She checked the wall clock and arched her back to ease a kink out of it even as the door chime resonated through the hall. Automatically, she reached to remove the red bandanna tying her hair out of her eyes, but thought better of it and just whisked a lock of hair from her eyes instead. There was too much left to do.

The large white van she glimpsed through the window appeared a shade lighter than the dismal January snow contouring the rolling lawn and dormant shrubs beneath the clear sky. Black letters along its side cut right through the caricature of a man in a lab coat and spelled out "Piano Man." *He's nothing if not prompt,* Josie thought.

A tall, muscular silhouette showed through the oval of colored glass. Josie turned the knob and opened the door.

Nothing could have prepared her for the shock that met her. That face, the chiseled features. . .those unforgettable eyes. For a moment she could not speak as she gawked at the man she hadn't seen for half a lifetime. "Gray?"

He seemed equally eloquent as he stood there, metal invoice box in one hand, leather tool case in the other. "Josie?" There was a momentary pause as he glanced down at his sheet. "You're the Mrs. Marshall with the sick piano?"

Josie felt color slowly returning to her face about the same time she recalled the ridiculous kerchief she still wore over her hair. She fought the impulse to reach up and yank the thing off. Squelching the hundred and one questions popping into her mind, she gathered her composure and purposely did not ask a single one of them . . .even the uppermost one. *How on earth can it be you, Graydon Richards?* "Yes. Come in," she heard herself say. "It's right this way."

He wiped his feet on the mat and stepped inside.

Even as she headed toward the living room, Josie was mildly conscious of the fact she'd forgotten to offer to take his jacket. From the corner of her eye she saw him shrug out of it and loop it over the doorknob. She gave herself a mental shake. *This cannot be happening.*

❧

"You're starting to burn," the jovial voice announced.

Josie bolted to a sitting position on her beach towel. Her fifteen-year-old gaze all but drowned in the most fascinating eyes she had ever seen. Too light to be blue, she decided. They were silver-gray, like clouds at sunset, just after the last mauve tint faded away. Realizing she was staring, she felt a warm flush flood her cheeks. She shifted her attention away from his strong, square face and curly brown hair to the choppy waves of Harvey's Lake licking the light sand of the beach in front of her.

"Hi," he said, plopping down beside her, all enticingly tanned and muscled six feet of him. "I'm Graydon Richards." A teasing glint sparked in those breath-catching eyes. "Gray, to my friends. I haven't seen you here before."

Josie had to remind herself to breathe. He had to be seventeen, maybe eighteen. No boy that old had ever bothered to look twice at her, much less speak to her! She swallowed. "I'm visiting my grandmother for a few weeks. The big white house, over there." She indicated the two-story clapboard mansion some fifty yards away, fronting the lake. Surrounded by screened porches, its emerald shutters complemented the dark green roof. A white and green motorboat with a canvas canopy bobbed at the dock.

He followed her motion, then turned, his straight brows hiked higher. "You're not from the lake, then?"

She shook her head. "Close, though. Just down the road, at Dallas. I'm Josie. Josie Prescott. You from around here?"

He shrugged. "Up the road, in the other direction. Tunkhannock. I've been a lifeguard the last two summers."

"Hey, Gray! Coming back?" a feminine voice hollered from a group of young people playing volleyball

14

near the lifeguard tower.

He waved and stood up, brushing sand from the seat of his swim shorts. "Well, I need to get back to work." He turned and started striding away. "Be here again tomorrow?" he tossed over his shoulder.

"Most likely."

"Good. See you then, Josie Prescott."

Josie drew her lips inward and hugged herself against the shivers that teased her insides. Then she rose and shook out her towel. She could hardly wait for tomorrow.

❧

"This is it," Josie said, gesturing toward the ebony grand piano dominating a large portion of the spacious parlor.

"What seems to be the problem?" Graydon asked, all business.

"You tell me. It's been mostly unused for the last eight or nine years. I just moved it from my mom's."

He gave a nod. "She still live in that big yellow house in Laurel Estates?"

"Up until last fall, when she passed away."

"Oh. I'm sorry."

Josie smiled slightly. "Well, I'll leave you to your work. I, um, have some stuff to do down the hall." Taking her leave, she rushed back to resume her chore in the spare room, grateful for the reprieve so she might get her still-churning emotions under control. But her mind continued to review the mental picture she'd just encountered.

He hadn't changed a bit. . .unless it was for the better. He had filled out a little, and that engaging grin of his had etched deep grooves alongside his mouth. The five-o'clock shadow which once seemed so prominent had lightened over the years, and his close-cropped curls were silver now at the temples. But those eyes—

Exhaling a shaky breath, Josie schooled herself to concentrate on her task, tuning out the sounds of his presence mere rooms away. She removed a heavy item from the open carton and began unwinding the newspaper enshrouding it, letting the crumpled paper join the growing heap on the mocha-hued carpet. She smiled, recognizing an ornate sterling wall mirror which had graced one of her mother's guest bedrooms.

Setting it aside, Josie caught her reflection in the glass and cringed. Two smudges of newsprint from her fingers crested her right cheekbone, and a similar blotch on her chin was even darker. The bandanna was off-kilter, too, allowing a wisp of chin-length hair near her ear to poke around it. *A vision,* she fumed in exasperation. *An absolute vision.* For a reason she didn't care to analyze, she set out for the powder room to repair herself . . .then caught herself midstep. That would be just a touch obvious. He'd already seen her anyway. Grimly she retreated to the growing stack of unpacked boxes.

"Er, Josie?" his deep voice called.

She jumped. "Yes?" She put down a china dish and went to see what he wanted.

Graydon's face, as she approached the parlor, looked stormy. "Did your mother have a *cat,* by any chance?" He all but spat the word.

"Yes. Two, actually. A friend gave her a pair of Persian

kittens after Daddy died. Why?"

"That would explain it," he muttered almost to himself. Agitated, he raked his fingers through his hair.

"Explain what?"

"The sad shape it's in."

Josie emitted a lungful of air. "I don't suppose you could possibly be more specific."

He rolled down the sleeves of his plaid flannel shirt and buttoned the cuffs, then picked up his invoice box, checking the long list of notations. "This vintage instrument of yours—which, by the way, any technician worth his salt would about kill to own—needs a ton of work to restore. The sound board is cracked, the tuning pins are loose, the hammers and dampers need replacing, and it needs to be completely restrung, thanks to those cats. In fact, even the keys need to be leveled—" He referred to the invoice again and shifted his stance, as if reluctant even to approach the subject of the grand total.

"So?" Josie interrupted, refusing to wither under his scornful demeanor. "Is anything wrong that can't be fixed?"

"No." His grimace softened. "Everything can be fixed."

"Well, then. I don't see the problem. You're a technician. Fix it."

"It'll cost a bundle," he challenged.

"Do what it needs. I want it to sound the way it used to. The best it can be."

His gaze swept over the surroundings, the costly floral-patterned sofa and matching love seat, the custom draperies and window treatments, the distinctive touches in the decor, all without comment. "And it'll take some time."

She tamped down her growing nervousness. "Do you have to take it someplace?"

He shrugged. "Most of the work can be done on-site. Some in my mobile workshop outside. Any parts we don't have in stock will have to be special-ordered."

"So what are we looking at here? What kind of time frame?"

"Three to four weeks, minimum. Month and a half at the outside."

"Is that all?" Josie felt much more hopeful. She relaxed. "And when can you begin work?"

"Tomorrow."

"Afternoon?"

"Morning. Is that a problem?"

She shook her head. "I work at home. I'm usually always here, unless I'm at church."

Gathering his gear, he stepped around her and headed for the front door, where he'd hung his jacket. "Then I guess I'll see you bright and early," he said, shoving his hands into the sleeves. He opened the door. "By the way. . . ." The semblance of a smile quirked the corner of his mouth. "Nice to see you again, Josie."

"Graydon," she nodded. Closing the door after him, she sagged against it momentarily. *Please, Lord,* she prayed silently, *let this be a dream. Let me wake up and find none of this is real.* But inside she knew it was all very, very real.

Chapter 2

Graydon inserted the keys into the ignition as he assessed the neat two-story Victorian home nestled among Pennsylvania's rolling wooded hills on the fringes of Dallas. Josie's home. Letting his eyes ramble over the pale yellow structure with pristine white gingerbread and black shutters, he smiled. She'd been well taken care of. He'd often wondered, often wished he'd known, but he'd never been able to bring himself to make inquiries.

She'd maintained her trim figure and had taken on much of her mother's handsome beauty over the years. Her stylish hair had warmed to a richer honey shade from its more flaxen hue of her teenage years. But her eyes were the same arresting jade he remembered. . .even if they had an elusive quality to them now. He started the motor and backed out of the curved drive.

❧

"You want to ask me out?" Watching her gaze up at him as if he were a movie star, Gray saw Josie's green eyes flare wider in the perfect oval of her face as she leaned in her one-piece swimsuit against a wooden leg of the lifeguard stand.

"Of course. Why wouldn't I?" he responded.

She shrugged a slender shoulder even as she flicked

her attention toward the group of boisterous young people at the concession stand not far away. "No reason."
She met his eyes again. "Sure."

"Pick you up at seven, then. We'll grab a foot-long
hot dog from the Ranch Wagon, then go for some soft ice
cream. Okay?"

She nodded. "You'll, um, have to come in and meet
Gram," she said hesitantly. "She doesn't let me go out
with boys she doesn't know."

"No problem. I kind of like to see what I'm getting
into myself."

Glad his light remark had put her at ease again,
Gray donned his sunglasses and grinned as she set off
toward home, her leather sandals dangling by fragile
straps from her index finger. He couldn't keep from watch-
ing after her; he could almost smell the fragrance of the
shiny shoulder-length hair feathered by the breeze as she
turned to smile. She seemed so unaffected by her grand-
mother's elegant house or her own expensive clothes.
And she had a way of making him feel like a king. Or a
knight, at least, ready to fight off any threat of danger for
her. But he couldn't help wondering if she'd be so eager
to date him if she knew he wasn't as cool as his shades
made him look. His best friend wasn't some guy who
hung out at the drive-in. His best Friend was the Lord.
Time would tell.

❤

That was some piano, Gray reflected as he drove home-
ward. A Mason & Hamlin, 1920s vintage. Satin ebony,
real ivories. How often he had basked in that long-ago

summer and the beautiful music the elderly Mrs. Prescott could so easily plumb from its depths. Josie had been possessed of no little talent herself, but her grandmother was a true virtuoso. He let out a silent whistle. And to think he'd been so brash in his youth that he'd plunked out "Heart and Soul" on that magnificent instrument, in a silly duet with Josie!

At first, when he'd come face-to-face with part of his past, out of the blue, he'd entertained thoughts of having Uncle Jake handle the job, hoping to eliminate the awkwardness he and Josie might feel being around each other again. But as he took stock of the fine piece to get an estimate of the work the piano would require, he knew he had to do the job himself. He'd only had the privilege of going on a service call on a Mason & Hamlin once in his life years and years back, when he'd been apprenticing. And that one couldn't hold a candle to this one. No way would he miss this chance. No way.

He hadn't heard Josie play for ages, but he could still envision that straight back of hers, the dreamy expression on her face as she lost herself in some moving piece. Blinking the picture away, he forced himself to mull the upcoming project over in his mind, planning what to do first as he turned onto Route 309, heading for Tunkhannock.

His stomach growled as he neared his aunt and uncle's house. Knowing Aunt Mavis, she'd have spent most of the day making his favorites—roast beef, mashed potatoes, and gravy. Maybe even pie and homemade ice cream. The old pair were happy to have him back from

Colorado—especially since his uncle's advancing years necessitated having help in his piano service business. And with Gray living only two miles or so down the road from them, they invited him to supper a few times a week. He was never one to refuse. They were one of the primary draws that had brought him back to his roots, needing to ensure that they, his last surviving relatives, knew the Lord. So far they hadn't claimed to set foot in a church except for the occasional funeral of someone they knew, but they seemed to have mellowed considerably in the time since he'd moved away to go to Bible school. Maybe it was parting with so many acquaintances that made them more open to what he had to say when the conversation turned toward spiritual matters.

Coming up on the simple ranch-style home with its white aluminum siding and brick trim, Gray maneuvered his van into the driveway, going slowly beneath the low-hanging elms and maples lining the way. The trees were bare and stark without their glorious crowns, and he didn't want any branches to snap.

Pal, their old collie, loped out to meet him as he swung down from the truck. He bent to ruffle the animal's silken ears. "How are ya, boy?" Then, accompanied by the dog, he mounted the porch steps and rapped lightly.

His barrel-chested uncle yanked the door open. "No call for you to be knockin', Sonny. May!" he yelled. "Sonny's here." Thumping Gray's back with a gnarled hand, he pointed to one of the huge throw-covered chairs that provided infinite comfort no matter what position one chose, then limped back to his own, puffing on the carved pipe that seemed an extension of himself. Pal curled up before the blazing hearth and laid his head on his paws.

"How'd the calls go today, Sonny?"

Contemplating the appointments, Gray glanced around at the familiar homey furnishings. From lamps to books to knickknacks, they were things he'd seen when he'd visited as a youth. "Not bad, actually. Two tunings and one estimate for major repair. A Mason & Hamlin, Uncle Jake. Can you believe it?"

The older man skimmed back the few snowy hairs on his balding pate with the palm of one hand. "You don't say. Don't think I ever worked on one of them old beauties but once in my life. Some lady down t'the lake had it. Didn't need much but a tunin'."

"It's probably the same one. Only it's in pathetic shape now. Cats."

" 'Nough said. To think people let them critters crawl up an' down the strings an' sleep in them is a pure shame."

The hearty aroma of roast beef mingled with the not unpleasant blend of pipe tobacco his uncle preferred, setting Gray's stomach to growling in a rather audible fashion. He grinned as Uncle Jake's keen blue eyes twinkled.

"Must say," the man went on, "it's a pure relief havin' you around to help out with my calls. This bursitis of mine gets worse with each winter, I swear. And now with a game leg, to boot—" He shook his head, then brightened. "I'd say that workshop on wheels you fitted out must make quick work of things. Havin' everything handy—or at least easy to get to."

"Yeah, it helps a lot."

"I've had to let the out-of-town calls pile up lately, what with the slippery roads."

"I'll get to them soon as I can."

"Supper's on," Aunt Mavis announced, peeking around the jamb, her thin face aglow as she caught sight of Graydon. She took her usual seat at the mahogany table laden down with an assortment of delectable foods and dipped her head toward the place she'd set for him, her small frame almost lost behind the edge of the crisp tablecloth.

"Mind if I do the honors?" he asked as his uncle took his spot.

The pair bowed their heads. They'd quickly accepted his saying grace at mealtimes.

"Gracious heavenly Father, we do thank You for this wonderful food and the loving hands that prepared it. We pray Your blessing on it and on this home, for we ask it in the name of Your dear Son. Amen."

"Help yourself, Sonny," Aunt May said, offering him the platter of sliced beef. "And tell us about your day."

As he began, he knew the part he'd leave out. Josie.

❧

The small house Graydon purchased upon his return to his old hometown, seemed deafeningly silent as he lay in bed staring at the ceiling. All he could see was Josie's face emblazoned across the darkness. Her voice had struck old chords inside him. Chords he'd thought were long dead.

The two of them had lots of catching up to do. He hoped he'd have opportunity to probe a little from time to time. He wanted to find out about her life and all the years they'd been separated. From the framed portraits that adorned her walls he could tell she had married, though he hadn't noticed any evidence regarding a male presence in the house. And she'd given birth to some children. One of the pictures bore a striking resemblance to her. A bittersweet ache crimped his insides.

❧

"Oh! It's beautiful! Thank you." Josie's eyes sparkled as she examined the herringbone chain with the delicate gold cross, his birthday gift to her. "Would you fasten it on, please?" Lifting her hair off her neck, she turned to allow him to do so. "I'll never take it off, I promise."

He just grinned. "Well, I'm sure that once in awhile you might prefer a different necklace. I plan to buy you at least a dozen myself. A fellow can't go steady with a pretty gal all summer without noticing she likes jewelry, you know."

She blushed in a way all her own, and his heart warmed. "Just the same, I adore this. Thank you." Scooting closer, she raised her soft lips to his, and he felt himself warm even more. "It was a great service tonight, don't you think?" he asked, choosing a safer subject.

"Wasn't it, though. I never thought the Bible could be so easy to understand—or so real and vital for today. I've read the one you gave me almost through already."

With a hug, Graydon held her against his side, working up the courage to broach the matter he'd been putting off discussing with her. He finally decided to get it over with. "What would you say if I told you I've been giving some thought to going to Bible school?"

She didn't respond immediately. Her expression sobered, and her lashes raised slowly to meet his gaze. "I. . . think you'd make a wonderful pastor. But wouldn't that mean you'd have to go away to study?"

He nodded. "But not forever. I'd come home on holiday breaks, and stuff."

Her countenance turned dubious. "You'd probably meet somebody else. Someone older, more sophisticated."

"Don't be silly. I love you. Remember that. How could I live without that pretty face to greet me every morning of my life?" *Noting her still-somber demeanor, he tried to lighten the mood.* "Besides, a minister needs a pianist. . .and those long fingers of yours sure do play a mean hymn."

She barely smiled. "I won't hold you back, if that's what you truly want to do with your life. Who am I to come between you and God? But that won't make it any easier to part with you. Even if it's not forever, it will seem like it."

"Well, we can write letters every day until next summer when I come home. And once you graduate, you could enroll there yourself. How about that? Never hurts for a pastor's wife to acquire a good knowledge of the Bible and develop her own gifts."

Appearing to consider the concept, Josie shrugged a shoulder in the manner he had grown so used to seeing her do. "I need some time to get used to this, okay?"

she finally pleaded. "Let's not talk about it anymore tonight. I'll go dish us some ice cream."

Going so far away from Josie, all the way out to the Midwest, was going to be the hardest thing he ever did. It would take a lot of prayer and studies to keep him there, that's for sure. But he'd already been accepted at Moody, and there was no turning back. Things would work out. Somehow they would get through the long years while he prepared for his life's work. They would have to.

❧

Rolling over, Gray punched his pillow, his mind still occupied in the past. He'd been the envy of the dorm that whole first year, what with the raft of perfume-scented letters that arrived so faithfully, the stream of home-baked cookies. A second summer of dating cemented his and Josie's relationship for the future. . .but after that, that's when everything had somehow gotten sidetracked.

What was that saying, about the best-laid plans? He sure had made a royal mess of things, not coming home to Pennsylvania and her as he'd intended. Funny how he'd never seen things with such clarity before.

Judging from what he could tell now, she'd had a good life, at least. For that Gray would be eternally thankful. Maybe things worked out for the best after all. And as for the present, well, it wouldn't take forever to whip that concert grand into mint condition. He just wouldn't drag his heels doing it, that's all.

Chapter 3

J osie checked over each page of her new children's book as it spewed out of the printer. At the last one, she straightened the pile and looked for a clear spot on the desk to set them. All that remained now was to put the finishing touches on the action sketches of Chester the Liberty Mouse and arrange the word art for the cover. Then it could be shipped off to her editor.

She sipped some coffee from the mug at her elbow and glanced at the clock. Nearly eight, already. Graydon would be here in a matter of minutes, if he was as punctual as he used to be.

What was it going to be like, having him around almost daily for—what had he told her?—up to a month and a half? Not that she had the slightest intention of allowing his presence to disrupt her life. Between the Chester series and the new line of young adult novels she was in the process of developing, she had projects enough to keep her occupied—thank heaven for deadlines. And once the piano was finished, he'd be on his way. There was hardly a reason for needless concern. A tiny part of her began wondering about his life during those missing years, and why he hadn't ended up in the ministry as expected. Most likely her premonition that he'd meet another woman had turned out to be right. In any event, the arrival of the van put a damper on her musings.

She wasn't expecting to see so many snowflakes swirling about crazily on the stiff breeze when she answered the door. . .to say nothing of Graydon's lopsided grin as he came inside on a blast of cold air.

"Morning," he said, stomping snow off his boots.

Josie smiled politely, certain she'd imagined the quick once-over from his eyes. But then, she did look considerably better today. Only sickness or death could have made her look worse than she had yesterday. "May I take your jacket?"

"Oh. Sure." Setting his gear down, he slipped out of his parka, and she hung it on a hook in the closet.

"Well," Josie said, for want of something better, "I'll get out of your way. There's fresh coffee in the kitchen, if you'd like some while you work. Help yourself."

He nodded his thanks.

Returning to the room she had fitted out as an office, Josie tried to leave behind that feeling of an almost electrifying current that seemed to hang in the air. *Back to work, Josie.* She took a deep breath and adjusted the blinds to allow as much light as possible across the surface of the drawing table. She had never considered herself much of an artist and had often regretted having submitted character drawings with the original series proposal—especially considering that she had intended them to be mere suggestions for someone with talent, someone who would add a more professional quality to them. But the publisher had liked the childlike appeal of Josie's work and quickly added them into her contract.

She held the cover sketch of Chester at arm's length in critical appraisal. Not quite as elegant as she wished she could render, but in Jessica and Susan's estimation the little guy was perfect. That must count for something. Josie envisioned it with the stylized text even as she sat down at the computer.

❦

Gray opened his case and spread out in meticulous order an assortment of special tools, many of which he had designed himself. Made of brass and fashioned on a grinder, each one performed a single tuning or repair function and suited his needs far more adequately than similar items available from piano supply warehouses. He then removed the music desk of the grand piano.

The gentle floral scent of Josie's perfume still lingered, as did her presence, in some indefinable way. Gray glanced toward the hallway and wondered what sort of work she did at home. Whatever it was, it obviously provided more than a few creature comforts. A classy stereo system took preference over television, since the former was visible and the latter most likely was housed behind those closed doors in the built-in wall shelves. No doubt her musical tastes were still as widely varied as they had been in her younger days.

He had noticed a simple wedding band on her left hand when she'd taken his parka, and he let his gaze drift to the framed portraits scattered about the walls until he found the one he sought. The only male portrait in sight. The somewhat-faded pose hung alone, yet was no less prominent than the more colorful grouping on the larger wall across from it. Hesitant to be caught blatantly scrutinizing the photograph up close, Graydon contented himself with what he could tell from his present position. The subject wore a dress uniform, and next to it hung a glass-fronted wall case displaying a trio of military medals. He drew his own conclusions. Her husband must have been killed in the service. Probably Vietnam.

His own ever-so-noble intentions had backfired. Josie had been alone for a long, long time. Who knows, all these years, he and she might have spent their life together as planned, shared that sweet love. Then caught by guilt that he was being disloyal to the memory of his late wife, Gray schooled his thoughts into line.

Putting a tuning hammer up on the plate, he set his pallet of tools within arm's reach and set to work on the fine instrument, releasing the tension and removing one by one the old strings, to prepare for the new. From time to time he heard Josie moving around, heard a printer running, or her muted voice answering a phone call. But she seemed to be making a determined effort to keep out of sight. Just as well, he decided. He had plenty to do himself, and only by keeping at it would he be able to finish the job in short order so the two of them could resume their lives.

But even as he labored at restoring the magnificent piano, he knew he could not bring himself to cut corners on such a treasure. It was worth his finest efforts. And he felt his plans and hopes for possibly catching up on the events of each other's lives begin to fade away. He relegated thoughts and memories of Josie Prescott Marshall to the back burner of his mind and focused his attention on the task before him.

❧

Josie knew she would have to leave the sanctity of her haven sooner or later. What she didn't know was how to handle the lunch situation. The last thing in the world she needed was to plop herself across the table from her First Love and chat over chicken salad sandwiches every day! Gathering herself together, at noon she clicked on the screen saver and exited the room.

Her fears, however, were swiftly put to rest as she heard the van driving away. A glance at the disassembled piano scattered about the living room revealed Gray had left the task in progress, likely to get a bite to eat. She exhaled a breath of relief and went to the refrigerator.

❧

At the sound of Gray's Jeep, Josie sprang to her feet and ran outside, flinging herself into his open arms. "I thought the term would last forever!"

He laughed and tightened the embrace, then eased her down onto her feet. "I missed you more than you'll ever know." His gaze all but devoured her. "Come here, little one," he murmured, drawing her close again. His warm breath teased the fine hairs on her neck as he raised her chin with one finger and pressed his lips to hers in a kiss that left her breathless.

Josie's heart tripped over itself. How had she endured the long winter and endless spring without him?

"Ahem."

Automatically, Gray released Josie.

"Daddy!" Josie gasped, struggling to keep her balance as her face flooded with warmth. "Gray's home."

"So I see." Her father's pleasant but guarded nod seemed to contain equal measures of both qualities. He came down the porch steps and extended his hand.

Gray clasped it, grinning. "Sir."

"Glad you made it back safely." The stern expression grew softer as a twinkle appeared in his clear blue eyes. "Well, come on inside, both of you. Mother's homemade peach cobbler is probably finished by now. You can tell us all how your studies went."

"Sure thing." Smiling down at Josie, Graydon draped an arm about her shoulders and the two of them followed her father into the house.

Josie couldn't help comparing her two favorite men. Gray was the taller by a head, and had a much more athletic build than did her distinguished-looking father, but whenever their gazes turned her way, they mirrored an identical quality. Love. Her heart swelled. And best of all, both her parents thought the world of Graydon. . .and so did she. She hoped the summer would never end.

❧

While Josie rinsed out the few lunch dishes after her light meal, the phone rang. "Hello?"

"Hi, Grandma," a sweet voice singsonged. "It's me, Jessica. Know what?"

"What, sweetheart?"

"I have a loose tooth. Pretty soon I'm gonna look dorky, like my friend Nichole. She has two teeth missing right in front."

"Well, your grown-up teeth will fix that pretty quick, wait and see."

"I hope so. Mommy wants to talk to you, Grandma. Bye. I love you."

"Bye, honey." She heard the phone change possession.

"Mom? Hi. What's happening?"

"Same old, same old. I'm just finishing up another episode of Chester and trying to come up with ideas for my Jessica stories."

"I sure hope you manage to get everything off your back before school's out. The girls are already counting the weeks till your visit."

The door chimes cut across the last sentence. Josie hadn't even heard the van, but knew instinctively that Graydon had returned.

"Oh. I'll have to call you back later, dear. The piano man is here to work on Gram's piano."

"Okay, Mom. Love you."

Smiling, Josie replaced the receiver, then hurried to admit Gray.

❧

"Play just the parts in this section, Josie," Brad Germain said. "Altos, use the music this time, starting on measure sixty-four—and remember to watch me for that crescendo." The lanky choir director nudged his glasses a notch higher on his nose, then started beating out the tempo desired.

Josie did as requested, then repeated the same portion

as tenors and basses joined in. The rich harmony of voices echoed in the confines of the practice room.

"Right. Right," Brad acknowledged. "Much better. Okay, once more, everyone, without the music. The accompaniment, Josie."

Finally satisfied when the piece ended, the director closed the scores on the music stand in front of him. "It's sounding great, you guys. This is our last practice before Sunday night's performance, so I need you to come an hour early for a sound check. Now let's close in prayer, and we'll call it a night."

Moments later, as the rest of the choir members mulled around visiting and putting their folders away, Dorie came to Josie's side, her fine brows crimped with concern. "I couldn't help noticing you seem a bit down, or something. Everything okay?"

Josie grimaced and gave a shrug. "I'm fine. Everything's fine." She began gathering the music sheets together and assembling them in order.

"You could fool most people with that tale, but not me. So you might as well come out with it." Dorie's foot tapped in impatience.

Meeting her friend's gaze straight on, Josie decided to confess and get it over with. "It's just a little. . . awkward."

"What is?"

"You know I'm having work done on Gram's piano, right?"

"Mm-hm."

Josie shook her head. "The technician. . .well, he, um,

turned out to be Graydon."

"Richards?" Dorie's mouth gaped for a second, then snapped closed as she tucked her chin.

"Yeah. Well, like I said, it's kind of awkward."

"I can imagine. I had no idea he'd come back to the area after all this time. Listen, couldn't you get some-body else?"

"It's a bit late for that. . .plus there aren't a lot of tuners qualified to work on a parlor grand—especially one that needs the extent of restoration Gram's does."

"Oh, well." Dorie looked thoughtful, then the hint of a smile flickered over her lips. "How's he look?"

"Excuse me?" Josie stared at her friend.

"You know. Did he go all fat and bald? Toothless?"

Josie fought an irrational urge to giggle but shook her head instead. "Actually, if you want the gospel truth, I would have to say Gray more or less improved with age." She paused to let the statement sink in. "Beat's everything, don't you think?"

"By a mile." With an empathetic pat of her hand, Dorie looped the long strap of her leather purse over her shoulder and turned toward the wooden music case, fil-ing her choir folder in its numbered slot. "Well, Jo, I sure do wish you luck."

"Thanks, but if it's all the same to you, I'd prefer prayer. I do not want things to get complicated, if you know what I mean. I don't have a clue what's happened in Gray's life all these years, and I'm not really sure I want to, for that matter. I only know what's gone on in mine. I'm quite content with the status quo, and I intend to keep it this way."

But even as she spoke, the words had a hollow ring, even to her own ears.

Chapter 4

The setting sun slipped behind the thickly treed hills around Harvey's Lake, scattering fragments of color among the choppy indigo waves. Awed by the wondrous display, Josie leaned her head on Graydon's shoulder, and he drew closer as they sat together on the sand.

"I wish you didn't have to go back," she said, finally giving voice to the words she had tried so hard to suppress.

He did not respond, but his fingers stroked up and down her arm, sending shivers through her.

She inhaled slowly. "It was hard enough to give you up that first whole school year, when I didn't know how lonely I would be without you. I don't know how I'll endure another."

"I know," he said softly, trying to steel himself against the tremor in her voice. "I feel the same way. But maybe once we're both busy with studies again it'll get easier. Pass more quickly. Your senior year will probably be pretty hectic, you know. All those extra activities."

Josie only sighed.

Gray tapped her nose in an obvious ploy to lighten the mood. "I'm going to pray that you enjoy this special year. I wouldn't want to think of you sitting home by *yourself mooning over my ugly mug. Not when you could be doing things with your friends, having good times. I'd rather picture you smiling and happy than gloomy and miserable. Promise me you'll try to have some fun, okay?" He paused, and Josie sensed some kind of inner struggle before he spoke again. "And that includes accepting invitations from other. . .classmates."*

Startled by such a request, she turned her troubled gaze up to meet his. "Other boys, you mean?"

He broke eye contact and looked off into the distance, then gave a determined, if reluctant, nod.

"But I—"

His gentle kiss silenced her words, then he held her tight for several seconds. "If our love is meant to be," he murmured against her hair, "it'll survive."

❧

Josie came awake and bolted upright in her bed, her heart hammering. She thought she had exorcised the memory of that last evening they'd been together. Thought she had worked through the heartbreak of the good-bye that had turned out to be forever. It had taken years to erase Graydon Richards's features and voice from her every thought.

What cruel twist of fate had brought him back into her life now, almost a lifetime later? It just wasn't fair. Well, one thing was for sure. She would not put herself in a position to be hurt by him again. Ever. She slid to her knees beside her bed and poured out her heart to God.

❧

Graydon couldn't help noticing that Josie practically barricaded herself in her office down the hall whenever he was there. Aside from letting him into the house twice every day, he scarcely caught a glimpse of her—despite having resorted to asking her to help him pull the action out of the Mason & Hamlin before he tuned the piano first thing every morning—a job he was more than capable of handling on his own. But there seemed no way to wangle any actual conversation from her.

Now as he tuned the strings yet another time to help set them, Gray tried to come up with a way to broach the subject of her husband, to learn what kind of man had married the girl he himself had once loved. . .the girl he in some ways had never stopped loving. But though Josie didn't seem to mind lending a hand, she never lingered a moment longer than necessary.

Well, hopefully, that was about to change, he assured himself. He finished weighing each key several times with his gram weights, regulating it to specifications and to the touch he remembered. But there was a much better way to do that. Smiling to himself, he slid a hand into his pants pocket and strode up the hall.

He stopped in the doorway of her office, taking in the overall tidiness that pervaded the efficient room even though she obviously was up to her elbows in what appeared to be a writing project. At the moment, however, she was seated at her oak desk, gazing fixedly out the window. He cleared his throat.

Josie's head snapped toward him, and a slow flush of rose crept over her fine cheekbones. "Yes?"

"I'd like your opinion on the tone. If you're not too busy, of course."

"Not at all," she answered. Her expression relaxed, and she got up to follow him.

"What do you do?" he asked on their way back to the parlor, wondering if she'd think him nosy.

"I write. Children's books."

"Ah. Seems I remember your mentioning once that you were helping in Child Evangelism. A Good News Club, wasn't it?"

"Yes. I taught for a couple years, actually. That was a long time ago. Now I just write stories. It's. . .fun."

"That's great. . .doing what you like."

"Aren't you?"

They had reached the living room. Turning his head, Gray caught her searching look and held it for a long moment. Then he gave an answering nod and gestured gallantly toward an upholstered chair as he took his place at the keyboard to voice the hammers.

Having the opportunity to observe Josie closely was something he relished more than he showed outwardly, and he had no qualms about feasting his eyes for as long as he could drag out this procedure. Watching her expression for the slightest indication of satisfaction or displeasure as he struck each key, he adjusted it accordingly, then rattled off a few chords, a run, a snatch of a particular song he remembered she had liked.

When he saw her begin to fidget, he stood. "Your turn. You're the one who needs to be satisfied with the new touch."

"Oh. Of course." Moistening her lips, Josie rose and took the bench, positioning her tapered fingers above the keys as she reflected on what to play. He wasn't surprised to hear the opening bars of "Clair de Lune." It had always been her favorite.

The years fell away as Gray lost himself in the bittersweet moodiness of the piece. Her face was alight with memories of her own as her body swayed slightly with the movement of Debussy's classic, a faint smile upon her mouth.

"I must have a dozen different renditions of that song in my collection," Gray mused when the final notes faded.

"Me, too." Clasping her hands in her lap, Josie glanced in the direction of her wall shelves. "Some things never change."

Neither spoke for a heartbeat or two, until Graydon broke the spell with a nod toward the military portrait. "Your husband, I presume?"

"Yes."

Against his better judgment, he had to ask. "Were you happy, Josie?"

Her features clouded over, and she stiffened, turning cooler even as he watched. "The middle register wasn't quite right. It's. . .stiff, or something. I'll leave you to your work." And with that, she all but bolted from the room.

Well, old man, did you actually expect you could elbow your way into her life again, after the history the two of you share? You blew your best chance a long time ago. You don't deserve her now. . .and she sure deserves better than you. Gray let out a shuddering breath. Then, slowly filling his lungs, he collected a few parts that needed to be glued and clamped, then set them aside to repair in his workshop. It was time to pack it in anyway. He stood and began putting the piano back together. When he finished, he cleared his throat. "I'm done for today, Josie. See you tomorrow."

Hearing no response, Gray hesitated for a few seconds, but she did not come out. He wasn't sure he'd expected her to. Donning his jacket, he walked into January's frigid darkness.

❦

"So, how's it going?" Dorie asked over another segment of the Toll House pie on her plate. "With you and Gray, I mean."

Glancing up from the check the waitress had just brought to their table at Truly Scrumptious, Josie felt her friend snatch the itemized paper out of her fingers. She swallowed her last bit of cheesecake. "How do you think?"

"Well," Dorie drawled as a slow smile crept across her lips, "you could always cure that problem, you know. Mike is still available. And I have it on the best authority that he's a real neat guy. Larry's authority. My husband does not give his approval lightly, you know. Mike could come by, drop in, and you two could—"

"No, thanks. As I've told you before, I don't want *or need,* for that matter, a new man. I like my life the way it is. *Or was,* she added mentally. She averted her attention, feigning a sudden interest in the tasteful surroundings of mint pastels and cream, the simulated candle chandeliers reflected in the mirrored walls.

"Well, that's the difference between us," Dorie admitted dryly.

"What is?"

"Being content with the status quo. I mean, here's this guy who pretty much *dumped* you a hundred years ago with hardly a word, and now he's back in the picture. If it were me, I'd march right up to him, get straight in his face, and have it out with him! Get some answers! If nothing else, at least you'd know what on earth happened."

Josie mulled over her friend's words, trying to envision herself being so bold, taking charge. Dorie was one of the few people close enough to her to know that her assured and confident facade was just that. Inside she was nothing more than a. . .blob of Jello.

"Besides," Dorie continued, "how do you know that God didn't bring Graydon back into your life to give you guys a second chance at romance? I don't believe you ever really got over him in the first place."

Peering at her over the rim of her coffee cup, Josie knew Dorie was right. Part of her heart had always belonged to Graydon Richards and perhaps always would. But still. . ."Romance!" she scoffed. "This part of life is not about romance. It's about a future of reading glasses and hot flashes, knee braces and heating pads. I fail to see anything romantic in that scenario."

"Honestly, you make us sound ancient," Dorie said on a laugh. "Well, you should take some comfort from the fact that he's even older than you, you know. He probably has the same qualms about the thought of starting over with someone again himself—especially a gal who knew him when he was Mr. Perfect, who all but worshipped the ground he walked on."

Josie had never even considered that Gray might suffer from similar fears. And truth was, she really did wish she knew what had kept them from getting together so long ago. But before she did anything foolhardy, she'd have to do some serious praying about the whole thing.

Dorie's voice interrupted her musings. "Has Gray nearly finished the project?"

Josie cocked her head back and forth. "It's coming along, that's all I know. I have no idea how much more remains to be done."

Dorie gave a thoughtful nod. "And the books? Your new Jessica series? How's that, now that our big choir program is but a dim and distant memory and you have all kinds of time to devote to your writing?"

With an embarrassed grin, Josie rolled her eyes. "You know, I haven't even been able to get it off the ground. I turn on the computer every morning, all fired up and ready to go. . .and then stare at that blank screen. I can't seem to concentrate. It's the pits."

"Oh, well, kiddo," her friend crooned with a comforting pat on Josie's forearm. "This, too, shall pass, and all that."

"Right."

"Talk to the man. What could happen?"

"I hate it when you say that."

❧

"You mean, some strange man has been coming to the house every day?" Mary railed incredulously. "And staying all day long? I sure don't like the sound of that!"

Josie cradled the receiver between her ear and her shoulder while she poured herself a cup of herbal tea. "Don't be silly, dear. The piano needs a lot of work. And I'm a grown woman."

"That's precisely what I mean, Mom."

"Anyway," Josie assured her daughter, "he's not exactly a stranger. I knew him a long time ago."

Obviously the remark did not have the desired effect. "All the more reason to be on your guard," Mary insisted. "People change, you know. He's probably figured out you're there all by yourself all the time, and—"

"Mary, Mary," Josie murmured in exasperation. "I'm fine. The very minute I think I'm in danger I'll call 911."

Her daughter didn't answer right away, then sputtered into a giggle. "You're right. I'm being paranoid. It's just, well, you know. We love you. And being so far away, we need to know you're safe."

"I'm safe, sweetheart. Very safe. Please don't worry, okay?" A tone sounded in the earpiece. "Uh-oh. . .I'm getting another call. Want to hold?"

"Naw, I'll catch you tomorrow. 'Night, Mom."

" 'Night. Kiss the girls for me." A click of the button picked up the second caller. "Hello?"

"Josie? It's Gray."

"Yes?" Her throat tightened. Trying to ignore her quickening pulse, she clutched the front of her chenille robe more snugly over her silk nightgown as if he could see through the phone wires.

"Sorry to call so late," he went on. "I hope I didn't wake you."

"Not at all."

"Listen, this is probably stupid," he went on, "but I was taking stock of my equipment, and—did I happen to leave my tuning fork on the piano bench, by any chance?"

"Hold on. I'll check and see." *Calm down, ninny,* she schooled herself with clenched teeth as she set the receiver on the counter and went to peer into the dim recesses of the parlor, then returned. "Yes, there does appear to be something on the floor under the bench."

"Oh. That's a relief," he said with an audible whoosh of breath. "Well, no problem, then. I was afraid I'd lost the fool thing. Thanks, Josie. . .and again, I'm sorry if I imposed on you."

"It's fine. I was still up."

"See you tomorrow, then," he added quietly.

"Right." Replacing the receiver on the cradle, she knew it would be some time before she would eliminate the sound of that voice of his from her last waking thoughts. Or the old flutterings which had begun cavorting about in her heart. Dorie's well-meaning advice had begun to get to her despite her every effort to the contrary. *This cannot be happening. I can't let it be happening.*

Chapter 5

"Morning," Graydon said, stepping inside. He slid his jacket off and hung it in its now-familiar place in the closet.

Josie smiled politely, the mug of coffee she'd been drinking still in her hand. "You know by now to help yourself, right? I usually always have a fresh pot on the warmer in the morning."

"Yeah. Good stuff, too." He grinned, then sobered as she started to walk away. "Josie?"

"Yes?" Halting, she glanced over her shoulder.

"I'm sorry about yesterday."

"Forget it, Gray. I told you, I wasn't asleep."

"No, I mean earlier. Prying into your life. I had no right to do that. You're entitled to your privacy. I just wanted to apologize."

She turned to face him. "Really, it's not necessary. If the truth were known, I'm. . .probably as curious about your past as you are of mine. Which, I suppose, is to be expected, considering."

Bending to pick up his tool case, he merely stared.

"In fact," she rushed on before her courage evaporated, "I've been thinking about it. Praying about it, really." She gulped a reinforcing breath. "We probably *should* talk sometime. Get things out in the open so we can. . .get on with life. Heal." She couldn't believe she had actually said *heal*.

"I agree. Totally." He raked his fingers through one side of his hair, his expression a mixture of amazement and puzzlement. "Doing anything for lunch?" he asked tentatively.

Josie shook her head.

"Well, it's been ages since I had one of those pork barbecues that were all the rage in the old days. . .shaved meat piled over an inch thick, sauce without comparison, all on a fresh warm roll. Anybody still serve those?"

Josie had to smile. "A few places. I haven't had one for quite some time myself. Sounds good."

He nodded. "You're on, then. Noon."

"Right. Noon." With a dip of her head, she returned to her own project. And the first order of the day would be to stop shaking. What on earth had she just done, for pity's sake? Here she'd been doing her best to keep out of his way, to maintain proper distance before things got out of hand. . .and for what? To throw herself at him? She needed her head examined for listening to Dorie's reckless advice—to say nothing of what Mary Ruth would think about this brilliant move!

But gradually Josie became aware of something far stronger, an indescribable peace that flowed through her being. In her devotions, earlier, the conviction came to her that this was the only way to deal with having Graydon Richards back in the area. Undoubtedly they would run into one another from time to time. Certainly two rational adults could talk honestly to one another. It didn't have to go beyond that. Anything was better than dwelling in limbo for the next forty years. Go back and finish that chapter of her life, then go on to the next one. If nothing else, it would at least eliminate some of the awkwardness this forced circumstance had caused.

Draining the last of the hot liquid from her mug, Josie tried not to think beyond the basics. Had he married? Did he have children? She would not permit herself to demand an explanation regarding why he had never come back to her. It could prove more painful than she could bear. He didn't have to know how his remaining in the Midwest had devastated her. . .and demonstrated how closely love is akin to hate. *Come on, old girl. Get off the morbid track. Life did go on, you know.*

Josie reaffirmed that fact in her mind, drawing strength from it. Right. She would get through lunch and through the rest of the day. . .and however long it took until the piano was finished. After that, things would go back the way they were. Orderly. Planned. Things on schedule. End of story.

❧

Gray had come dangerously close to confessing he had left the tuning fork on purpose, simply to have a reason to call. But he thought it best to keep that little matter to himself. Squelching a guilty smile, he focused his attention on the middle register Josie had been concerned about, hoping to get it more to her liking. He knew it needed only the most minute of adjustments, if any. In her mad dash to freedom, she had probably blurted the first thing that came to mind. The strings had stabilized well, as expected, much to his gratification, so he retrieved the gram weights again and set to work.

But his mind kept playing probable scenarios of the

upcoming lunch. He realized that if anyone would have told him he'd be taking Josie out to eat today, he wouldn't have believed it. But he, too, had been devoting considerable time to praying about the situation, and something about the lunch suggestion sounded. . .right.

This time he'd soft-pedal it, though, not plunge recklessly ahead in his quest to fill in the missing years. No sense rushing things. If the Lord was giving the two of them this chance to catch up, they'd better take it and use it wisely, at least give closure to the past. Gray sent a silent prayer aloft that God would help him guard his words, his actions, his motives. He would count it a blessing just to be able to renew his and Josie's friendship. Neither of them, it seemed, needed any more at this stage in their lives.

❧

Josie tamped down the nervous flutterings inside her with a vengeance, chagrined to be feeling like a sixteen-year-old. After all, it wasn't as if this was a date. She was just grabbing a sandwich with an old friend. As they sat opposite each other in a corner booth at Ralph's Place, a forceful mental shake helped her dredge up some of the ease she had felt so long ago with Graydon.

"Who'd believe this?" Gray asked, his gaze sweeping the dated interior of the restaurant. "Looks just like I remember it. Same floor, same tables—almost the same old seats, except for the color change in upholstery. And isn't that the old jukebox in the hallway? Is it possible such a relic could still work?"

"Relic?" Josie teased, observing the familiar twinkle in his eye. "You wanted some old standby menu items, as I recall, so I wouldn't be too critical. And you did come here for a memory, you know."

"Absolutely."

The change in his tone, the intensity lying just beneath the surface. . .Josie was relieved when a thin redheaded teenager approached, writing pad in hand.

"Ready to order?" she asked on a crack of gum.

"We'll have two number sevens," Josie replied before Graydon could respond.

"Anything to drink?"

A renewed surge of merriment accompanied a sudden recollection of former habits. "Cherry cokes. Please," she added as an afterthought.

Gray absolutely gawked, his jaw slack.

"Don't be stuffy," Josie said, tucking her chin. "Yesteryear, and all that."

He nodded slowly, a peculiar frown connecting his straight brows.

When their order arrived, he nearly laughed aloud. "As I live and breathe. A real, authentic pork barbecue." He placed a hand over his heart and looked heavenward. "May fast food never take root in this place."

"Hear! Hear!" Josie chimed in.

After a second's hesitation, Graydon reached across the table and covered her fingers with his palm as he bowed his head.

Josie did her level best to ignore the wild slammings of her heart and closed her eyes for prayer.

"Thank You, Father," he prayed, "for this incredible food. We ask Your blessing upon it and upon our conversation, in the name of Your precious Son."

They both bit into their food at the same time. Josie enjoyed hers well enough, but the pure delight that registered on Graydon's face doubled her own pleasure. She smiled and gave a satisfied nod as he took his time, obviously savoring every bite and every sip of the drink.

"Fit for a king, pure and simple," he said when he finished. He brushed a stray crumb off the edge of the table. "Come here often?"

"I used to. Hardly ever now, though."

"We'll have to remedy that," he said lightly. "Support our national treasures, you might say."

She could only smile. "I'm glad you've enjoyed it. Any other local delicacies you've been pining away for?"

"Maybe a twin kiss," he responded, referring to their favorite soft ice cream cone, a creamy swirl of vanilla and chocolate. "Does the Dairy Bar still exist?"

"Yes, but under a different name. The twin kisses are probably pretty close to what you remember, though. We just have to go inside to get them in the winter."

"Good. Let's go there before we head back."

Josie nodded and led the way to her car.

Half an hour later, after devouring their cones, they returned to Josie's car, and she turned onto the lake highway, heading for home.

"In a particular hurry?" Gray asked.

"No, not especially. I thought you might be in the middle of something."

"Nothing that can't wait. We were supposed to talk, as I recall."

Josie swallowed. Nearing Dallas and the cutoff to her place, she bypassed it and continued on toward the lake instead, wondering all the while how to start, where to begin. She decided on the direct approach as the dreary winter landscape sped by, and forced herself to speak without emotion. "You asked yesterday if I'd been happy. The answer is yes. For two wonderful years. Chad was very good to me. A gentle, considerate, loving husband. I was glad the Lord brought him into my life."

"And after that?" he asked quietly.

"After that, I survived. Our daughter, Mary Ruth, never knew her father. He was sent to Vietnam not too long into our marriage. His helicopter was shot down. His. . .body was never recovered."

"I'm sorry. That must have been. . .hard."

"Yes. Extremely. But I had a lot of friends praying for me, which helped. Plus Daddy and Mom to lean on. The Lord sustains His own. And time, as they say, does heal." *And I've had a lot of time, Gray. A lot of time.*

Several moments of silence came to an end when she spoke again. "How about you, Gray? Were you happy?"

"Pretty much. I was in my element for awhile, being offered what I considered an unbelievable opportunity— to apprentice under a true master. That kind of chance comes along once in a lifetime. Funny," he added evenly. "Looking back now, I see that decision in a different light. Kind of selfish."

"You never went into the ministry, then?"

"No. Never had peace about it. I wasn't gifted at preaching, and I felt the Lord was leading me into a different field. Music. Not playing it myself, of course. . . more in the background. Enabling others to showcase their talents, while I tended the instruments. That's. . .

54

how I met Valerie."

"Your wife?"

From the corner of her eye, she saw him nod. "Her father was the man I idolized, the man I hoped to be. He had a real gift for bringing out the very best in pianos. Played like a prince, while Valerie sang. An angel's voice, she had. I. . .became enamored with her."

The news disturbed Josie measurably less than she had expected. Surprisingly, she didn't even hate the girl who had stolen Gray away. "What. . .happened to her?" she had to ask.

"Leukemia. She passed away two years ago."

"I'm very sorry," Josie whispered, always touched by another's loss.

"She'd always had a kind of fragility about her. It's what drew me, I guess." He paused. "Strange, though, I never—" As if suddenly aware he was on the verge of saying more than he'd intended, Graydon quit talking and gazed off at the rolling snow-covered hills and forests in the distance. "Anyway, that's when I began outfitting my mobile workshop and decided to come back to. . .my roots." He turned to Josie. "So, what about your daughter? Mary Ruth, was it?"

Josie nodded, glad for a cheerier subject. "She's married now, living in California. She and her husband have two little girls, whom I adore spoiling rotten every chance I get. You and. . .Valerie. . .never had any children?"

"None. I suppose that was for the best."

Not knowing how to reply, Josie chose not to. She had no idea where else this conversation might lead, or if it would go anywhere at all. She had said her piece.

"Gray—"

"Josie—"

Having spoken at the same time, they both smiled. He tipped his head in deference to her, and Josie forced aside the throbbings of her heart as she rounded a curve ahead, then slowed and pulled off the road. She killed the engine and spoke quietly, staring straight ahead. "It feels. . .strange. Having you back."

Only the sounds of their breathing disturbed the still moment. Then Gray gave a thoughtful nod. "I can relate to that. But please, let me assure you that I didn't come with the intention of disrupting your life. I'm fully aware that I hurt you years ago—"

Josie cringed at the understatement, but remained composed.

"—but I can only say I thought I was doing what was best."

"For me?" she whispered, blinking away a sudden threat of tears as she searched his eyes, then averted hers. "Or for you?"

With a gesture of futility, he shook his head. "I thought it was for both of us. Now, in hindsight, I seriously don't know. I. . .only wish I hadn't hurt you, above all people in this world. I have no right even to ask you to forgive me, yet I can't not ask."

Never in her wildest dreams did Josie conceive he'd have come back after such a long, long, time. . .much less actually be here, now, asking her forgiveness. For quite a few of those years she would not have been able to give it. But life's experiences and partings had taught her to accept the hard lessons and go on, "forgetting those things which are behind, and reaching forth," as the apostle Paul had put it. Eventually she had gathered up all the bitterness inside and given it to the Lord. . .and He had replaced it with a desire to write, to bring happiness to children, which had fulfilled her in ways she could never have been otherwise.

She breathed out slowly and cocked her head. "I do. I forgive you, Gray."

The greatest visible relief she had ever witnessed in her life erased years of creases from his face as he took her hand in both of his and pressed it to his heart. "I can't ask for more. Thank you. Then. . .dare I hope we can be friends again, Josie?"

She smiled slightly. "I don't see why not. Everybody needs friends, right?" Withdrawing her hand from his grasp, she turned the key in the ignition and made a U-turn, heading for home.

Not all of her confusion had been cleared up regarding Graydon and their shattered dream, but her spirit felt immeasurably lighter. Only the Lord knew what might transpire in the future, and she was content to leave it with Him.

Chapter 6

"This should generate a few more calls, Sonny."

"Hm?" His uncle's voice recaptured Graydon's attention.

The older man whacked the lower corner of the newspaper he'd been flipping through during their after-dinner coffee. "I had the gal at the paper run my old ad for the next couple weeks." A huge grin spread across the weathered face.

Gray raised his mug to his lips, only to discover it was empty. He hadn't remembered drinking any of it. "I thought we were running behind as it is, Uncle Jake. With that Mason & Hamlin, I haven't been able to think about other calls yet."

"Yeah, yeah, I know." The crackling blaze in the fireplace cast a golden sheen on his uncle's balding head as he set his pipe down on the lamp table next to his chair. "But you must be prit' near done with that by now, and anyways, I'm feelin' better. Startin' to get antsy sittin' around all the time. Figure I could get two or three tunings done tomorrow. Winter's good for business. People are stuck home, you know. They need to play their pianos, and the pianos need to be tuned proper."

"Whatever."

Filling his pipe from the ever-present pouch at his elbow, Uncle Jake continued to scrutinize Gray as he packed down the tobacco with his thumb. "You okay, Sonny? You seem quiet."

Gray smiled. "I just have a lot on my mind. I mended a bridge today, and was just reminiscing."

"Oh. That explains it."

"Actually, though, since you brought it up, Aunt Mavis didn't seem her usual bubbly self at supper. Is anything the matter? I didn't want to pry."

"Yeah, well, it's just one of her friends is bad off, and had to be taken to the hospital today. The old gal's worryin'."

"Oh. Sorry to hear that. I'll be sure to pray for her friend tonight."

His uncle regarded him thoughtfully. "You really put a lot of stock in those prayers of yours, eh?"

"Sure do. I've seen the difference the Lord can make in many situations."

"I suppose." Uncle Jake expelled a soft sigh. "You know, May an me, we've never been the type to darken the door of a church much, unless we had to. But we've read those books you sent us from time to time. Read 'em clear through, and I don't mind tellin' you, some of 'em made us think. 'Specially now it's gettin' so we know more dead folks than live ones. Who knows but one of these days we'll be in the same boat ourselves."

"How do you feel about that, Uncle Jake?" Gray asked quietly, immensely encouraged that a lifetime of prayers on their behalf might at last be drawing their hearts toward thoughts of eternity.

"Not too comfortable, to be truthful. I been with friends as they lay dyin', seen their pain, listened to their fears. Can't say I'm all that eager to be put under myself."

"Well, you know, I've been present at a few deaths, too," Gray replied. "But my experiences were just the opposite. I watched them anticipating the joy of coming face-to-face with their Savior. Some of them even caught a glimpse of heaven and died peacefully, with smiles on their faces. They had nothing to fear."

"Think it could be like that for us? Even if we didn't take to livin' for the Good Lord all these years?"

Gray smiled gently. "When a person makes his peace with God, the past is erased. What counts is now, this moment, and what you do with it. God provided the way for all of us to get in right standing with Him, and He did it by sending His Son to die on the cross to pay for our sins. All that's required of us is to accept that priceless Gift. Nothing more."

"Sounds too easy, Sonny. Seems we should clean ourselves up first, be more deservin', or something."

"There's no way to clean up enough to deserve what God has done for us. His love takes care of everything, just the way He planned it. Jesus' blood alone has the power to wash our sins away and make us clean before God. Like I said, it's a gift. A miracle of a gift."

"Hmm." Kneading his chin in thought, the older man nodded his head. "May needs to hear this, too. Got time to answer some questions?"

"You two are the only family I have left, Uncle Jake. I've got all the time in the world for you." Gray's calmness astounded him, when what he would have liked was to jump up and shout for joy. First, Josie's forgiveness, and now this. A benchmark day for sure.

Putting his pipe aside, the older man looked in the direction of the kitchen. "May!" his big voice boomed. "Let the dishes go, and come on in here. Sonny's got something to say."

"Be there in a jiffy."

At his aunt's soft reply, Gray breathed a silent prayer of thanks, then asked for wisdom as he prepared to speak to his loved ones about the Lord.

❧

Josie read the Ninety-first Psalm over again, relishing the passage that had been her mother's favorite, and one of her own as well. For some reason, it had seemed easier to concentrate on her Bible reading and prayer this evening. So much of the turbulence that had plagued her since Graydon's appearance had somehow evaporated during their talk. In its place was a peace she hadn't known for ages.

Life had not turned out anything at all like she had envisioned it in her romantic girlhood dreams. Thinking back on how innocent and naive she had been then, upon how passionately she had declared she could never live without the man she loved, she smiled at the realization that she had done exactly that. All these years, working through the pain of first one heart-wrenching loss and then a second, she had discovered that true happiness was not dependent on someone else. It came from within. And foremost, from God.

She wasn't the same person now, and neither was Gray. They had different memories to cherish, different priorities and goals. . .and ahead lay an entirely new kind of relationship. The deep, abiding, honest friendship of soul mates. Closing her Bible, she hugged it to her breast and offered a joyful prayer to the Lord.

The bedside phone interrupted her in midthought. Josie sighed and picked up the receiver. "Hello?"

"Hi, Mom. Just called to say hello. How's everything?"

"Actually," Josie breathed, "I'm glad you asked, because it's wonderful. Absolutely wonderful. And I am extremely glad to have someone to tell that to."

"Why?" Mary's voice rose in alarm. "What happened?"

"Nothing, dear. Nothing. Wait, that's not quite true. Everything! Oh, I don't know. . . !"

"Mom. . .you're scaring me. It's not that man, is it? Tell me it's not. I knew this was going to happen, I just knew it."

"Knew what?" Josie asked, aware that her giddiness had obviously caught her daughter off guard. But she couldn't help feeling so happy. "I'm fine, Mary. In fact, everything's great. I've had the most wonderful day. . . ."

"With *him?* The piano man?"

"Well, actually," Josie hedged, "y–yes. But not the way you think, I'm sure. We only talked."

"Only talked. Right. That's how everything starts

out, you know. Then, before you know it, things get—out of control! Oh, I wish I were there, to make sure you . . .you don't—"

Fighting the urge to giggle, Josie smothered it behind her hand and composed herself. "Really, dear, you've gotten the wrong impression. Gray and I, we're just friends. That's all."

"Gray and I? *Gray and I!* Oh," Mary Ruth wailed, "it's worse than I thought! Mother, please don't go doing anything rash. Will you just promise me that? Please?"

It had been quite a few years since Josie had known her daughter to become so flustered over something so inconsequential—but the girl had, after all, grown up with the sole companionship of her mother. Her possessiveness was probably natural. Josie had to laugh.

"Motherrrr. . . !"

"I'm here, sweetheart. And you have nothing to worry about. Listen, I hear the teakettle boiling. I'd better go now."

"But—"

"I'll talk to you tomorrow, okay? Kiss the girls for me."

Laughing to herself, Josie hung up the phone and padded out to brew her tea. Mary and her notions. She'd soon discover how silly they were. . .

Chapter 7

January drew to a close with a roaring wind that awakened Josie one morning an hour before dawn. Old Man Winter was not to be ignored, she concluded wryly, despite such a deceptively mild November and December. The entire past week had held nothing but unsettled weather and snow squalls, but obviously those had only been a prelude to a real storm waiting in the wings to wreak havoc on the entire northeast coast.

Sliding her feet into her slippers, she moved to the window, where the outside floodlight glowed through the white fury of a blizzard, a sight which magnified the chilly draft seeping through the sash. Shivering, she picked up the chenille robe draped over the foot of the bed, snuggled into its thick, warm confines, and padded out to the kitchen to put on some coffee.

More than likely, Graydon wouldn't venture out on the treacherous roads between Tunkhannock and Dallas this morning as he had during the less severe storms. She realized how quickly she had grown used to having him around every day, now that they had taken to sharing lunch either out or at Josie's home. They had many lively conversations regarding current events, common interests, even spiritual concerns. Rarely, however, did the subject touch on the past. Josie could only assume he was as reluctant as she to rehash the old hurts or disappointments.

Oh well, it was all water under the bridge, and besides, a day all to herself would be welcome too. A perfect opportunity to don comfortable old clothes and sort through more boxes from her mother's attic.

A few hours later, with the partially unpacked cartons forming a semicircle around her in the spare room, Josie propped her back against the bed and sat thumbing through the old high school yearbooks, report cards, and candid photos of her teenage years. Some ridiculous shots of her and Dorie in assumed bathing beauty poses brought a laugh. Was it possible they had ever been so young? Still smiling, she delved deeper into the box.

A small chest decorated with decoupage brought instant recognition. *My private treasures!* Nibbling her lower lip, Josie raised the lid, eager to see what her ever-so-young self had deemed noteworthy enough to save forever.

Opening a heart-shaped trinket box her grandmother had given her at age ten, she recalled being awed by the loose pearls and rhinestones from old jewelry. It also housed Josie's class ring, which, she discovered, still fit her finger.

Moving aside the padded folder containing her diploma and the tassel from her graduation cap, she saw in the very bottom of the chest a faded envelope, lying facedown.

A shiver ran through her. She had buried, burned, or torn up everything that would remind her of Graydon a long time ago. All but this. . .a valentine he had made her the first year he had been away at school. Not even when her shattered heart was aching most had she been able to part with that.

Josie twisted her head and peered over her shoulder, as if unwilling to be caught peeking at the personal memento of her old love. Then with a shake of her head to remind herself she was alone, she picked up the envelope and turned it over, knowing exactly what she would see.

He had fashioned the letters of her name to form a flower, a unique design which even now, decades later, awed her. She pressed it to her heart and closed her eyes momentarily against the pain of remembered loss.

When the burning behind her lashes subsided, she lifted the flap and drew out the card whose hand-drawn entwined hearts had been burned into her memory long ago. She couldn't help but gaze at the verse he had penned. Her heart had never forgotten it, since the first letter of each line also spelled her name:

> *Just when I think of life without you,*
> *Or the world devoid of the sunlight of your smile,*
> *Something reminds me how empty it all would be*
> *If I didn't have you in my life . . .*
> *Every moment, every hour, until forever.*

A rush of tears clogged Josie's throat as she closed the valentine. *Why, Graydon? Why did you forget promises you made me? The words you wrote from your heart? I thought true love was never supposed to end.*

But the answers which had escaped her a lifetime ago eluded her still.

Maybe rekindling this friendship with Gray wasn't the wisest thing to do after all. Clamping her lips together, she slid the card into its worn envelope and dropped it back inside the chest. Then she dumped the other mementoes in on top of it and closed the lid, the carton, and finally, the door to the room. She didn't want to look at it or think about it anymore.

❧

When the impassible roads had prevented Graydon from going to Josie's yesterday, he had felt frustrated, and even a little lonely. But now that the endless hours of forced solitude were over, he couldn't help whistling as he navigated the snow-lined roads to Dallas.

After arriving at her house, however, he sensed a definite change in the atmosphere. A polite smile, and she vanished from the room. Gray frowned and disposed of his jacket, then took his tool case into the parlor.

The project was nearing completion. The resonance produced by the combination of new strings and the repaired soundboard rivaled that of most newer pianos currently sold for home use. He brushed his fingers over the precision-balanced keys, barely grazing them, appreciating all the more the fine craftsmanship which had gone into this vintage instrument so long ago. Then he gave the hammers a final voicing, evening the tone from bass to treble, bringing out its mellowest tones.

A little before noon he strode to Josie's office, hearing as he approached the clicking of computer keys, the quiet hum of the hard drive. She had a CD playing as she worked, but the volume was so low it was nearly indiscernible. Today a pair of half-glasses were perched on her nose, a pencil tucked behind one ear, and she appeared totally engrossed in her work.

Watching her for a moment while he debated whether or not to disturb her, he finally threw caution to the wind. "Excuse me?"

"Hm?" She looked up.

"It's lunchtime. Would you care to go out for a bite?"

"Oh." She checked her watch. "I think I'll pass today, if you don't mind. I need to finish this. My editor had a slot open up out of the blue, and wants me to fill it. Thanks, though."

Nodding, he took a step away, then stopped and turned. "Is. . .everything all right, Josie?"

She stiffened slightly, and a hint of pink tinged her cheeks. But she was all efficiency and composure as she lifted her eyes to his. "Of course. Why wouldn't it be?"

With a shrug, he slid a hand into his pocket. "No reason. Well, I'll see you later." Gray felt that something was definitely bothering her, and it had nothing to do with any children's book. He sent a wordless prayer aloft that God would lift her troubled spirit.

❧

"I might as well tell you," Dorie confessed after choir practice, "Mary called *me* a few nights ago. She was worried about you."

Josie's mouth gaped. "You've got to be kidding."

"Nope. She must have asked me a zillion questions

about the 'piano man,' as she termed him, about how often he's at your place, about whether you're getting involved with him. You know. She's so afraid you'll be hurt."

"And what did you tell her, if I might ask?"

"What's to tell? Only that you two knew each other from before, that you seem pretty happy. . ."

With a moan, Josie slid the accompaniment music into her tote and zipped it shut. "I can just imagine what she thought of all that. You don't know my daughter the way I do."

Dorie gave an offhanded shrug as she and Josie walked to the music file, where Dorie slid her practice folder into its slot. "Sorry. She caught me off guard, know what I mean? I was only trying to be honest, to put her mind at ease."

"Well, no point in worrying about it now. I'll just call her when I get home. Most likely the lines that were down because of all the storms are in working order again now."

But when the snow tires on Josie's car crunched over her gravel drive, she found it more than a little alarming to see every light in the house ablaze. Pulling into the garage and closing the door behind her with the remote, she gathered her things and went into the house through the connecting door.

Two little pairs of arms immediately snagged her around the waist. "Grandma! Grandma! Surprise!"

Josie bent to hug her granddaughters, and they smothered her with kisses even as their willowy mother came into the kitchen.

"Hi, Mom," Mary Ruth said. "We took the first flight we could get, once the storm system cleared."

"But why? What are you doing here?" Josie asked, flabbergasted, her arms still around Jessica and Susan as she peered in confusion at her daughter.

"Because, Mom. I was worried about you. Really worried. I couldn't stay away." Beneath a wave of flaxen bangs, Mary Ruth's fine brows dipped.

"Mary." There seemed nothing but sincerity in Mary Ruth's stance, the particular tilt of her head, the concern in her blue eyes. Josie raised a hand to knead her own throbbing temples. "I cannot believe Craig would be a party to your flying all the way out here from California on the spur of the moment! With the girls, no less, when the weather is so unpredictable. And especially when there is absolutely no reason to do so! And what about Jessica's school?"

"Mama said it's okay to miss a day or two," Jessica announced in six-year-old exuberance, innocent blue eyes wide in her fair face. "And anyway, we wanted to surprise you."

"You have lots and lots of snow!" Susan toyed with a lock of her golden hair as a huge yawn made its appearance.

Josie exhaled in exasperation. "Well, let's get the beds made up, at least. The kids look sleepy."

"I did that, Mom," Mary said. "While we were waiting for you to come home." She paused. "Where were you, anyway?"

70

I absolutely refuse to account for my comings and goings as if I'm the errant teen and my daughter's the parent! Josie affirmed inwardly, seething as she patted her granddaughters' heads. "Go brush your teeth, sweeties, and put on your jammies. Then we'll come hear your prayers, okay?"

As they nodded and scampered off, Josie swung her gaze to their mother's. "You know I have choir on Wednesdays." She purposely did not elaborate further.

A guilty smile tweaked Mary Ruth's lips. "After the girls are in bed, could we talk, Mom? Please?"

Josie gave a reluctant nod. There had to be worse things than being loved by one's child, she admitted to herself. A lot of parents these days had kids who barely uttered a civil word to them, much less actually cared about their welfare. With that realization her anger began to subside.

While Mary settled her girls for the night, Josie put on the teakettle, got out some china mugs, and arranged a few cookies on a plate, then went to listen to some bedtime prayers. It really was a treat, this spontaneous visit, but with winter being so capricious, she wouldn't breathe easy until she knew the precious threesome had arrived safely back home after they left here.

Over steaming tea, a short while later, she and Mary Ruth clasped hands and prayed together, a habit carried over from their years together, just the two of them. At the close of the prayer, Josie moved the cookies a bit closer to her daughter.

Mary helped herself. "You must think I'm really

obsessive, Mom," she began. "But the last time we talked on the phone you sounded so. . .weird. Then with the storm, when I wasn't able to get through to you at all, I started going bananas, worrying that something might have happened, you know, with that workman here every day. And talking to Aunt Dorie didn't help much."

Smiling that Mary's childhood habit of calling Dorie her aunt had held on so long, Josie gave her daughter's hand a comforting pat. "Well, dear, I can only say that your worries were completely ungrounded. The fact that I happen to have had a prior acquaintance with the man who happens to be restoring your great grandmother's piano is just a coincidence."

"But you sounded like—like a silly teenager!"

"I was just in a funny mood. The piano man—his name is Graydon Richards, by the way—and I had just gone out for lunch to some of the old places he'd known years ago before he moved out of the area. And it was just *fun*. What can I say?"

"Then you aren't. . .involved? Or maybe *getting* involved with him?"

Josie didn't answer the direct question right away. Maybe she had been on the verge of letting herself trust Gray again, letting herself become too dependent on his presence, letting old dreams get the best of her. But now she was more in control of her feelings and had gotten her head back on straight. She opened her mouth to speak, but Mary beat her to it.

"You know, Mom. . .it isn't really that I want you to live alone your whole life. I've always wished you would find someone who would love you the way you deserved to be loved. . .but I can't help remembering that widower Morris Peters, before I married and moved away. He seemed oh, so charming, yet only really wanted someone to support him and wait on him hand and foot the way his late wife had. You came so close to falling into that trap!"

Josie could not dispute that statement.

"I know you date other men occasionally—Aunt Dorie still sees to that, I'm sure. But the fact that you've never formed a relationship with any of them—well, it's kind of scary now that I live so far away and have to deal with the possibility of your falling in love with someone I've never even met, a virtual stranger. Do you know what I'm saying? That probably sounds stupid, but I don't know how else to say it. I'm just trying to be honest."

Nodding, Josie smiled. "Well, perhaps I should be honest with you, then. The truth is, Gray and I knew each other long before I ever met your father. We spent a lot of time together when we were younger. In fact, we were almost engaged when he left Pennsylvania to go to Bible school out in Illinois. Only he never came back."

The color drained from Mary's face. "You mean, you guys were actually in love?"

"Yes. He was my very first love. I was devastated when he broke my tender little heart."

The attempt at levity rolled right off Mary Ruth. "Then it really is more serious than I thought."

"No, it is not," Josie assured her. "Just because we were close as teenagers does't mean we still have feelings

73

for each other now. We're different people. People who just want to be friends again and are happy with just that."

"Are you sure, Mom? Are you really, really sure?"

Josie looked deep into her daughter's eyes. "At the moment, I am very sure. I do not see that ever changing . . .but I am still praying earnestly about it. Naturally, what I truly desire is God's will. . .whatever that is."

With a nod of acceptance, Mary reached over and squeezed her hand. "Well, I can accept that. I guess I'll just have to trust you, then." Her lips curved into a smile. "But I sure hope I get to meet this Graydon Richards before the girls and I leave to catch our returning flight . . .just in case. Either way, I do have some curiosity that needs to be satisfied!"

Josie had to laugh.

"I do love you, Mom."

"I know."

But later as she lay awake in bed, Josie felt a few degrees less confident about the situation. Now that she had purposed in her heart not ever to be vulnerable again, was it really God's will she sought. . .or her own?

Chapter 8

It seemed almost comical to Josie the way Mary Ruth hovered about, acting as if she weren't the least nervous waiting for Graydon's arrival. Jessica and Susan, completely oblivious to the underlying tension, could talk of nothing but playing in the snow. Right after breakfast they begged to bundle up in the winter clothes they so rarely got to use, then dashed outside.

Seeing her daughter check the wall clock for the dozenth time as they washed up the morning dishes, Josie had to smile when the van pulled into the drive precisely at eight.

"He's here," Mary announced, laying aside the dish towel.

"Graydon is always punctual." Moments later, as he wiped his boots and came inside, Josie was more than aware of her daughter's scrutiny of the poor man as the two met him side by side in the entry. Always impeccable, he looked especially nice today, she noted with satisfaction. Fairly new jeans molded enticingly to his muscular frame, and a burgundy-and-charcoal checked shirt lent a slate shade to the grayness of his eyes.

Suddenly realizing that the three of them were staring at each other, Josie seized control. "Gray, there's someone here I would like you to meet. This is my daughter, Mary

Ruth. She popped in for a surprise visit. Mary, Graydon Richards."

He immediately offered a hand. "Well, I'm glad to meet you, Mary. Your mom talks about you a lot. She's very proud of you."

"How do you do?" Uncharacteristically speechless after her polite greeting, Mary withdrew her hand.

"You've come all the way from. . .California, isn't it?"

"Y–yes. It was a kind of a spur-of-the moment thing. We're flying back this weekend."

"Ah. Well, I hope you have a great visit. I assume the little early birds building a snowman belong to you, then."

She nodded. "Those two consider snow the eighth wonder of the world."

The smile he flashed doubled his appeal and charm, Josie conceded. "Then I hope they enjoy this supply we special-ordered just for them," he said lightly, his amiable grin now including Josie. "Well, I'll try not to intrude on your time together. I only have a final tuning to do, then I'm out of here."

Josie had observed the nearly imperceptible way he had looked between Mary Ruth and herself, as if making a comparison. And she couldn't help sensing in his fleeting smile a measure of approval of her offspring—and something else she couldn't quite put a finger on. It sent a pleasing surge of warmth through her.

Mary Ruth stared after him as he strode to the parlor, her expression turning gradually to one of acceptance before she slid a glance to Josie. "He seems nice enough," she whispered.

With a smile, Josie motioned with her head in the direction of her office, and they went there to talk privately.

"Well, I must admit, he's nothing like I pictured him," Mary confessed quietly. "I thought he'd be old, dowdy, maybe even bald, with a paunch. Instead, he's— handsome. . .considerate. And something about him seems . . .I don't know. Honest. Worthy of trust. I felt it the first second I saw him."

"Now do you agree you have nothing to worry about?"

Nodding, Mary gave her a hug. "I sure hope I didn't make you rue the day you gave birth to me. I should have known anyone who could raise such a wonderful daughter on her own—" her eyes sparkled with mischief— "not to mention establish a career in her favorite field, should be able to take care of herself, too."

"Well, it did seem a bit much, thinking you had to approve of everyone I associate with."

"Sorry, Mom." Mary's demeanor revealed she had more to say, and was struggling to find the words. "May I barge in with my opinions again? I know you're pretty content with having Mr. Richards for a friend. But his returning to town after all these years a master piano technician, just when Grandma's piano was in need of extensive work—are you sure it's coincidental, and not the Lord's doing?" A knowing brow arched over her smirk.

Josie averted her gaze while she mulled over Mary's

suggestion. "No, I'm not sure. Not completely. I only know the Lord got me through two very crushing experiences in the love department. . .the hardest of which happened to have been wrought by Graydon Richards personally. I don't know if I could let myself be so vulnerable again. I could not survive pain of that magnitude a third time."

Mary gave her mother's shoulder an understanding squeeze.

❧

Graydon took all the time required to give the Mason & Hamlin a proper concert tuning. He envisioned Josie sitting down this evening to play, that unique touch of hers nearly a caress, and he determined that she'd find the instrument at its absolute best. A large part of him wished he could be here to listen, for the sheer enjoyment of it. But she already had company.

His thoughts wandered to her guests, to how different all of this might have been had he not let the love of his life slip through his fingers. Mary Ruth could very easily have been his and Josie's, those little girls their granddaughters.

Come on, old man, he grated inwardly, *the love you and Josie shared was as pure and beautiful as any melody. But you're the one who ended it. She's given every indication—and deservedly so—that it's too late now. Don't make a fool of yourself.* Expelling a breath rife with regret, he hoped he'd never be as *smart* again, or as noble, as he thought he was at twenty.

❦

Seeing her dear ones off at the Scranton airport, Josie gave hug for hug, and kiss for kiss, then watched and waved until the departing jet was swallowed by the overcast sky. The few days they had visited had been a real treat, whatever the reason.

This time when she returned to the house, it would be empty again. Really empty. The work on the piano had been officially finished, and there would be no more daily appearances by Graydon taking up the better part of every day. He'd scheduled a follow-up tuning two weeks from now, but until then she would have the place all to herself. Peace and quiet. Total solitude, the way she liked it, she avowed. Everything orderly, on schedule. The way entire years of her existence had been since Mary Ruth had left home, for more years than she cared to remember.

Popping a classical piano CD into the car stereo, she willed her mind to concentrate on nothing but the familiar piece as she took the shortest route home.

At least it was still daylight, she thought with relief as she pulled into the garage. Nothing was worse than returning to a dark, empty house. Grabbing her purse and keys, she went inside and put on a pot of tea.

It would be a long two weeks. Graydon had spent so many hours here, she still felt his presence in some almost tangible way. But meandering to the parlor, she saw the big room was as empty and oppressively silent as it had been before he'd come that first day.

With a sigh, she brushed the satin ebony finish of the piano with her fingertips and sat down on the padded bench. Playing a few runs and improvisations, she reveled in the perfection he had wrought from the old treasured instrument. Its rich mellow tones were as she remembered. Her heart swelled with gratitude.

That he'd made a favorable impression on Mary Ruth was extremely comforting. After all, if things had been different, he might have been Mary's father, would have shared all the triumphs and sorrows of her growing years. Only he had not. Nothing could change that.

Time to get on with life again, Josie. You've done it before, you know the routine. With renewed determination, she sloughed off the remembrance of wasted dreams and shifted her concentration to the reams of new choir music that needed to be practiced. She opened the bench and took out the large envelope containing the upcoming numbers.

As she withdrew the folder, a small white envelope fluttered to the floor, landing facedown.

She frowned in confusion, picked it up and turned it over. Her heart thudded to a stop when she saw the familiar floral design which had spelled her name on the treasured memento so long ago. Scarcely able to breathe, she carefully opened it and drew out another valentine, one depicting a Victorian parlor scene with an old piano. Inside, the handwritten verse also bore the unique style of before:

Just in case you're ever lonely,
Or need someone on whom you can depend,
Sure as morning follows night,

I'd give the world to be more than a friend.
Eternally. I promise to get it right, this time. . .

He had signed it with just an initial. Josie's eyes misted over as she traced the single letter with her finger. "Oh, Gray," she whispered. No further words would come.

How long she sat there holding the tender message, Josie had no idea. Valentine's Day was still a few days off, but she knew he'd purposely left the card for her to find. . .to give her time. Time to contemplate his words before his next scheduled visit. Instinctively, because she knew him, she knew he would follow her lead. But before she could make any sort of concrete decision, major questions needed to be answered. Gathering all her courage, she went to the phone. Her fingers trembled as she dialed his number.

"Hello?" came his resonant voice.

"Hi. It's me."

"Josie." A pause. "Is something wrong?"

"I. . .found the valentine you left."

Another pause. "And?" he prompted.

"We need to talk."

"I'll be right over."

Her nerves almost got the best of her after she hung up. What would she say when he got here? Quivering inside, she went to the fireplace and lit the gas fire, then curled up to take advantage of the warmth. Waiting. Unable even to form a prayer.

❧

Graydon did his best to fend off the trepidation setting

his nerves more on edge with each mile. He could still hear Josie's voice—the words that offered no clue to her state of mind. The years had stolen some of the way he had once been able to read her moods, her inflections. He could only guess whether he would find her receptive, angry, or indifferent. Yet nothing would have kept him from her side. Since the day their paths had crossed again, it had been the deepest hope of his heart —a prayer he could not even voice—that somehow they might find their way back to the love they once shared.

He knew he did not merit any such happiness. Yet his spirit still felt so drawn to hers, as if neither of them was truly complete without the other. And considering all the other wondrous works God had done before his very eyes lately, he was not about to question the possibility of one more miracle. He breathed a prayer that the Lord would guide them both, help them know His will. Covering the icy roads to her place in an amazingly short time, he pulled into the drive.

❧

As Josie admitted Graydon into the house, she wondered if her smile appeared as tentative as his. "Thank you for coming."

"How could I not?" he asked softly, doffing his parka.

With a nod of agreement, she forced her legs to move, leading the way to the parlor, where she perched on one end of the couch and gestured for him to take the other. Swallowing a huge lump in her throat, she again took the direct approach. "There's something I've avoided asking you. I tried to convince myself it was no longer important, that we could just ignore the past and pretend you're just an old friend who's just moved back to town. But I can't. Not after your valentine. I have to know what happened to us, Gray. The real reason why you never came back to me."

He inhaled deeply, and a muscle worked in his jaw. "You're right. You deserve an answer. I acted inexcusably —despicably—to you, the woman I loved. Still love," he corrected without missing a beat. "I don't know what makes a guy consider his motives for doing something stupid as *noble*. But I deceived myself into thinking that."

Josie was still puzzled, but she did not interrupt.

"One thing I loved about you was the way you made me feel like a champion. A hero. Believe me, it does wonders for a man to have a woman who has that kind of faith in him. Anyway, I had led you to believe I was going away to study for the ministry. Then when the calling from God just wasn't there, I felt like a failure, that I'd failed you—and after I'd already kept you waiting so long. So when the opportunity came up for me to apprentice under Valerie's father," he continued, "which involved signing a two-year contract, I couldn't bring myself to ask you to wait that much longer."

He gave a helpless shrug and spoke again, his tone much flatter. "I guess the truth is I couldn't bear the thought of being less than a hero in your eyes. So I did what seemed the *chivalrous* thing and released you from your commitment. I can only say that if I had it to do over again, I'd have used the brains God gave me, and allowed Him to work out the details."

83

Josie's gaze fell to her lap. This was so much to take in.

Exhaling a ragged breath, Graydon slowly shook his head. "I have no problem understanding why you don't trust me. Why should you? But just know that the Lord never let me completely erase the guilt I felt whenever I thought of you. But I am supremely thankful He provided you with at least a measure of happiness."

As she considered all the ramifications of Graydon's explanation, Josie felt the chains of yesteryear unlatch and fall away, one by one, and hope began to take its place. The utter sincerity in his expression, in his eyes, confirmed that he felt it too. . .the fragile hope that what had been lost was on the brink of being found, rekindled, given life again.

She held his gaze for a timeless moment, then reached up to touch his face.

Graydon caught her hand and kissed her open palm. With a sigh, he gently drew her, unresisting, into his arms.

Josie melted against him for several heartbeats, eyes closed as he rocked her softly. A never-forgotten sweet ache of longing filled her being, banishing all time, taking her back to their beginning. It had felt so right to be in his embrace then, felt so good now. The years in between had lost their power to bring pain. All that mattered was the present.

"How could I ever have let you go?" he murmured against her hair.

Easing away a little, Josie smiled up at him. "Both of us had a lot of growing up to do back then." She moistened her lips. "Did–did you really mean what you wrote in the card?"

"Every word. I would never lie to you. And I'll gladly spend the rest of my life making up to you for my immaturity and utter stupidity. . .if you'll give me a chance."

She echoed one of his replies. "How could I not?"

In the circle of his arms, Josie watched his smiling eyes darken as he lowered his head ever so slowly, still giving her the chance to call the shots. To tell him to back off, if that was what she wanted.

It wasn't. This had been something she had dreamed of even when it seemed impossible, and she would not have moved away for anything. She raised her lips to the tenderest, most reverent kiss she had ever known. "I love you, Gray," she whispered.

"And I have never *stopped* loving *you*." Still smiling, he tightened the embrace for a long moment before inching back, his expression peculiar. "Did you hear that? I could have sworn I heard music. Come, my love." He led her to the parlor and drew her down beside himself on the piano bench. The grin broadened as, with a spark of mischief in his eyes, he struck the lower chords of "Heart and Soul."

It was so easy to enter into his jubilation. Perhaps it wasn't the most romantic song in the world, she conceded, making up an innovative melody to accompany his chording. But hopefully, it would be the first of a great number of duets.

For the rest of their lives.

Sally Laity
An accomplished writer of contemporary and historical romances, Sally's novel, *Dream Spinner*, contained in the *Inspirational Romance Reader–Historical Collection No. 2* (Barbour Publishing), is a bestseller. She recently coauthored an inspirational romance series set during the Revolutionary War entitled "Freedom's Holy Light" (Tyndale House Publishers). Sally makes her home in Bakersfield, California and is married with four children and nine grandchildren. She enjoys writing inspirational romance because it is an avenue for her to openly share her faith.

Reluctant Valentine

Loree Lough

Prologue

Buddy Poulet propped both cowboy-booted feet on his desk and leaned back in his overstuffed leather chair. "Well, don't this just beat all," he said, grinning, "Dr. Jake McCafferty, having a panic attack." Gray-white brows rose high on his well-lined forehead. "What would your listeners say!"

Jake took quick inventory of himself. Pacing like a caged tiger, arms waving wildly about his head, he *did* look like a man who'd lost control. Pocketing both hands, he tucked in one corner of his mouth. "If my listeners knew you'd replaced my producer with a, with a *rookie,* they'd say you've been chewing too much chicken fat."

Chuckling good-naturedly, Buddy aimed a bony finger at his employee. "I hope that isn't a chicken joke; you know how I hate chicken jokes."

Slumping onto one of two tufted chairs facing Buddy's massive mahogany desk, Jake smiled despite himself. "It was more a reference to the condition of your mind, 'cause hiring Casey Wallace has got to be one of the most birdbrained ideas you've ever—"

But Jake didn't complete his explanation. Sam Bell, with twenty-five years in the business, had practically single-handedly built the show's audience. What would happen to ratings, now that Sam had decided to retire— and Buddy had replaced him with a greenhorn?

On his feet again, Jake flapped his arms. "What were you thinking, hiring a kid with no radio experience to replace a guy like Sam?"

Buddy sat forward and leveled a one-brow-up gaze at his employee. "Park it, Jake, before I call the Baltimore Zoo and have you written up for impersonating an ostrich."

Employees often called Buddy "Santa Boss", as much for the minuscule bulge above his belt as for his gift-giving tendencies. But Buddy Poulet hadn't become the nation's largest producer of poultry products because of his jolly demeanor. He'd earned his reputation as a savvy, hard-edged businessman by being tough, gutsy, straightforward. When that left brow slid closer to what used to be his hairline, folks knew better than to get in his way.

Jake parked it.

"I hired Casey Wallace," Buddy began, "because I have a good feeling about her." He tapped a fingertip to his temple. "Got a lot on the ball, that one."

Jake shrugged a shoulder. Like it or not, he had to admit Buddy had never steered him wrong.

"Have I ever steered you wrong?"

He raised a brow of his own, grinning at the boss's intuitive powers. Buddy was much more than the guy who signed his paycheck. In the years they'd worked together, he'd become a close friend. "No," Jake said. "At least, not yet."

"Look Jake, 'Lovesick' is WCHK's best-selling program. You don't honestly think I'd do anything that would jeopardize our ratings. . .?"

It amazed Jake, the way this diminutive man could make him feel ten instead of thirty. Ten years old and as foolish as when he'd belched into the microphone in the middle of his first choir solo. "Of course you wouldn't."

Buddy slid a manila folder toward Jake. "Take a gander at her résumé. Casey may not have on-air experience, but she's well-rounded."

"So, it's 'Casey' already, is it?" Buddy's wife had died ten years earlier, and during the past five, old "Santa Boss" had had a steady stream of attractive young ladies accompany him, primarily as social fixtures rather than intellectual companions. He hoped Casey Wallace wasn't one of them.

"For your information, she didn't want the job. I had to talk her into taking it."

"You talked her in—" He scrubbed a hand over his face. "But *why?*"

"Same reason I talked you into doing the 'Lovesick' show."

Buddy's statement hung in the air between them like an invisible spider web, capturing Jake's full attention and binding him to accept the honesty of the words as well. The boss had, after all, hornswoggled Jake into going on-air with his counseling sessions. "There are a lot of lovesick people out there," Buddy had insisted, "who don't have a clue how to fix what's wrong with their love lives, and you can't possibly help enough of them in your fancy suite of offices in Ellicott City."

Jake had tried to point out that without face-to-face

contact, he couldn't do the would-be listeners a bit of good.

"Your book was on the bestseller list for months. Folks all over the country are still claiming you saved their marriages. . ." Faced with Buddy's in-your-face logic, Jake had agreed to give the show a trial run.

Nearly three years later, "Lovesick" was still on the air. In that time, the show had won several prestigious awards, had been touted by a *Baltimore Magazine* critic as one of Charm City's most popular talk shows. The phone lines were jam-packed every afternoon between two and five o'clock with men and women hoping, praying that Dr. Jake would have a solution to their relationship problems. And thanks to the cooperation of his soon-to-be former producer, Sam Bell, he often *could* resolve those conflicts.

But could he continue helping people to the same degree without Sam—and with a novice in the production booth?

"I know what you're thinking," Buddy said.

Jake waited for the boss to read his thoughts yet again.

"Quit worrying whether or not 'Lovesick' will stay on top with Casey at the helm." With a jerk of his thumb, he gestured heavenward. "I don't make decisions—not even small ones—without consulting the Big Guy first." Buddy sent Jake a fatherly smile. "He wouldn't steer me wrong. I trust Him, and so should you."

Jake stood and headed for the door. "Okay, boss," he said, pulling it closed behind him. He stuck his head back into Buddy's office. "I'll try, 'cause I'm not chicken," he added, grinning mischievously, and quickly ducked out.

A dull *thud* left Jake wondering which of the books perched on the corner of his desk Buddy had thrown at the closed door. "You *know* I hate chicken jokes!" came his muffled shout.

Hands in his pockets and smirking over the fact that he'd more or less gotten the last word, Jake nodded politely at Buddy's secretary and headed for the studio. *Yeah,* came his silent retort, *and I hate surprises, so I guess we're even. For now.*

Chapter 1

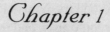

C asey's mouth dropped open in disbelief. "You expect me to do all that—with just one day's training?"

Buddy patted her hand reassuringly, then headed for the door. "It'll be plenty of time, you'll see," he said from the hallway. "You're a smart kid; I have nothin' but confidence in you."

Her grandpa had a favorite saying: "Don't bite off more than you can chew." *It's good, sound advice,* she told herself, *and if you had taken it, you wouldn't be in this fix now.* Casey clucked her tongue. *You'll be lucky if you don't choke on this mouthful,* she thought, looking around her.

It was a small room, no more than fifteen by fifteen feet, with a semicircle desk dominating the space. She stood behind one of three chairs, which would at times be occupied by as many guests, and swung the long-armed microphone stand aside to peer over the salmon-colored counter.

That's where your new boss will be sitting, she told herself, glancing at the oversized black chair. And as she shoved through the heavily padded door beside the console, Casey gave an involuntary shudder. *I wonder if he'll be as bold in person as he is on the air.*

The thought died a quick death as she glanced around the control room. Surrounded on three sides by panels of knobs and dials and blinking lights, she peered through the window behind the control board. From here, Casey realized, she'd have a bird's-eye view of the intimidating Dr. Jake McCafferty. Would he be a reasonable boss—at least until she learned the purpose of each gizmo and gadget? Or would he be a tough taskmaster who'd demand perfection, right from the start? *If that's the case, you're in trouble, girl.*

Running both hands through her curls, she closed her eyes and tilted her face heavenward. *Dear Lord, only an angel of mercy can save me now.*

"It's not as scary as it looks," came a cheerful, masculine voice.

Turning to face it, Casey grinned. Her "angel," as it turned out, was a tall, thin man in his early sixties. "Then how scary is it?" she joked, hoping he was as merciful as his friendly face made him appear.

He dumped a battered briefcase onto the table near the door. "Exactly as scary as you make it," he said matter-of-factly. "Name's Sam," he added, touching a forefinger to the orange bill of his black Baltimore Orioles baseball cap. "Sam Bell. You must be Casey Wallace. I've been hearing good things about you."

Sam wrapped her hand in his own and gave her arm a thorough pumping, then flopped unceremoniously onto the seat of the chair behind the console and rubbed his palms together. "Now, what say we get busy?"

Casey grabbed a tablet and pen as she wheeled a

low-backed chair into the cramped space beside Sam.

"You're in luck, because it just so happens I'm sitting in for Stuart's producer today." He poked a few buttons, and the console came to life, blinking orange and yellow as needles wavered within their business-card-sized windows. "Stu does a restaurant review show," he went on to say, "and he's only on for an hour." Sam flipped a switch. "It's not generally a call-in show, so it's less frantic than Jake's."

"Frantic," Casey echoed. "Just what I need to hear right about now."

"Think of this as a ship," he said, arms spread as wide as the tight space would allow. He nodded toward the empty chair on the other side of the window. "The host is the captain, and you're the navigator."

Sam pointed to a shelf across the way where dozens of narrow cardboard boxes, filled with computer disks, stood side by side. "Would you hand me the box marked 'Food'?" When she did, he flipped through the contents. "So, did you get your FCC license?"

Casey nodded. "Buddy must have pulled some strings. From what I hear, *nobody* applies for—and gets—a license in less than a week."

Chuckling, Sam shook his head. He pulled a disk labeled "Dinner Music," and one stamped "Kitchen Noise" from the box. "Sound effects," he explained, and added a disk called "Restaurant Sounds" to the stack. "Never underestimate the power of the Chicken King," he said.

Casey laughed. "That guy has more nicknames than

I have hairs on my head! Am I the only one who calls him 'Buddy'?"

"Jake does, along with anybody pushin' for a raise or a promotion—or both." He flicked on the computer. "You know what this is for?"

Casey shook her head. "I don't have a clue."

"Stuart does get an occasional call, and I need to be ready, just in case. If somebody wants to talk to him, I'll find out who's calling, see, and what suburb they live in, and put 'em on hold. Then I'll type the info here, and it'll show up on a screen in the studio." He typed in a dummy call: John Doe, from Annapolis, Maryland. "If it's a so-so call, I'll just let it slide into the regular lineup, but if it's somebody I think oughta get on-air pronto, I'll put 'Talk Now' beside the name."

She made a mental note of the fact that the computer kept track of how many minutes the caller had been on "hold," and scribbled the rest of Sam's lesson on her tablet. "How many calls does 'Lovesick' get, compared to 'Food for Thought,' I mean."

"No comparison," Sam said. "Stuart doesn't get as many calls in a month as Jake gets in an hour. We log anywhere from fifty to a hundred calls a show."

Casey's arms hung limp at her sides. "Please God," she prayed aloud, "let him be joking."

Chuckling, Sam leaned back to get a better look at her. He placed the logbook beside the phone and tested his ballpoint pen. "Half a hundred calls per show, minimum. I'm dead serious."

She only rolled her eyes.

"You won't patch that many through," he said, anticipating her objection. "You'll hear some of 'em out, choose the ones that'll incite more responses, and hand 'em over to Jake. He'll take it from there."

"But. . .but how will I know who he'll want to talk to, and who he won't?"

"Aw, after your first dozen or so lovelorn listeners, you'll get the hang of it." Sam shrugged. "Took me five, maybe six calls to tell the crackpots from the serious callers."

Casey sighed. "I'll be lucky if I can do that in five, maybe six *years!*"

His grating laughter filled the small cubicle. With a wink and a nod, Sam added, "I have a good feeling about you, Casey Wallace."

She could only shake her head. "Buddy said the same thing. So how come I'm not more sure of myself?"

"Hey, if you weren't a little nervous on your first day as producer/engineer, you'd need Jake in a professional capacity." Snickering, he winked. "So where's that FCC license of yours?" Sam pointed to his own framed permission to operate. "It's gotta be on display, in case an inspector decides to pay us a, ah, visit."

Casey lifted her overstuffed shoulder bag from the floor and slid the document from a side pocket. "Got a thumbtack?" she asked, holding it against the bulletin board beside the console.

Sam cut her a sidelong glance. "I see you're not one who stands on ceremony, eh?"

"If I have to stand on anything," she responded,

grinning, "I'd like it to be my own two feet."

He wiggled his eyebrows. "It ain't your feet you oughta be worryin' about; you're gonna be spendin' most of your time sittin'. Hang your license with staples for now. But do yourself a favor. Buy a cheap frame down at Wal-Mart, 'cause having the thing reissued—if anything should happen to it—will be a lot tougher than getting it in the first place. Ask me how I know."

He scribbled something in his logbook. "Relax, will you? You're gonna do fine, just fine."

She turned sideways, so he wouldn't see her staring at the eight-by-ten glossy of Dr. Jake McCafferty on the pegboard in the studio. *He's easy on the eyes, I'll give him that much,* she admitted. *But with my luck, he'll be one of those stuck-on-himself guys who buffs his fingernails and keeps a comb in his shirt pocket.*

Whatever kind of man he was, Casey wanted to impress her new boss, wanted him to have as much confidence in her ability to learn the job quickly—and perform it efficiently—as Buddy and Sam seemed to have.

So, Dr. Jake, she asked the framed color photo, *will you give me a chance to prove myself?*

Dr. Jake's smile, though wide and handsome as any actor's, never quite reached his eyes. Casey shook off a chill. *Well,* she thought, *a girl can hope.*

"You'll do just fine," Sam said, heading for the door. And on the other side of it, he mumbled under his breath, "Not. . ."

❧

Jake took the shortcut from Buddy's office to the studio

through the production room, and immediately felt a strange kinship with Papa Bear from the Goldilocks story: *Who's that sitting in my chair?* he asked himself.

Both hands wrapped around the microphone, brows furrowed and eyes squinted, it appeared the young woman who was all snug in his seat had no idea what to make of the instrument. Jake sighed and rolled his eyes. *She doesn't even know what a* mike *is.*

Habit made him give a quick knock before shoving the door open. "You must be Casey," he said, forcing a smile he didn't feel, extending a hand. "Jake McCafferty." He made a mental note of her hearty handshake, and unconsciously began a "Reasons to Like and Dislike Casey Wallace" list.

"It's nice to finally meet you."

She had a pleasant voice, too—another item for the "plus" side of his list.

Then, as if it were a national secret, she pointed at the microphone. "There's catsup on your mike."

Jake leaned in for a closer look and got a whiff of her perfume instead. He didn't want to like her. Not her bouncy auburn curls, not her big brown eyes, not the wonderful way she smelled. "Stuart can be such a slob," Jake said, frowning as he straightened. "He does the show before ours, a restaurant review called—"

" 'Food for Thought.' Sam told me all about it." Casey plucked two tissues from the box on the countertop and wrapped them around her forefinger. "I've always wondered," she said, dipping the fingertip into her water glass, "if those noises coming through the speaker were Stuart eating on the air." She blotted the excess moisture with a third tissue and tossed all three into the trash can. "Now I know." Grinning, Casey propped her chin on a fist. "So, what are we gonna do about it, boss?"

Only one other person had ever called him 'boss,' and Marsha hadn't said it good-naturedly. He shoved away the bitter memory of his ex-fiancée and repeated Casey's question in his mind. "There's not much we *can* do about it. Stuart's a slob, but he's got a heart as big as his head." Jake shrugged. "We've all kind of learned to put up with his messes."

Casey's pucker slid to the right side of her face. "Is that so?" she challenged, a playful glint in her eyes.

Jake sat across from her, in one of the chairs reserved for guests, and pushed the swing-arm mike aside. He'd been reading faces for nearly a decade, a talent he'd honed to assist him in deciphering patients' responses to his questions. And unless he was mistaken, *this* pretty little face was gearing up to perform some sort of mischief.

"How'd you and Buddy meet?"

"I was catering a party at his house about two months ago. Afterwards, a couple of us were cleaning up the deck—and admiring his view of the bay—when he came out and started gabbing. Before I knew it, I'd practically told him my life's story—where I grew up, where I went to college, what I majored in. He said I had a lot on the ball. When he called last week to offer me the job—he sure is persuasive—anyway, he said I'd be a perfect replacement for Sam."

That remains to be seen, Jake thought. But he smiled politely and said, "What *did* you major in?"

"Actually, I double-majored—Education and Home Economics."

She tucked a lock of hair behind her ear, and Jake added "pretty ears" to his list. If he was aware the list had become lopsided in favor of the "plus" side, it didn't show on his own face.

"The original idea," Casey said, a forefinger in the air, "was to teach Home Ec at the high school level. Only—"

She blushed. The last woman to do that in his presence was his mom, who'd blamed her red cheeks on a menopausal hot flash. Jake thought Casey's flush was charming. His grin broadened. "Only, what?"

"Only I found out there was a lot more money in cooking than in teaching it. I started working for my sister's catering company, and—" She held out her hands, palms up, and left Jake to figure out the rest of the story.

"Why did you need 'a lot' of money?"

Casey's friendly grin took on a "just for company" edge. "This and that," she said after a moment of thought.

What is it with women? he asked himself. *Why do they* all *need to have secrets?* Well, he'd been down that road, had crashed headfirst into heartache, and didn't intend to go in that direction ever again. "Covert" became the first item on the "minus" side of his list.

Jake stood and walked around to the other side of the console. "Sam agreed to stick around, train you, at least for a while, right?"

She waved his concerns away. "We went over a few

things before you arrived." With a nod, Casey indicated the door. "Didn't you pass him on your way in?"

Jake found himself looking in the direction she'd nodded. "No, I didn't see him," he complained. "The traitor," he muttered.

Her brow furrowed. "You sound as though you expect the ship to sink."

His mouth formed a tight line. "That depends on—" *On you, Casey Wallace,* he started to say. How would he pick up, monitor, and log phone calls, listen to and answer callers' questions, and read "live commercial" blurbs, when his so-called producer had no more than—

Jake ground his molars together in an attempt to summon self-control. "Exactly how much time *did* Sam spend with you?"

Casey pursed her lips and narrowed one eye. "Couple of hours, give or take thirty minutes."

Shaking his head, he blew a stream of air through his teeth. *Couple of hours,* he repeated, *to learn what it took Sam two and a half decades to master. This oughta be a humdinger of a show.*

"So, what's the topic of the day, boss?"

Jake took a deep breath and pocketed both hands. "Hmmm?" he asked, distracted by means and methods by which he'd get even with Sam for leaving him in the lurch.

"Sam said you always come to work with a subject in mind that you'll focus on for the show."

"Oh. Topic." *How 'bout "Coping with Abandonment?" "Dealing With Desertion?" "Going On After*

Your Partner Has Gone On?" Another exasperated breath escaped his lungs before he snarled, "Ironically, today we're discussing 'The Unrealistic Expectations of New Partners'."

"Sam didn't give you much notice, did he?"

Jake ran a hand through his hair. "Called me at home last week, said he'd be finishing up the week, and—"

"And today's Friday," she finished.

Their eyes met. Was that understanding he read there? Compassion? *Naw, can't be,* he corrected. *She's a* woman. *And if you haven't learned anything else in your miserable life, McCafferty, it's that women are coldhearted!* "And today's Friday," he repeated, none too gently.

She raised both brows and folded her hands primly in front of her. "Well, boss, seems you bit into a wormy apple, all right. Sam should have given you more notice, but he didn't. The way I see it, we have two choices."

Casey held up a forefinger. "Stand around, wringing our hands," a second finger joined the first, "or dig in our heels and make the best of a bad situation." She raised her chin a bit to add, "Want me to start by plugging 'partnership' into the Internet to see what we come up with?"

Who does she think she is, Joyce Brothers? His life of late had made him the King of Coping Skills. If he needed advice, he'd go to a professional, not some young, inexperienced—

Jake gave some thought to telling her he had a third choice. He could call Sam and appeal to his loyalties

Linda,

These are Christian
mystery/fiction.

Easy to read - not too
heavy on religion - good
plots.

Mary Sim

and beg him to come back. But her last question side-tracked him. "Internet?"

Casey gave him a "how long have *you* been hibernating?" look. "The Internet. You know, on the computer? I can log on, type in your topic, and see what the rest of the world has to say about it." Shooting him a sideways glance, she headed for the monitor across the room. "Don't tell me you've never 'surfed the net'," she said, settling into the squeaky chair at the computer station.

He hooked both thumbs into his pants pockets. "The only surfing I've done was in Hawaii, 1972, on the back of my dad's rented board, in three feet of water."

Her merry giggle filled the studio. "You didn't enjoy it?"

He'd empathized with Papa Bear earlier, but now he felt like the Big Bad Wolf. *My, but what a lovely laugh you have, Casey*—he stopped himself midsmirk. *Watch it, McCafferty; this is how things got started with Marsha.* He crossed both arms over his chest. "Not particularly."

"Why not?"

He shrugged. "Couldn't swim at the time, for one thing; and there wasn't much call for seven-year-old wild surf-riders in Fargo, for another."

Casey tilted her head to ask, "Can you swim now?"

"I'm no Bruce Jenner, but—"

Again the delightful laughter floated around the room. "You mean, Mark Spitz?"

He hated to admit it, for fear of being branded un-American, but Jake had never been much of an Olympics fan. "Oh. Yeah. Spitz."

Smiling flirtatiously, she asked, "Do you like wild rides, now that you're all grown up?"

The Big Bad Wolf had obviously paid no attention to his earlier warning: *My, but you're a sassy li'l thing,* he told her silently. "They're all right, I guess. I earned myself a T-shirt once that says 'I Survived the Sooper-Dooper-Looper.' "

"I have a Hershey Park shirt, too! I guess while you were surfing with your dad in the Pacific, my pop and I were riding that roller coaster." Casey gave a proud little bob of her head. "I rode it six times in a row, I'll have you know."

Don't doubt it for a minute, he thought.

"Well, pull up a chair, boss. Don't worry—this ride won't earn you anything but information." With that, Casey leaned over the keyboard, chin-length hair all but hiding her face as her fingers pecked out their destination in cyberspace.

"Do me a favor, Casey?"

She never even looked up to say, "Sure, boss."

"Call me Jake. Call me Doc. Call me late for dinner, just don't call me 'boss,' okay?"

"No problem."

He wasn't even sure she'd heard him. *That must be how Beethoven looked,* Jake mused, *creating his great symphonies.* He pulled up a chair and sat down to watch her work. *Naw,* he added, chuckling to himself, *even on his best day, Beethoven couldn't have looked* this *good.*

Chapter 2

"I think you're doing okay—for a greenhorn."

Casey tucked in one corner of her mouth. "Just can't bring yourself to pay me a compliment, can you?"

Jake frowned. "What are you talking about? I compliment you plenty."

Casey snickered. "Yeah. Right. 'That's some tidy handwriting you've got there, Casey,'" she said in her best "Dr. Jake" impersonation. "'How 'bout another cup of that terrific coffee, Casey?'" She shook her head. "For your information, I only deliver the coffee, I don't brew it."

He felt the heat of embarrassment color his cheeks. Buddy had been right—Casey *did* have a lot on the ball. Granted, it would take time to get used to her way of doing things, but she *was* doing things, and doing them well. So why couldn't he admit it, to *her?*

"Well, you always put in just enough milk," he said in a lame response to her coffee comment, "and you've never spilled a drop that I know of."

"Good to the last drop, huh?"

"What?"

Scowling, she handed him a slip of paper. "According to that, we're working this weekend."

Jake took the memo from her and gave it a cursory

read. "Buddy signed us up to emcee the Independence Day festivities at the Inner Harbor." He met her eyes and grinned. "You up for that?"

"Up for what? Standing around, watching folks eat hot dogs, waiting for the fireworks display—"

It was Jake's turn to snicker. "Boy, have *you* got a lot to learn about a WCHK Fourth of July!" He gestured to the empty chair beside him, and once she'd filled it, explained: "We'll have to get there by noon, and we'll be there 'til midnight, at least. And knowing Buddy, we'll be responsible for setting up the booth." He leaned back in the chair and shook his head. "We'll hand out ball-point pens and refrigerator magnets 'til our fingertips are numb, all while shooting the breeze with passersby 'til we're hoarse, and then—"

"I think it sounds like fun."

He held up a hand to silence her. Jake propped both feet on the counter and linked his fingers behind his neck. "And then we'll introduce the rug rats who'll compete for the 'Baltimore's Most Beautiful Baby' trophy, and—"

Casey's brow furrowed. "Rug rats? Can't you think of anything nicer to call them besides—"

"And *we*," he interrupted her interruption, pointing first at her, at himself, back again, "have to pick the winner."

Jake watched as she rolled her big brown eyes.

"I can't pick one; I think *all* babies are beautiful."

"Trust me. A few will march by who don't deserve to—"

She scooted her chair closer to the computer terminal and typed in the topic of the day. "What's the matter? You don't like kids?"

Truth was, he liked them fine. Liked them a lot, in fact, and had once looked forward to the day when he'd have half a dozen of his own. Jake shrugged, feigning nonchalance. "Sure. I like 'em."

Casey harumphed. "Could have fooled me," she muttered, staring at the screen. Suddenly, a directory popped up on the monitor. "Wow," she said, "there's enough material here for *ten* shows. You want me to print all of it out?"

Jake walked around to her side of the counter. One hand on the back of her chair, the other flat on its arm, he squinted at the list.

But he couldn't read a single word. She smelled like apples and sunshine and line-dried sheets. Jake closed his eyes and made a feeble attempt at gathering his wits. "Use your own judgment," he answered. "You've been doing fine so far."

"Whoa," Casey proclaimed, turning to face him, "a genuine, bona fide compliment!" She began rummaging in a drawer. "I'm looking for a pen, so I can write this on the calendar."

"What," Jake retorted, "that I said you're doing fine—"

"For a greenhorn," their voices echoed.

Chuckling, and without giving it a second thought, he gave her hair what should have been a brotherly tousle. It turned out to be anything but.

Somewhere, deep in his subconscious, he'd been wondering if her hair would feel as thick and luxurious as it looked. It was, and then some. Reluctantly, he pulled his hand free from her soft, bouncy waves and stuffed it in his pocket.

Casey, concentrating on the pages sliding from the laser printer, seemed not to have noticed that he'd touched her at all. With a distracted pat, she repositioned the curls he'd mussed, and made a tidy stack of the information she'd gathered for him.

Something warned him that the feelings bubbling inside him, good as they felt now, were nothing but trouble waiting to happen. Practically from the moment he'd first set eyes on her—had it really been just three months ago?—he'd been biting back the compliments she so richly deserved, afraid they'd come out sounding like some schoolboy's crush-induced exaltation. If he had a nickel for every time he'd wanted to touch her hand, tuck a tendril of hair behind her ear, brush her rosy cheek with his fingertip, there'd be several dollars' worth of coins jangling in his pocket by now.

What's wrong *with you, McCafferty! You're a shrink; if* you *don't know better than to fraternize with an employee, who does!*

But Casey Wallace had quickly become far more than an employee. He thought about her day and night, it seemed. At first, he'd chalked it up to loneliness, since there hadn't been a woman in his life since Marsha left, a year ago last Valentine's Day. Oh, sure, he'd been out a few times, but never with the same woman twice, never more than once a month. "Physician heal thyself," Jesus had said. Well, shrink or not, he simply hadn't healed enough to risk giving his heart away, only to have it returned, mashed flat.

Yes, Casey was another matter entirely.

With seemingly little effort, she often made him laugh. In the past, it had been up to him to put the fun into his man-woman relationships, professional and personal. She'd done things for him, too, extra things that weren't part of her job description. Take the way she'd made it her business to know exactly how much cream he liked in his coffee, precisely where he preferred to keep the 'Lovesick Show' script on his desk, how many calls he could handle without getting a headache.

Right from the start, he'd felt comfortable around Casey, free to speak his mind without fear of recrimination or judgment. It was a good feeling—being liked for who he really was instead of his on-air persona. Gratitude had, on more than one occasion, made him want to wrap her in a hearty hug and—

"What're you staring at, Jake?"

"Hmmm? Oh, ah, sorry," he stammered, "was I?"

Casey nodded. "Lost in space," she exclaimed, then hummed the old TV program's theme song.

"You're too young to remember that show," he said, glad for the change of subject.

"So are you." She grinned, handing him the printouts. "Reruns—the Eighth Wonder of the World."

Man, but she's adorable, he told himself, pretending to read the data. *How are you gonna continue working with this woman, feeling the way you do about her?*

Jake watched Casey putter around the engineering console, preparing for the day's show. *And just how do you feel about her?* She hadn't turned off the intercom button that allowed them to communicate while 'Lovesick' was on the air, and he could hear her in there, humming softly to herself.

She's adorable, smart, funny, with the voice of an angel and eyes you could drown in, he thought, a wistful smile plastered across his face. *She's about as perfect as a woman can get,* he admitted, *from the top of her brown-haired head to the toes of her size five feet.*

Now she was lightly tapping a pencil against her chin as she read something that put a scowl on her face. *Adorable,* he repeated, *but. . .how do you* feel *about her?*

A somber expression replaced his smile as Jake acknowledged what he'd been fighting since shaking her hand, three months earlier:

You're falling for Casey Wallace.

❧

Since Jake had been nothing but professional since her first day as producer of "The Lovesick Show," Casey didn't know what to make of the way he'd run his fingers through her hair. She could have chalked off the affectionate gesture as a casual pat on the head, something he might do with a friend's cute kid or a well-behaved nephew—if it hadn't been accompanied by that little-boy-lost expression.

If anybody had asked her—and thankfully, no one had —she'd have been forced to admit that she was attracted to him. And Casey knew she wasn't the only woman who felt that way about Dr. Jake McCafferty. He shrugged off the amorous attentions of the receptionist and the saleswomen, but it seemed to Casey that something sizzled between Jake and Lucy, Buddy's secretary. Whenever the tall blond was around, he stood straighter, smiled wider, and laughed louder, like Charlie Brown showing off for the little red-haired girl.

Whenever Casey spied a group of women, chances were good that Jake would be in the middle of the crowd, inspiring girlish giggles from mere youngsters, middle-aged matrons, and blue-haired grandmothers alike. Women were naturally drawn to him, and who could blame them? Tall and muscular, with flashing, thick-lashed green eyes and a head full of wavy, cinnamony hair, he could have been a *GQ* model if he'd had a mind to.

But he was more than handsome, so much more. From the very start, Casey had sensed something good and decent in him, and time had increased her admiration, because no matter how ridiculous his callers' problem sounded, Jake treated every predicament with seriousness and respect.

It had surprised her that his on- and off-air personalities were so different. During the show, he fast-talked, used five-syllable words, said things like "hmmmm" and "ahhhh" and "interesting". When the mike was "live," he nodded and frowned, tapped a beefy forefinger on the desktop. But once the red-on-black "On Air" light above his head dimmed, Jake became his true self.

She'd have chosen the real man over the radio man

113

any day. Because, for one thing, his smile seemed to generate from deep in his soul, surging up and out through those dazzling green eyes like a current of electricity.

Casey stirred sugar into her black raspberry tea and held the spoon up, letting it drip into her mug as she stared out the window above the sink. Two purple finches peeped and fluttered to see which would control the bird feeder's quadruple perches.

She'd heard talk around the water cooler about Jake's country house. Did he, too, have a feeder outside his window, where he whiled away the hours, watching the birds compete for sunflower and thistle seeds?

She wondered if his house was as eclectic as the collection on his desktop: A green-shaded brass lamp stood on one corner, a variegated ivy plant on the other. Between them he kept a framed photo of a golden retriever, a wolf calendar, a chunk of fulgurite, and eight polished rocks in an onyx box.

A chickadee flew in, nabbed a seed and carried it to a nearby branch, setting the finches into a new feathery flurry. The activity roused Casey from her mental wanderings, and she dropped the spoon into the sink. *He occupies far too many of your thoughts,* she scolded herself, *because if he's thinking of any woman, it's probably that Viking, Lucy.*

She glanced at the clock, and despite the warning to herself, the thought flitted through her mind: *Half an hour 'til you leave for the Inner Harbor; forty-five minutes 'til you see him again.*

The chickadee returned for another seed, hid behind

114

a clump of leaves, and pecked the shell to reach the tender meat inside. He was so intent on getting his prize that he never noticed the jay that soared in and perched atop the feeder. "My territory," the blue bully seemed to say, reminding her of the way Buddy's secretary behaved when Jake was nearby.

Jealousy jolted through her veins. Narrowing her eyes and lips, she dumped her tea down the drain. *If he wants a woman like that—all flash and no substance—more power to him!* She stuffed her mug into the dishwasher. *Get a grip, girl,* she thought, closing its door, *before you make a complete fool of yourself—again.*

Already sour thoughts now turned corrosive as she recalled how Marlow had pursued her, like a house cat stalks a mouse. He had taken her to Baltimore's best restaurants, to the opera, the symphony, the ballet. He brought her Godiva chocolates and long-stemmed roses. Marlow refused to buy greeting cards with preprinted verses, saying, as he looked adoringly into her eyes, that he preferred to create his own poetry to express his love for her. His actions and his words gave Casey the impression he thought she'd hung the moon. So was it any surprise when, two Valentine's Days ago, she expected him to pop the question?

He'd told her to wear her best dress, and handed her a bouquet of roses when he picked her up at five-thirty in a rented limousine. Marlow slipped the maitre d' a twenty-dollar bill to seat them at a corner table overlooking the Chesapeake Bay at The Narrows in Annapolis. The waiter hadn't even delivered their appetizers before Marlow placed a small, black velvet box on the white linen table-cloth.

"I wanted tonight to be perfect," he said, smiling, his hand atop hers, "because you're so special to me." The smile had faded as his hand covered the box. "I. . . I don't know quite how to say this, but. . ."

Casey remembered the way her heart had thumped as he struggled to choose the right romantic words. Though he'd been wooing her, so it seemed, for over a year, in those last few months, Marlow hadn't left one sonnet on her answering machine, hadn't given her flowers, and she'd thought perhaps his ardor had cooled, his interest had waned, once the mouse had been caught. But obviously, she told herself as he stumbled to phrase his proposal in just the right way, she'd been wrong.

"I feel so close to you," he'd said. "You've become such a dear, dear friend. . ."

She supposed friendship *was* an important part of a good marriage, but found herself hiding a frown, because should the subject be such a big part of his marriage *proposal?*

"I find myself wanting to share everything with you, Casey," Marlow had continued, "all the good, all the bad, all the joys. . ."

He opened the box, exposed the beautiful, glittering solitaire diamond that nestled in a bed of white satin. "I've met someone in Italy—"

"You mean, all those nights you weren't available, you were in *Italy?*"

Marlow had neatly sidestepped the question by

saying, "She's very special, and I'm going to ask her to marry me tonight. It's Valentine's Day, and I thought it would be romantic if—"

Casey hadn't heard a word after "special." She felt as if someone had picked her up out of the red leather wingback chair in that fancy restaurant and chucked her headfirst into the Chesapeake, and from there, under the cool bay waters, his voice came to her: "I'm going to ask her to marry me."

Trembling from the mother of pearl comb in her hair to the heels on her pumps, she'd risen slowly, tossed her napkin on the tabletop. "Excuse me," she'd said, hoping he hadn't heard the tremor in her voice, and walked purposefully toward the maitre d' station. "Would you call me a taxi, please?"

The tuxedoed fellow had quirked a brow and shot a quick glance at Marlow. Casey followed the man's gaze. Marlow was looking at her now, a sneer curling his upper lip, a glint in his eye. He knew exactly what he had done to her, his expression told her, and he was enjoying it.

"Of course, miss," the maitre d' said. "Would you care to wait in the lounge until it arrives?"

"No." *Too public,* she thought, *and I want to hide.* "I believe I'll just wait in the ladies' room."

Those next ten minutes were the longest, most humiliating of Casey's life to date. *Valentine's Day,* she'd told herself then, *is for the birds!*

Thankfully, she wouldn't have to face another hearts and flowers celebration for seven whole months. And if God and the angels had heard her prayers, this one would be easier than the last.

Slamming her front door behind her, she put Jake's tender touch out of her mind, and headed for the harbor.

Chapter 3

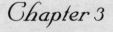

"And we're live today from Baltimore's Inner Harbor," Jake said into the microphone, smiling at the audience that had gathered in front of WCHK's booth, "so if you're 'Lovesick,' give us a call at four-one-oh, five-five-five, one-two-one-two."

His gaze locked onto Casey's, and he raised both brows—his silent signal that he wanted to know how many callers were on hold. Sometimes, it amazed her, the way they had so quickly learned to read one another's thoughts with a glance, a grin, the quirk of a brow. She held up two fingers and mouthed "Line One."

Her pulse rate doubled when he winked and sent her that flirty grin. *Better watch out,* she warned herself, *he could do more damage to your heart than Marlow ever could have.*

In the studio, Jake usually wore Italian loafers, jeans and a collarless shirt with one of his many sports coats. Today, in honor of the holiday, he'd chosen dark blue shorts, a red T-shirt, and well-worn Converse sneakers, making him look like an oversized kid—or an American flag. Casey made a mental note of the way his hair gleamed in the sunlight, the way his smile seemed wider, more carefree under the cloudless blue sky. His amber-lensed sunglasses blocked the bright light, but not so much that she couldn't see his long-lashed sea-green eyes.

Oh, how she loved those eyes! One minute, they flashed with wit and intelligence, the next, they glowed with passion as he delved into a phone-in patient's relationship problems. He was frowning now, nodding with understanding as the caller on line one explained the way her boyfriend had emptied her bank account, and disappeared. "Chalk it up as an expensive life lesson," he advised; "you can always earn back the money, but self-confidence, once it's gone, is hard to replace."

He's wearing that "been there-done that" expression again, she noted. A lot of the time, as she listened to his repartee with callers, Casey got the feeling Jake's counsel came, not from some highbrow psychiatric manual, but from personal experience. And it was *how* he dispensed the guidance, rather than the words themselves, that made her believe he'd been deeply wounded by love —and fairly recently, if what she read on his face was accurate. *Ironic,* she thought, *that Jake is "lovesick," too.*

The station went into commercial. Next up, a traffic report, then straight into the news. He had ten minutes to kill before having to return to the mike. Jake held out his hand to her. "Let's get out of this hot sun."

He'd taken to doing that a lot lately, and pleasant as it was, Casey didn't for the life of her know what to make of it. She hesitated, but only for a second, before giving him her hand.

"I saw a lemonade stand a couple of booths down," he said, licking his lips. "How 'bout I buy you a glass?"

Unconsciously, she licked her own. "Sounds great."

They walked along in companionable silence for a moment or two before he stopped. "Are you planning to go to Buddy's party after the fireworks?"

She shrugged. "Hadn't given it much thought, really."

Jake squeezed her hand. "Say you'll stay. I more or less have to go, since a couple of my sponsors will be there. Sure would be nice if I could look over and see a friendly face across the room from time to time."

A friendly face. Marlow had called her his friend. Casey swallowed. She couldn't bear another humiliation like that. *C'mon, Case, face facts,* she told herself, *Jake hasn't bought you flowers and candy, whispered poems into your ears, made you feel like you hung the moon.* But if he *had,* she admitted, she wouldn't have minded a bit. The gentle touches he'd been giving her lately didn't mean a thing. *He doesn't* want *anything more than a friendship with you.*

"So, what do you say? Will you stay?"

Casey's gaze slid slowly from his lips to his high cheekbones to his lightly freckled nose, and settled on those glittering green eyes. How could a thirty-two-year-old man so resemble an innocent boy? How could she say no, if he continued to look at her like *that?*

Casey sighed. "Where's the party supposed to be held?"

"On top of the Science Center." He wiggled his eyebrows. "Buddy says they're having hot crab dip—"

Why in the world had she told him about her weakness for crab meat? "I'd give my eye teeth for anything

121

with crab in it," she'd admitted at lunch, no more than a week ago. Her tongue made another swipe across her lips. *Sure,* she answered silently, *I'll go to the party with my* friend, *and we'll dip Triscuits in the hot crab dip* together.

"They say the view of the harbor is great from the Science Center roof." Jake tilted his head slightly, raised both brows, and looked at her from under those long, lush lashes of his.

She'd known for some time that what she felt for Jake was more than a workplace crush. *This is the "head over heels" stuff, and when you start singin' the blues, you'll have nobody to blame but yourself.* "I'll go," she said, "if you promise to walk me to my car afterwards." She thrust a thumb over her shoulder. "I had to park blocks away. I may as well have driven to Pennsylvania and hiked south."

Still holding her hand, Jake managed to bow from the waist and, with a grand sweep of his free arm, said, "Escorting you will be a pleasure, m'lady."

Oh, to be able to bracket that face with both hands and plant a big kiss on that sweet, smiling face! She took another deep breath. It may well be unrequited love, but Jake had not done or said anything to inspire it.

He squeezed her hand just then, and leaned down to press a soft kiss to her cheek. "Thanks, Case. You're a lifesaver."

Or had he?

The spot where his lips had touched her skin tingled. She resisted the urge to lay her fingertips over it, close her eyes and caress it to preserve it in her memory.

Casey sighed again. "Guess we'd better get that lemonade and head back to the booth. Tim is probably halfway through the news report by now."

He glanced at his watch. "You're right," Jake said, grimacing. "Let's make tracks."

And with that, he darted forward, tugging her along behind him like an errant child. "Two large lemonades," he said at the counter, "with extra ice and a slice of lemon." He turned to Casey. "Want a peppermint stick in yours?"

Unable to speak, she smiled feebly and shook her head. Why did she suddenly feel like she might start to cry?

But she knew why. *Because you're falling in love with the "Lovesick" doctor, like every other woman in Baltimore. How appropriate.*

Lucy chose that precise moment to strut toward them. In her cutoffs and off-the-shoulder peasant blouse, Lucy reminded Casey of Daisy Mae.

Lucy's eyes locked onto Jake's as she sidled up to him. "Hi, Jake," she purred. Turning her blond mane, her eyes narrowed as she added flatly, "Casey."

Her "get lost" clearly delivered, Lucy turned back to Jake who stood blinking and slack-jawed, a paper cup in each hand.

"I've been looking for you two—ooh, lemonade! May I?" Lucy helped herself to a long sip. "Mmm. That *is* delicious, isn't it, Jake?"

How would he know? was Casey's silent question.

He hasn't had a chance to taste it! She was reminded of her moments at the kitchen sink that morning, when the blue jay flew in and took over the bird feeder.

Casey relieved Jake of the other cup. "Thanks for the lemonade."

"Hey, what's your hurry?" he asked as she turned to leave.

"I. . .I'm suddenly feeling too much like a chick-adee."

The look on his face told her he didn't have a clue what she was talking about. She didn't understand it well enough *herself* to explain it. "See you back at the booth," she said, and left them standing there in the sun.

"A chickadee?" she heard Lucy ask.

"Chickadee?" Jake echoed.

Despite herself, Casey grinned.

❧

The full-color picture on the "Today" section of the *Baltimore Sun* nearly took up the whole top half of the front page. It was a profile shot of Jake, beaming like a proud papa as he held a giggling two-year-old above his head. The caption read, " 'Baltimore's Most Beautiful Baby' adopts Dr. Jake."

The report explained how and when the contest had originated, and that the winner received not only a toddler-sized trophy but a ten thousand dollar scholarship to the University of Maryland as well. Of the fifteen hundred or so words that told the story, one line stood out: "They need to change the title," the reporter quoted Jake, " 'cause, like my producer Casey Wallace says, '*All* babies are beautiful.' "

She'd accused him of not liking kids when he'd called them "rug rats." But as Casey had watched him during that competition, she realized nothing could have been further from the truth.

Like a department store Santa, Jake had taken each contestant in his arms and settled them on his knee. There hadn't been a single tear, a quivering lower lip, not one attempt to wriggle free of his embrace. The children seemed to sense, as he held their eyes with his steady, caring gaze and spoke in that soft, reassuring voice, that he genuinely enjoyed their nearness. They left the stage carrying a "Barney" coloring book and a small box of crayons, purchased at Wal-Mart by the "Lovesick" doctor himself, and Jake left with one hundred twenty sticky kisses stuck to his cheeks and chin—Popsicle-and-fruit-punch-red proof that ten dozen kids had fallen in love with Dr. Jake.

She didn't know how long she'd been sitting there, staring at the photograph when the trill of the telephone interrupted her thoughts.

"Hey," came the now-so-familiar voice, "how would you like to see an Orioles' game with me today?"

Casey was still holding the "Today" section, still looking at his picture when she grinned and asked, "What time is kickoff?"

His deep chuckle grated into her ear. "Kickoff, ha! You're a nut," Jake said. "Game starts at one thirty-five. I'll pick you up at noon, so we'll have plenty of time to find a parking space and a couple of Super Dogs."

"They're calling for rain," she warned.

"Yeah? So what? Sweet as you are, you're not made of sugar; you won't melt."

"I suppose I could wear a hat, my slicker, carry an umbrella—"

She heard his snort, and knew from experience it had accompanied a slanted, dimpled grin. "Gee, if you hide yourself under all of *that,* how's anybody gonna know I took the most gorgeous girl in Baltimore to the ball game?"

Casey's heart beat like a parade drum. She was tempted to say, "Another compliment? The calendar's gettin' mighty full." Instead, she said, "I'll be ready at noon."

"How will I recognize you—under all that rain gear, I mean?"

I'll be the one with my heart on my sleeve, she told him silently. "Maybe Lucy will loan me her Fourth of July outfit. You're sure to recognize me in *that.*"

She listened to the seemingly endless pause. *Smart, Case,* she scolded herself, *real smart. Now you've gone and* reminded *him of her!*

His voice came pleadingly into her ear. "Do me a favor, Casey?"

For you, she thought, biting her lower lip, *anything.* "Shoot."

"Just be yourself, always. Promise me, okay?"

Casey held the phone away for a moment, stared at the ear end of the receiver. Had what he'd said meant what she hoped it meant? *Please, Lord,* she prayed, *let it be true.*

"Besides, Lucy's outfit would hang like a potato sack on you."

You sure do have a talent for taking the air out of a girl's party balloon, she thought dismally, shaking her head. *Why do you have to balance every compliment with one of those frustrating qualifiers!*

But then, she had no proof the favor he'd asked had *been* a compliment. "See you at noon, then," she said. "And Jake?"

"Hmmmm?"

"Thanks for the invite."

Another deafening pause. What sort of insult would balance the compliment that invitation had been? "Hey," he said, "I'm a Birds fan from wa-a-ay back when. I'd rather die than let a Camden Yards ticket go to waste."

Nodding, Casey rolled her eyes. "Few things in life are as despicable as waste."

"That's just one of the things I love about you, Case, you're so practical and down-to-earth! I'll be there at twelve, straight up," he said, and hung up.

Casey focused on the first half of his sentence. "That's just one of the things I love about you, Case." She pressed a palm to her chest in an attempt to still her fluttering heart. Then, grinning like a lovesick fool, she zeroed in on a single word:

Love.

Chapter 4

Jake stood in the foyer, slack-jawed and wide-eyed, surveying the damages. An overturned philodendron and a toppled candlestick lay on the antique telephone table near the door. The ancient Persian rug, a flea market find, was heaped at the foot of the curving staircase, all but hiding an oval-framed portrait of his great-grandfather.

He held out his arm to bar her from entering, but Casey pushed past him. At first sight of the disarray, she gasped and pressed her hands to her cheeks. After a moment, she lay both hands on his forearm. "Oh, Jake," she said, looking up into his face, "I'm so sorry."

He wanted to hug her—tell her it was all right—because she seemed even more distraught by the destruction than he was. Jake shrugged instead.

Casey stepped away from the rubble, grabbed the gleaming brass doorknob. "Well, at least they didn't damage the door to get in," she observed, opening and closing it. Propping a fist on her hip, she squinted one eye and nodded. "They must have come in through a window. It happened to my sister a while back. Her husband battled the insurance company for weeks to get a replacement."

"Who's 'th—"

"It's just unforgivable, the way they tear things up. Isn't it enough they violate your space, without—"

"Who's 'they?' " he managed to get in.

She looked at him as if he'd just popped out of a fire-red flying saucer. "Why, the burglars, of course." Casey started to pick up the remnants of a shattered figurine, then carefully put each piece back where she'd found it. "I'd better not touch anything until the police get here. They might want to dust for prints."

"Burglars?" he repeated, chuckling good-naturedly. "Ruben, here, looks mighty guilty. I'd be willing to bet he had something to do with it."

The golden retriever sat at Jake's feet, raising first one, then the other doggy brow. He whimpered.

Jake squatted and slung one arm over his shaggy pal. His free hand lifted the dog's chin, to assure eye contact. "So tell me, Rube, was it something from your puppy-hood that caused you to act out this way?"

Casey giggled and Ruben cocked his head, as if to say, "Yeah, and who psychoanalyzes *you?*" then slathered his master's cheek with a sloppy kiss.

A loud crash destroyed the first lighthearted moment they'd enjoyed since coming into the house. Casey ducked behind Jake and Ruben got onto all fours, head low and ears flat as he aimed a low, menacing growl at the hall-way.

"Easy, boy," Jake whispered, rising slowly.

Jake moved slowly toward the curved archway be-tween the foyer and the parlor, crouching slightly. He turned to warn Casey to stay back. She'd been standing so close, he nearly knocked her over in the process. Jake grabbed her shoulders to steady her. "Stay behind me," he whispered, touching a fingertip to her nose, "I mean it."

She clicked her heels together. "Yessir!" she whispered back, and snapped off a smart salute.

Shaking his head, he eased into the parlor. There, as in the foyer, the signs of a destructive intruder were everywhere. Lamps teetered precariously on their tables, books and photo albums had been unshelved, sofa cushions and pillows were scattered across the oval area rug, a section of brocade drapery hung by a single hook above the French doors, the hem puddling on the hardwood.

From the corner of his eye, Jake caught a glimpse of Casey, fingertips hanging from her lower teeth, eyes wide with disbelief. *Lord help me,* he prayed, *she's even adorable when she's terrified.*

But he couldn't comfort her right now. Right now he had to find the miserable jerk who was responsible for this mayhem—and the crashing sound. He looked around.

Nothing.

Jake strained his ears, listening for footsteps, whisper-soft breathing, anything that might lead him to the intruder.

Again, nothing.

And then he noticed that Ruben's ears had pricked forward. Instinct made him crouch lower as the dog put his nose to the ground, sniffing out the bad guy's trail.

He skirted the room weaving between chairs and sofas, ducking under tables, climbing over fallen knickknacks. Jake grabbed the poker from the hearth, and followed him, wrought-iron weapon raised and at the ready.

With a clumsy lurch, the dog dove under the highboy Jake had rebuilt to house stereo equipment. The retriever's rear end swung to and fro like a furry pendulum as his thick, golden tail swept back and forth across the floor.

"What is it, boy?" he asked, on his hands and knees beside the pet. "What's under there?"

Casey, from the other side of Ruben, squinted into the darkness. "Well, at least we know it isn't packin' heat," she said, sighing with relief.

He straightened his arms to look at her over Ruben's back. " 'Packin' heat?' " he echoed. "You read too many mysteries during your lunch breaks," he pointed out. "Maybe you ought to switch to something lighter. Romance, maybe."

Rolling her eyes, she waved his comment away.

The thing under the cabinet moved slightly, drawing their attention back to the floor. Jake and Casey hunkered down and looked into a pair of beady black eyes. The gray-furred rodent cowered against the wall, trembling paws pressed tight to its hairy chest. "Ruben," Jake grumped, "how'd a *squirrel* get in the house?"

Ruben licked his lips and answered with a quiet snap of his jaws.

"Your mama must have forgotten to teach you to fight fair," Casey said, ruffling his thick coat. "Can't you

131

see the poor thing is only a tenth your size?" She
grabbed Ruben's collar and stood. "Come on, ya big
bully. Let's put you some place where you can't do the
li'l fella any harm."

Jake scrambled to his feet, prepared to rescue Casey
from the jaws of his beast. Most retrievers were friendly,
outgoing animals who welcomed each guest like a member of the family. Not Ruben. Ever since Jake had rescued the dog from the pound, he'd been a one-man animal. As long as folks kept their hands to themselves,
they were safe, but the moment anyone made a move to
touch him—

Jake's eyes widened in amazement as Ruben flashed
Casey his best doggy smile and trotted willingly along
beside her.

"Okay if I put him in the kitchen?" she asked, pointing to the door across the hall.

Jake shrugged. "Well, ah, sure, I guess." But he
tagged along, just in case Ruben returned to his normal
behavior and decided to sample a taste of Casey.

His worries, he soon discovered, were well-founded.
Ruben got a taste of her, all right.

"Ugh," she said, giggling as Ruben slobbered all
over her face, "haven't you ever heard of an invention
called a toothbrush?" She gave him a friendly hug. "And
something called toothpaste? They're making it special
for doggies these days, you know."

She stepped back into the hall, secured the lower
half of the Dutch door behind them. Paws on top of the
gate, Ruben whimpered. "Now, don't get all wimpy and

whiny on me," she said, patting his head. "We'll just be in the next room, trying to catch Rocky the Break-in Squirrel."

Jake had crossed both arms over his chest and leaned against the wall while she chitchatted with his dog.

She seemed startled when she turned and found him staring at her. "What's that half-baked smirk all about?" she asked, hands on her hips.

"It's not smart to get so friendly with strange dogs, y'know. He might have—"

"I've never been the type who judges a book by its cover," she said, one brow high on her forehead.

He'd been all set to give her a stern lecture about the dangers of touching unfamiliar pets. He rubbed his temples. "What on earth has judgment got to do with anything?"

Casey shrugged, and when she did, a shining auburn curl fell over one brown eye. She shook it back into place. "Well, just because *you're* strange doesn't necessarily mean you'll have a *dog* that's strange. I simply meant I was willing to reserve judgment until—"

Jake rolled his eyes, held his hands up in mock surrender. "Sorry I asked," he said, smiling.

She bobbed her head and grinned like the Cheshire cat, as if she'd won a major victory. Odd thing was, he hadn't realized they'd been in a contest. *You just gotta love her!* He resisted another of those urges to pull her into his arms, squeeze her tight, and lay a big kiss on her lips.

Dear God in heaven, he prayed, *help me, 'cause I'm*

getting in deeper and deeper here.

Jake fished the phone book out of the telephone stand and looked up the number for Howard County's Animal Control.

"Well," Casey said, "since we didn't find any blood, we can assume there wasn't a homicide committed in here after all, so—"

Still pressing the receiver to his ear, Jake grinned. "You sound disappointed."

Feigning a malicious sneer, she shook a fist under his nose. "That can be remedied." Without skipping a beat, she completed her sentence. "I may as well start cleaning up this mess."

"Wait, and I'll—"

"What if Ruben jumps over the gate and cuts a paw on the broken glass? *Then* you'd see some blood."

He'd started to tell her that if she'd wait 'til he got off the phone, he'd help, but the moment he opened his mouth to speak, a human voice broke through the recording he'd been listening to. Briefly, Jake outlined his dilemma for the Animal Control agent. Nodding, and slipping in an occasional "mmm-hmm" and "yes, but," he listened.

After a moment, he scowled and flexed his jaw. "I'm a doctor. I understand what 'euthanasia' means." His free hand high above his head, Jake growled. "What I *don't* get is why you say you'll kill the—"

He went back to nodding and mmm-hmmming. "So let me get this straight," he said after a bit, "you're telling me that although you're understaffed and underfunded you're gonna call in an off-duty officer and pay him overtime to give this squirrel a hundred dollar dose of death, rather than put him in a cage and turn him loose in the woods?"

More mmm-hmmming and nodding. "All right, then, *I'll* catch it. And if the little varmint bites me—" He stared, sneering, at the earpiece. "I don't believe it; the jerk hung up on me!" He slammed the phone down so hard, the fallen candlestick rolled onto the floor. When he bent to retrieve it, he thumped his head on the table.

"Ow!" he complained, grimacing.

Casey was beside him in a heartbeat. "Jake, are you all right?"

"Yeah," he grumbled, standing as he fingered the injury, "it's nothing."

"Let me be the judge of that; you can't even see it," she scolded in a motherly tone. Standing on tiptoe, she gave the injury a careful once-over. "Well," she said, standing back, "it's not bleeding, but you'll probably have a gorgeous goose egg in the morning."

Jake pressed his palm to the sore spot, and winced. Casey smiled. Then giggled.

"What's so funny?" he asked, checking his hand for blood. "And be careful how you answer," he warned, grinning, " 'cause I know a little something about—"

"The hard knocks of others?" Then, "I'm not laughing at *you*—exactly. It's just that, well, Stuart told me you gave him a house tour awhile back; he said it was one of the most boring experiences of his entire life." The giggle became a full-fledged laugh. "I've been to Bruce

Willis movies that weren't this exciting and we haven't even left the foyer yet!"

Her laughter was contagious, and soon they were both blotting tears of enjoyment from their eyes. "What a perfect end to a perfect day," she said.

If he were honest with himself, he'd have to say it was Casey who'd made the day perfect. He loved the way she'd gotten involved in the ball game, throwing her little fist into the air when Ripken snagged a ball on the third baseline, chanting "Moose, Moose, Moose" with the crowd when Mussina missed delivering a no-hitter by just one hit. She was on her feet a dozen times an inning, cheering the team. How she managed to stand at all amazed him, since she'd put away two cotton candies, a Super Dog, and a plate of nachos before the seventh inning stretch.

Jake had been going to Orioles' games since he was old enough to walk. They were a friendly lot, those O's fans, but he didn't remember having as many conversations with seatmates as he had that afternoon. And every powwow had been incited—and encouraged to continue —by Casey Wallace. Everyone who'd been sitting within earshot delivered their own version of "See ya, Casey!" when the game ended.

"I'll give you this much," she said, still trying to catch her breath, "you sure know how to show a girl a good time."

Jake looked into eyes still damp from tears of laughter. Oh, how he loved her big brown eyes. How many times had he told himself a man could get lost in them?

Too many times. His gaze traveled to her sweet, smiling lips.

When she'd stepped up to inspect his injury, Casey had gotten close enough to kiss. His arms had slid around her as if he'd been doing it most of his life. Holding her close seemed as normal as inhaling, as natural as exhaling.

Now, she seemed to sense that his mood had changed, and tilted her head up to study his face. What made her paint those pretty lips with the tip of her tongue, he wondered. Instinct? Or the same yearning that burned in him?

She was still close enough to kiss.

And so he kissed her.

"What about Ruben?" she asked when they came up for air.

Jake nuzzled his chin into her soft waves. "He's fine."

"But he's whining; maybe he needs to go outside."

He couldn't hear anything over his own heartbeat, hammering in his ears. "He's got a doggy door."

Jake held her face in his hands, his thumbs drawing slow, lazy circles on her cheeks. *Soft as satin,* he told himself, *smooth as silk.* His hands crept back, then up, until his fingers disappeared into her mass of thick, coppery curls. Then closing his eyes, he pulled her closer, so close that not even the summery breeze filtering in through the front screen door could have passed between them.

He'd held other women in his arms, but it had never felt like this, had never felt so good, so *right.*

Jake looked into the face so near his own, into eyes

that usually flashed with wit and high-spiritedness—eyes that now glowed with warmth and tenderness for *him.*

Pressing a gentle kiss to her forehead, he looked at the ceiling. *Dear God Almighty,* he prayed, *I know You've promised to give me the strength to survive anything, no matter how painful.* He thought for a fleeting moment of Marsha, and how she'd so callously battered his heart. *If it's all the same to You, I'd just as soon not go through that again. I want to do Your will; if Casey isn't the woman You intend me to spend my life with, show me a sign and then hand me a dose of superhuman strength, so I'll be able to live without her.*

Jake held his breath, hoping the Lord's answer would be the one he wanted to hear. He waited, listening for God's response as the grandfather clock in the hall counted the seconds—*tick, tick, tick.*

His grandma used to say, "Sometimes *no* answer is God's answer."

Heart swelling with newfound joy, he felt a need to celebrate.

And so he kissed her again.

Her voice was shaky and husky when she asked, "What about. . .what about the squirrel?"

He dotted her face with kisses. "Let him get his own girl."

"Jake," she said, a half-grin on her face.

Chuckling, he said, "He found his way in, he'll find his way out—eventually."

"But. . . ," she mumbled as he kissed the corner of

her mouth, "he's probably *crawling* with fleas and lice and mites and—"

"Aw, they're small. How much damage could they do?"

Casey pressed her palms against his chest, held him at arm's length. The maternal tone she'd used earlier returned when she said, "They could infest *Ruben.*"

At the mention of his name, the dog started yowling and scratching at the Dutch door that held him prisoner in the kitchen.

"Now look at what you've gone and done," Jake admonished, a teasing glint in his eyes. "I know that hound; we won't get a minute's peace until I let him out."

Her eyes widened. "But you can't do that. The squirrel. . ." She bit her lower lip. "Actually," she said, a finger in the air, "I haven't heard a peep from the parlor in awhile." She wriggled free of Jake's embrace and darted through the doorway.

He stared after her for a moment, then followed, found her on her hands and knees in front of the highboy.

"Well, he's not under here," she said, sitting back on her heels. "We can only hope you're right, that he traced his steps backward and found his way out."

Still on her knees, she planted her hands on her hips. "Now, about this mess; if you'll get me a big trash bag, I'll help you clean up." She began scooping up photographs that had fallen from an unshelved album. Casey frowned slightly as she looked at one picture, then rose and carried it to the lamp, as if to view it in a better light.

"Who's the blond?"

He joined her near the window. Dread drummed in his heart when he saw which picture she held—the one taken at his parents' house, the Christmas before Marsha dumped him. What would Casey think if she knew how he'd let that woman dupe him?

"She's my ex-fiancée." Jake flushed, jamming his hands into his pockets. "Well, that's not entirely true. I was about to pop the question when she dumped me," he corrected, shrugging, "so I guess she's just an ex-girlfriend."

Casey tucked in her chin. "Doesn't look like 'just' *anything* to me. Why, she's stuck to you like Super Glue." She pointed at the photo, where Marsha had draped herself over him like a six-foot afghan.

He didn't want to dwell on his past. But if he knew Casey, she wasn't about to let this drop, at least not yet. To his amazement, she handed him the picture and walked away without another word on the subject. Standing amid the squirrel debris, she dusted her hands together and pursed her lips. "So, where's that trash bag?"

Chapter 5

W hat *is it about you,* Casey asked herself, that makes you choose men who are all wrong for you? She rolled onto her back, stared at the ceiling. "You didn't ask for God's guidance," she said into the darkness. "That's why you kept picking losers."

Sighing, she rolled onto her side. She couldn't very well pray for God's guidance in a relationship with Jake, could she? He was her *boss,* for goodness' sake! And besides, it was perfectly obvious that, despite the slow, easy mood of his cozy house, he was a fast-lane man. If the way he reacted when women gathered around him wasn't proof enough, the picture of him with that big blond sure was!

On her back again, Casey tucked her hands under her head and tried to focus on the shadows dancing across the ceiling. With every soft sigh of the late summer breeze, the leafy branches swayed outside her window, like ballerinas on a stage, their heaven-stretched limbs painting streaks of silver-bright light across the drywall "sky" above her.

But neither the lustrous beams of the moon, nor the inky shadows it created could distract her from Jake.

She untucked one hand from behind her neck and

lightly pressed its fingertips to her lips. If she closed her eyes she could almost inhale the very male scent of him, that pine-forest-musky-bath-soap scent that she'd only been aware of when they got up close and personal.

And that kiss was about as up close and personal as it gets! she told herself. At first, she'd tried to fight it, thinking it a very stupid move between a boss and his employee. But walking in on what had appeared to be a burglary, seeing the distress written all over his handsome face when he saw what had happened to his treasured keepsakes, seeing *pain* flash in his eyes when he'd bumped his head—

Oh, who are you kidding? she asked silently. *It wasn't stress that inspired it; you've been wondering what it might be like to kiss him, practically since the moment you met!*

In all honesty, his kiss hadn't been anything like she'd expected. The way he behaved around women? Why, she'd fully expected the touch of his lips to be like the kisses she'd seen in movie theaters, where the hero grabs the heroine, brings her close in a swift, almost-vicious yank, and after a too-long stare-turned-glare, he roughly mashes her lips with his own. *Nothing romantic about* that, Casey had always thought.

But Jake's kiss hadn't been anything like that. Rather, he'd kissed her the way she'd always dreamed of being kissed, first taking her in his arms, gently, sweetly, drawing her near in a way that made her realize he saw her as delicate, fragile, easily broken. They'd never had occasion to discuss their romantic pasts, so how could he have known that, despite her attitude of resiliency and strength, she *could* be broken, in spirit at least? He'd looked into her eyes for what seemed an eternity. *What's he searching for,* she had wondered, *proof that I want to be kissed as much as he wants to kiss me?* Almost at the moment she'd concluded the thought, his green eyes sparked with a luminescent glow. The only proof he was looking for, he seemed to be trying to convey, was proof that she wouldn't hurt him. In that instant, in that quick tick in time, she had seen a flash of pain. Pain, and yes, fear.

But what's he afraid of, she'd asked herself, *big strapping guy like Jake? What does he think a woman my size could do to him?*

A barely noticeable furrow had creased his brow just then, and Casey had realized that, though he likely outweighed her by seventy-five pounds and stood a full head taller, she *could* hurt him, deeply just as that blond apparently had. She'd been so moved, so touched by the vulnerability she'd read in his eyes that Casey had forgotten her vow to steer clear of men, especially handsome, sweet-talking ones. The only thought in her head at that moment had been to comfort him and to reassure him.

She'd placed a hand upon his cheek, and when she did, he'd gasped, wrapped his hand around hers. Closed his eyes and held his breath, then tenderly pressed her fingertips to his lips and held them there as the clock in the hall ticked off the seconds—one, two, three.

His glittering green gaze bored into her eyes for a full twelve-count. Only then did Jake kiss her, at the exact moment when her heart was hammering and her pulse was pounding and her head was reeling in reaction to the gentle gesture that had seemed so genuine, so loving. She felt, wrapped in his big, muscular arms, like a small girl encircled by a protective parent's embrace—and yet, felt like a full-grown woman, surrounded by the love of a good man. And that kiss—

Casey had been kissed before. Her first? A snickering third grader who had darted up and planted a wet one on her cheek as she played hopscotch on the playground. Then at sixteen, a mere peck from Bobby Grimes, while standing on her parents' front stoop in the dim yellow glow of the bug light. Nearly two years later, Carl What's-His-Name, after he'd walked her home from a party on campus, barely more than a peck, but a kiss all the same.

And then Marlow.

Suave and sophisticated, he'd swooped down upon her like a bird of prey, never letting her out of his shadow, never giving her a moment to ask whether or not their relationship was something *God* had intended for her life. He kept her distracted by phone calls that lasted far into the night, thoughtful gifts, evenings out—kept her far too busy to get to know the real Marlow. How many times had he said "I'll win your heart one day, Casey Wallace, you'll see!"? Too many times to count! Now and then, the voice of reason had broken through, telling her to be careful, to stay a safe distance from Marlow, warning her that to get too close meant certain heartache.

But she hadn't listened to that voice. Instead, she'd

listened to Marlow's poetic words and had looked at the things he gave rather than the man who gave them, and eventually, he *had* won her heart. Like the well-fed house cat, he didn't stalk her because he was hungry for her; the fun was in the chase, and once he'd caught her, the game abruptly ended.

Marlow had been able to stare longingly into her eyes.

Marlow had given her kisses that made her dizzy.

Marlow had made her feel protective and motherly, flirty and female, all at the same time.

Casey sat up in bed and threw back the covers. *Oh, you're good, Jake McCafferty,* she told herself, climbing out of bed. *You're smooth as silk, all right.*

She'd seen that photograph—the way the camera froze a smitten expression on his face, and the way he looked at Lucy, in her Daisy Mae outfit.

He likes tall blonds, she told herself, filling the teakettle at the kitchen sink, *and you're anything but. You're obviously not his type, so what makes you think he feels anything for you?*

That kiss, *that's what,* she admitted as she turned on the burner. It had seemed so earnest, so heartfelt.

She stamped a bare foot on the black and white tiled floor. *Don't do this to yourself!* she warned. *Don't dwell on the kiss, or you're doomed for sure.*

Casey leaned against the counter, folded her hands in front of her chest and closed her eyes. "Dear Lord," she prayed aloud, "guide me, help me, show me the way." *Is Jake sincere?* came the silent addendum to her prayer, *or is he just another slick trickster, like Marlow?*

The kettle whistled, and she took a mug from the cupboard. *Is he the cultured man-about-town, or is he the real McCoy?* she added, filling the cup.

Absentmindedly, she dipped her tea bag into the steaming water in her mug. Was her lifelong dream to be a wife and mother the reason she so readily saw more good in a man than he possessed? Had media hype about her ticking biological clock and the lack of marriageable men turned her into a desperate, needy female who'd settle for any guy who even *looked* like he might make her dream come true?

Tough questions, she admitted, but they needed to be asked. She hoped the answer to both was "no." Still, she had been fantasizing about weddings and babies more than usual lately.

Since meeting Jake.

She sighed and admitted, "I can't survive another heartbreak, Lord, so if he isn't the man You intend me to spend the rest of my life with, show me a sign."

And if he isn't my intended, give me strength as You've never given it before, because I'm going to need all the strength I can muster to face a future without him.

Because, like it or not, right or wrong, she'd already fallen in love with him.

He wandered around the darkened house, unable to distinguish the ticking of the clock from the ticking of Ruben's toenails on the hardwood floors. It was as if he'd developed a four-legged, furry shadow that followed him from room to room, from window to window, looking *for what?* he asked himself.

Jake flopped heavily onto the family room sofa in the exact spot where Casey had sat earlier, sipping lemonade from a tall, frosted tumbler.

She'd stayed more than an hour after helping him clean up the squirrel's mess, but only because he'd grabbed her hand, and forced her to endure a house tour. At first, she'd resisted, tugging to free her hand from his grasp. A moment or two after his history lesson began, she relaxed and allowed herself to enjoy the stories that were part and parcel of his home.

"The house was built in 1772," he'd told her as he unlocked the front door. "All the woodwork is original, though I've refinished every board."

"I've never seen a porch quite like this," she'd said. "I feel a little like Scarlett O'Hara!"

Though she'd oooh'd and ahhh'd in all the right places, as everyone who'd seen the house before her had, Casey seemed to experience each room, noticing things no one else had. She had been fascinated by every nook and cranny, by every board, every wooden dowel that held it in place. If he walked through those same rooms now, Jake would have been hard-pressed to find a place she hadn't touched.

The thought made him smile. He rather liked the idea that she'd left her imprint everywhere in his home. He smiled wider, remembering what she'd said when the tour concluded:

"I never would have thought you lived. . .like this."

He'd shrugged. "You knew I had a country house; I

told you on the Fourth of July."

Casey had nodded. "Yes, but I pictured something contemporary, set *in* the country. You know, high ceilings and walls of glass, like those architectural marvels in *House Beautiful.* And inside, I expected everything would be very modern and sleek."

"Why did you see me in a place like that?"

She'd pursed her lips before saying, "Maybe because you're a celebrity. Maybe because you're such a ladies' man." She'd giggled when she added, "I've been hearing for *ages* that bachelors invite women home to see their, ah, etchings." She struck a pompous pose, holding a pretend cigarette between her thumb and forefinger, pinky up and one brow high on her forehead. " 'Won't you come with me, dah-ling,' " she exaggerated a foppish British accent, " 'and have a teensy peek at my . . . at my ahn-*tiques?*' " Giggling, she'd added, "Doesn't fit the stereotype, that's all."

"I'm *not* a ladies' man," was all he could think to say.

But she'd already headed for the next room, saying over her shoulder, "Uh-huh. Right. And ducks can't swim."

Of all her reactions to rooms in his house, Jake's favorite happened in the kitchen. She'd stood in the middle of the floor, hands clasped under her chin, turning a slow circle as she took it all in: the butler's pantry, the back stairs, the mud room, the wall-to-wall fireplace. "Oh, Jake," she'd sighed, stooping to stroke the hearth's aged brickwork, "it's. . .it's. . ."

Straightening, she'd bitten her lower lip, as if trying

to hold back her words. "It's what?" he'd coaxed.

"It's perfect." She'd gone to the window above the sink, stood on tiptoe and pressed her palms to the counter-top. "In the daylight, I'll bet you can see forever, can't you?"

He hadn't had a chance to describe the view from his window, because she'd faced him, smiling, the overhead light dancing in her brown eyes and said, "If this were my house, the first thing I'd do every day would be to thank God for allowing me to live like a fairy princess."

And as though she'd found her own words too silly, too sentimentally feminine, Casey blinked and walked toward the mud porch. "What's out here?" she'd asked, a hand on the doorknob.

"A small porch, some shrubbery, big old trees," he started to say. But the knock to his noggin stopped him cold. He'd been living in this house for nearly a decade, had been ducking through this five-foot-high doorway every day of it. No one but Casey Wallace, he'd decided, could have distracted him enough to start walking into walls.

In response to the echoing *thud,* Casey's maternal instinct kicked in, just as it had earlier, in the foyer. "For heaven's sake, Jake," she'd said in a mock-scolding tone, "I know exactly what to buy you for Christmas: a crash helmet." She slid a hand behind his neck and drew him near. "Here," she'd said, "turn this way, into the light." Gently, her cool fingertips grazed the throbbing bump. "You hit the exact same spot. What are the odds of that?"

And without another word, she'd marched to the

refrigerator and scooped up a handful of ice cubes from the plastic bin in the freezer. With her free hand, she tore off three sheets of paper towels, before he could tell her they were hidden behind the canisters, and wrapped them around the ice. "Sit down," she instructed, pulling a Windsor chair away from the trestle table.

He'd willingly obeyed, and she immediately pressed the compress to the lump on his forehead. "It's a good thing you're on radio instead of TV," she'd remarked, smoothing a lock of his hair back into place, tucking another behind his ear, "or you'd have to explain to your audience how you got a bump the size of Rhode Island on your head."

For the next fifteen minutes, she'd chattered like a magpie as she stood, holding the ice in place, never missing a beat in her nonstop conversation. With a firm yet gentle hand on his shoulder, she'd pushed him back onto the oak seat of the chair every time he made a move to get up. The clock in the hall was striking ten when she dumped what was left of the ice into the sink, nonchalantly tossing the soggy paper towels into the garbage. "Fifteen minutes under the ice pack ought to be enough."

How had she known which cabinet the trash can would be in? Most folks kept a container directly under the sink; Jake stored his in the cupboard to the left, instead.

It seemed as though she belonged in this kitchen.

As though she belonged in this kitchen. Not in the cliché sense, but as if it belonged to her—was made for her. Jake rolled it over in his mind another time or two.

It sounded good. Felt right. He said it again, out loud this time, adjusting the verb tense: "She *belongs* in this kitchen."

Ruben nuzzled Jake's hand. "You liked her, too, didn't you boy?" he asked, ruffling the dog's fur.

Ruben blinked and cocked his head. "What, are you kidding?" he seemed to say. "What's not to like!"

"You've got a point, there, pal," Jake said, grinning as he read the dog's face. "There is definitely a lot to like."

151

Chapter 6

He leaned forward in the chair, balanced his elbows on his knees. "I can not," he said, strangely unable to meet Buddy's eyes. "Get somebody else to do it." He clamped his hands in the V between his knees. "Have you asked Stuart?"

"Jake, Jake, Jake," Buddy chanted, closing the aluminum blinds behind his desk with a metallic *snap*. "Stuie is a swell guy, works hard, does a fine hour of airtime." Perching on the corner of his desk, he measured the air with his thumb and forefinger. "But his audience is this big."

Walking around to the other side of the desk, Buddy tucked his finger between two of the miniblind slats and peered through the opening. A narrow shaft of winter-bright light pierced the semidark room, slanting across Buddy's hawklike profile. "Besides," the boss added, settling into his chair, "Stuart isn't right for this gig. I know it, and so do you."

Jake hung his head, more so that Buddy couldn't read his face than because of the turn this conversation was taking. Without looking up, Jake said, "You know how I feel about—"

A finger in the air, Buddy silenced him. "And you know how I feel. This is a solid idea that'll make us a bundle. If—"

"You have more money than Donald Trump." He saw the beginnings of insult brewing on Buddy's face. "Well, more money than Donald Trump *used* to have," he corrected himself. On his feet now. He pulled a leather-bound volume from Buddy's bookshelf. Balancing it on an open palm, he flipped through the gold-edged pages. "Passing up one moneymaking scheme isn't going to break you financially."

"And doing a Valentine's Day show isn't going to break *you.*"

There was a note of finality in Buddy's voice that Jake didn't like. He realized, as he slid the book back onto the shelf, that he'd lost this argument long before he'd walked into the office. He planted both hands on a shoulder-high shelf, and dropped his head in defeat. "You've got a mean streak as wide as your head," Jake said, facing the boss. "You know this won't be easy for me. Why force the issue?"

"Two reasons: You've wallowed in self-pity long enough, in my opinion. Marsha was a hyena, and you oughta be glad she dumped you before she got *really* hungry, 'cause she'd have eaten you alive." Shrugging, Buddy spread his arms wide. "Your callers are daily proof that you're not the only man who feels like a fool 'cause he let a woman use him. C'mon, Jake. Get over it."

He'd heard all this before, the morning after, when he'd made the mistake of going to work as if nothing had happened. Buddy had been in the restaurant that night, seated at a table on the other side of the partition. He'd heard every word out of Marsha's mouth. The boss's advice then may as well have been a recording of what he was saying now. Jake hadn't liked hearing he'd joined the rank of fools then, and he didn't like hearing it now.

"You said there were two reasons," he interrupted, careful to keep a respectful tone in his voice. Buddy's advice may not have been on-target, but Jake knew he'd doled it out with the best of intentions.

"The ticket money will go to a good cause. It's earmarked for Children's Oncology down at Johns Hopkins." Buddy folded his hands over his minuscule belly bulge and narrowed his eyes. "You tellin' me your ancient heartache is more painful than what those kids are going through?"

Jake drove one hand through his hair, pocketed the other, and took a deep breath. He'd done half a dozen or so volunteer stints at the hospital, no fewer than three in Children's Oncology. Seeing those kids hooked up to monitors and attached to a myriad of tubes—some whose chemo treatments had left them bald and others who were so weak that even making eye contact seemed a painful strain—had clarified how precious every healthy breath was. Buddy was right; cancer had done far more damage to those youngsters than Marsha could do to Jake, even on her best day.

He felt like a heel. Those kids were handling their pain far better than he'd handled the breakup with Marsha. They were brave and stoic, and for the most part, uncomplaining. Some of them would recover, but others knew their time on this earth would be severely shortened. Still, each had found his or her own reasons to find joy in life, in little things.

He met Buddy's eyes and shook his head. "You sure know how to make a man feel small."

Another shrug. "I call 'em as I see 'em."

"All right. I'll do the show."

Buddy all but sneered as he lifted the telephone receiver. "There was never a doubt in my mind that you would, m'boy. Not even for a minute." He punched a few buttons, then listened as the phone on the other end rang. "Wilhelmina," he cooed into the mouthpiece, swiveling his chair and putting his back to Jake, "it's Buddy."

Jake quietly left the office and headed straight for the elevators. He wondered how many times Buddy's heart had been broken by callous females. *Never,* he decided, *because Buddy is too smart for that.*

Jake hadn't spent all these years studying human behavior for nothing. In his professional opinion, Buddy's behavior wasn't all that difficult to figure out. *I oughta write a paper and present it to the AMA,* he thought, punching the elevator's "down" button, *defining a new disorder—GBS, for "George Burns Syndrome."*

The elevator doors hissed shut and, as he rode toward the lobby, Jake nodded. Like Buddy, George Burns had surrounded himself with a bevy of empty-headed beauties, and the reason was simple: Old George, knowing he'd never replace his Gracie, adopted a "why try?" attitude. *A rare thing, that kind of love,* he mused.

His footsteps echoed in the big, marble-floored lobby. Pushing through the revolving door, Jake inhaled the crisp cold air. Hunching his shoulders, he leaned into the powerful winter wind. If he hurried, he could get to the church and back before he went on the air. But even if the trip made him late, Jake didn't see as he had much choice.

He had a lot to discuss with the Almighty.

❦

"What do you mean, he went to church?"

Lucy repeated it slowly, as if Casey were too dense to understand plain English.

Under other circumstances, Casey would have loved the opportunity to tell Viking Woman exactly what she thought of her unprofessional behavior. Today, she had more important things on her mind.

She repeated Lucy's words in her head, and could hardly believe it. Jake had less than half an hour to air-time. What could be so important that he'd leave the building and risk getting caught in traffic during Baltimore's horrific lunch-hour snarl!

Fortunately for her, Sam had stopped by the station to deliver a gift for Jimmy Watson's new baby. She snagged him in the hall outside Jake's office. "Sam, you have to do me a huge favor."

The lanky older man grinned paternally down at her. "Well, I don't *have* to, but I *might,* if you'll slow down and tell me what's got you so riled up."

"Jake has left the building and—"

Sam's nonchalant expression turned serious. He glanced at his wristwatch. "With thirty minutes to show time? Is he out of his ever-lovin' mind?"

"Lucy said he went to church. Do you have any idea wh—"

"Holy Redeemer," Sam lifted his baseball cap long enough to pass a palm over his bald spot. "Awhile back he'd stop in there now and then." Wearing a lopsided grin, he added, "Well, who do you s'pose a shrink talks to when he needs *his* wig picked?"

"Thanks, Sam. I'm going to get him," Casey said, ignoring Sam's snickering. "Will you cover for us, in case we don't get back in time?"

He lay a reassuring hand on her shoulder. "You bet I will, honey. I think this station's ready for a 'The Best of "Lovesick" ' show." He headed for the studio. "You still keep the recorded shows on the shelf under the window?"

"Everything is exactly as you left it." Shoulders up and hands out, she added, "If it ain't broke, why fix it?"

Sam grinned. "No need to butter me up now, I've already agreed to be your stand-in."

He disappeared into the studio as Casey stepped into the elevator. "Lord, let me find Jake and bring him back in time," she prayed aloud. It had been one of those "in the right place" moments. She'd been in WCHK's kitchen, refilling her coffee cup when Buddy came in with three men in suits. "Casey," he'd said, drawing her to him in a sideways hug, "I want you to meet Bob Richmond, with the network. He's here to listen in on Jake's show." Leaning near her ear, he pretended to whisper, "The bigwigs up in New York are thinking of putting 'Lovesick' on CableCast. Whaddaya think of that?"

I think it could be his big break, she told herself now, *and no one deserves it more than Jake.* He'd worked hard to balance patients he helped on the radio show with the patients he saw in his Ellicott City office. They'd never know what it cost him, in time and energy, to make the job seem effortless, but Casey knew. If he missed this chance at the big time, she'd never forgive herself.

Casey prayed all the way from the twelfth floor to the garage, continued to pray as she wove in and out of traffic on Charles Street, and prayed even harder as she slid into a parking slot in the lot behind the church. Not even bothering to lock the car door, she dashed across the blacktop and up the many-tiered concrete steps.

Despite her previous state of agitation, a peaceful hush fell over her as she stepped inside. Candle flames flickered, winking into the semidarkness like golden stars. Though the sun shone bright outside, its light, muted by stained glass windows, poured into the space in rainbow shafts, puddling on the worn tiles in pools of liquid color.

Artwork, no doubt created by parishioners' kids, hung on the walls, giving the place a cozy, homey quality. The carved wood altar rail gleamed under a thousand coats of furniture polish. Casey could almost see the ladies of the parish, wearing flowered aprons and yellow rubber gloves, spritzing Pledge—

She spotted him then, kneeling at the altar. He'd bowed his head, and above the soft whir of the furnace fan, she could hear his whispering voice. Should she make some noise, so he'd know he wasn't alone? Or sit quietly, give him a few more moments to do whatever he'd come here to do?

If it was me up there, she thought, *I'd hate it if someone eavesdropped on a private prayer.* Casey let the door bang shut behind her, then walked purposefully up the center aisle, the soles of her tennis shoes squeak-squeaking on the polished linoleum.

"What in the world were you thinking, Jake McCafferty? Do you realize we have a show to do," she checked her watch, "in less than twenty minutes?"

He stood, hesitated a moment in front of the altar, as if he didn't want to leave. "I, ah, had a few things to hash out with—" Jake cut her a sidelong glance, then slumped onto the front pew, his slouch rumpling his trench coat, his hair windblown. He reminded her of the kid she'd seen at the Columbia Mall last week, who'd somehow gotten separated from his mama. Jake had always seemed so sure of himself, so confident. Not now.

"Is there anything I can do?" she asked, her soft voice whispering in the rafters.

He shook his head. "This is something I have to work out on my own." He looked at her, laid a hand atop hers, and patted it a time or two. "Thanks for asking, though. You're a pal."

His touch reminded her of that kiss. Had it really been six months ago? She thought about it so often, it sometimes seemed like yesterday. At moments like this, when he referred to her as a "pal," it seemed ages ago. She wanted to be more than his pal. Much more. Sure, she'd taken a tough line with herself after that kiss, saying he was a typical man, a Marlow in sheep's clothing.

But she'd known better. Jake was nothing like Marlow. He was nothing like any man she'd ever met, if she were honest with herself. And in the wee hours of the night, as she lay alone thinking about him, about that kiss, she *had* been honest with herself: She loved him.

She had hoped he might feel the same way, because that night in his foyer, Jake seemed to want her, too. But the very next day, and every day after, he'd kept a careful, professional distance. Casey surmised he must have pigeonholed her in the "friend" compartment of his life.

She'd gotten to know him well in the nine months she'd produced his show. Their eyes would meet through the glass panel that separated studio from production booth, and she'd know, instantly, what he needed; a commercial, a bit of banter to fill dead airtime, an indicator that things were going well, or affirmation that they weren't.

During their second or third week working together, he took to scribbling black Magic Marker messages on sheets of white copy paper, things he wanted her to say on-air to lighten a too-heavy mood. It was their version of Martin and Lewis. If only his listeners could have known that the jokes that so often inspired gales of hearty laughter had been written by none other than the serious and somber Dr. Jake McCafferty!

"Odd as it seems," he was saying, interrupting her thoughts, "what's bugging me now is going to affect you, too, indirectly."

His voice, laden with sadness, echoed in her ears. "Me? How?" Not that it mattered. All that mattered now was giving him comfort.

"Buddy has us lined up to do a Valentine's Day remote from the National Aquarium; all the money collected at the door will be donated to Hopkins Children's Oncology."

She sandwiched his hand between hers and smiled reassuringly. "That doesn't sound so bad to me."

"It's not. . ." Jake exhaled a breath of vexation. "It's just. . .why did it have to be Valentine's Day?"

"Well, if it's any comfort to you, it's not my favorite holiday, either."

Jake sat up straight. "Well, what're you waiting for?" he coaxed. "I'm all ears."

Titling it "The Saint Valentine's Day Disaster," she gave him an abridged version of her last night with her would-be husband. "Top that," she challenged, grinning wearily.

"I don't think I can." And after a moment, he punched his own palm. "What's the jerk's name, and where can I find him?"

"It isn't important." And then, "Well," she quoted, "what're you waiting for? I'm all ears."

"Why don't I tell you as we head back to the station, since we're so pressed for time," he suggested, getting to his feet.

"What about your car?"

"I walked here." He shot her a sheepish grin. "Thought the fresh air might clear my head."

Casey led him to her car, turned the heat up full blast to warm it up. "I guess I shouldn't complain," she said, teeth chattering in the late January chill. "It could be snowing."

"I like driving in snow."

"That's because you own a four-wheeler. Try maneuvering this old tub around on two inches of ice."

"You know how unpredictable Maryland winters can be. What were you thinking, buying a big old boat like this?"

"I didn't," she protested. "My grandpa left it to me in his will. 'Waste not, want not,' or so the sages say." She steered into traffic. "Enough stalling. Start talkin,'" or I might get all agitated and crash into something—and I haven't bought you that crash helmet yet, don't forget."

He snorted. "We're safer in this tank than folks with air bags."

Casey tucked in her chin and narrowed her eyes.

"Okay, okay," he said, hands up in mock surrender. Jake took a deep breath, let it out slowly. "I've never told anyone this story before."

"There's a first time for everything."

Jake clasped his hands between his knees tapping the thumbs together, as if the action might lend a syncopated rhythm that would encourage his words. "I'd been dating Marsha for years before I popped the question. Almost from the start, she told people we were 'unofficially engaged.' After five years of hearing it, I sorta believed it myself.

"Anyway," he continued, "we somehow got this tradition started, where I gave her a long-stemmed red rose every Valentine's Day. One year she stuck her nose into the flower, took a big whiff and came up saying, 'Maybe one day there will be a beautiful diamond engagement ring tucked into the blossom.' "

"Ugh. Please. Stop," Casey interrupted, feigning nausea. "I have a loose filling; this sweet-talk is making my tooth ache."

"Do you want to hear this or not?"

She gave him a wide, upside-down smile. "Ex-cu-u-u-she *me,*" Casey said, doing an early Steve Martin impression.

"Well, to make a long story short—"

"Too late for that."

Jake shook his head and grinned despite himself. "As I was *saying,* it was just about this time two years ago, when the Valentine's ads started popping up. By that time, Marsha and I had been together forever—or so it seemed."

Casey gave him a minute to ruminate. "Didn't your mother tell you it's rude to leave curious people hanging?"

He chuckled. "Telling you this isn't as tough as I thought it would be. You're a good friend, Case."

Casey ignored his second reference to her status in his life. "Time wounds all heels, eh?" she joked, deliberately messing up the age-old cliché.

"Guess so," he agreed. "Anyway," he said again, "about a week before Valentine's Day, I made ten o'clock reservations at Sabatino's—"

"Mmm. Little Italy. My favorite place to eat."

"And put a down payment on a two-carat solitaire, set in platinum. I picked her up, and drove downtown. The waiter brought our appetizers. We ordered and I took the ring box out of my pocket."

Jake abruptly ended his rat-a-tat recitation, shaking his head. "I don't know—maybe this isn't such a good idea."

"You made me tell my tale of woe. Way I see it, you owe me one."

"Touché," he said. "So I put the ring box on the table, took her hand, looked into her eyes, and said, 'Darling, this has been a long time coming, but. . .'

"Then she held up her left hand, and flashed a rock big as her head in my eyes." When he took Marsha's part, Jake spoke in an exaggerated falsetto: " 'Remember when I got back from Italy this summer, I told you what a lovely time I had?' And like a numbskull, I said, 'Ah-ha.' And she said, 'Well, the man who made it such fun—' I interrupted her. 'You mean, all those times you couldn't see me, you were with *him?*' And she said, 'Ah-ha.' 'And you're engaged now, to *him?*' And she said. . ."

" 'Ah-ha,' " they harmonized, laughing as Casey wheeled into a parking space in the WCHK garage.

"What's the jerk's name, and where can I find him?" she said copying him as they walked side by side toward the elevators.

"Marlow."

Casey stopped walking. It took Jake a few steps to realize he'd left her behind. Halting, he looked over his shoulder, and when he saw the look of complete astonishment on her face, understanding dawned in his mind.

"No. It can't be."

She nodded. *If this is the sign I prayed for, Lord, there's no doubt You have a terrific sense of humor!* "Well," Casey said, hitting the elevator's "up" button, "I don't know whose tale is sorriest, yours or mine, but I know this—"

"I hate Valentine's Day!" they hollered together.

Epilogue

The pace was flurried, the atmosphere frenzied, there in the lobby of the National Aquarium. WCHK's makeshift studio would broadcast to hundreds of thousands of listeners throughout Maryland, Pennsylvania, Delaware, Virginia, and Washington, D.C. Hundreds of people milled around, their voices creating a low din that reminded Casey of bees in a hive.

"So, are you ready to make your big announcement?" she asked, adjusting her headset over her ears.

He grinned. "Ready as I'll ever be."

She wondered about the mischievous gleam in his green eyes, but chalked it up to excitement. Starting today, the "Lovesick" show would be seen by cable TV viewers in addition to the usual listening audience. "Don Imus and Howard Stern, move over," she said, winking.

Jake smiled. "How 'bout you? Ready for the big time?"

She sighed. "Ready as I'll ever be," she quoted him.

"You look gorgeous today, by the way."

Since no one but the station's employees had ever seen her at work, Casey had always worn comfortable clothes to the studio; jeans, loafers, casual blouses, and blazers. Today, she'd chosen a snappy dress of navy blue with matching high-heeled shoes. "Thanks," she said. "You don't look half bad, yourself."

In response to the compliment, he tugged at his tie's Windsor knot. "I'm thinkin' I should lose the noose. What do you think?"

"I agree. The shirt and jacket are plenty professional. Why make yourself miserable?"

"You guys sound like an old married couple," Buddy said, joining them on the stage. "She fixes your lunch, you rotate her tires; you ask her advice on your wardrobe, and she gives it." He looked toward the ceiling and rolled his eyes. One hand on each of their shoulders, he added, "Do you realize how much money you'd save if you got hitched? Two *can* live cheaper than one."

"Money ain't important to Jake anymore," Sam said. "He's gonna be rich and famous, startin' today."

"Sam," Casey injected, "what are you doing here?"

Shrugging, he grinned. "Thought it was only fair to lend my support, since I kinda left him in the lurch back in April."

"Hey, if I had known then what I know now," Jake said, winking, "I would have fired you years ago." He looked at Casey. "She's ten times the producer you are, you old buzzard."

She waited for the qualifier that usually balanced his compliments. When none came, she felt the heat of a blush creep into her cheeks.

Jake faced his boss and ex-producer. "Get out of here, you guys," he ordered, grinning. "We have a show to prepare for, and you're blocking our creative thought processes."

Buddy started down the stairs, Sam followed close behind. "I made lunch reservations at Chiaparelli's," the boss said, "to celebrate the new show. Don't dillydally when you go off the air, 'cause I didn't have breakfast."

Once they were out of earshot, Jake faced her. "Can I ask you a question, Casey?"

"Sure. Anything."

"I was just wondering. . ."

Normally, she could read his expressions, but not this time.

"If you ever get married, will you want to continue producing my show?"

The question stunned her into silence. "I, ah, hadn't thought about it, really."

"Well, think about it. I need to know."

Ten minutes to airtime, and he needs to know this now? "I suppose I'd work, if we needed the money—my potential husband and I, that is—otherwise, I'd rather stay at home and be a full-time wife and mommy."

"You want kids?"

"You bet. A houseful!"

"Me, too. But I'm not sure I'd be a good father."

"Are you kidding? You're Santa Claus and the Pied Piper all rolled into one. Kids love you."

"Thanks, Case. I needed to hear that." He hesitated. "Although, I'm gonna miss you—when you leave to be a full-time wife and mommy, that is."

"I wouldn't leave you in a lurch, like Sam did. I'd give you plenty of notice. I'd even help train my replacement."

"You're a real trouper."

"What're friends for?"

Casey had decided weeks ago, on the day he'd told her about this Valentine's special to be exact, that the best way to handle her feelings for him was to focus on their friendship. Eventually, she hoped, the wishful-thinking part of her, the part that wanted a long, happy future with Jake, would be overtaken by the practical side—the side that said better friendship than nothing.

❧

Don't look at me like that, Jake thought, *or I'm liable to jump the gun.* He'd suspected for quite some time that her feelings for him ran deeper than she pretended. The way her eyes lit up when he told her she looked great today, the way they'd flashed when she said he'd be a good father, he more than suspected—Jake *knew* she loved him, too.

He'd been up half the night, honing his plan. And at precisely two minutes before they went off the air, he'd put it into action.

The show started, as always, without a hitch. One caller shared the way her husband had rented a sky plane, to write his proposal over the crowd at Memorial Stadium back in 1969. A woman in the live audience said she'd wear caps on her front teeth for the rest of her life thanks to the engagement ring her then-intended had shoved into the underside of a piece of Valentine's candy. And then there was the guy who said his wife had proposed to *him* from the peak of Mount Everest.

When they went into commercial, Casey left the stage to refill her water cup. While she was gone, Jake slid a sheet of copy paper from his briefcase, grabbed the Magic Marker from an inside pocket, and printed the message he'd get her to read when they went back on the air.

Traditionally, she'd always had so much to do, what with monitoring the phones, logging calls, plugging in commercials and announcements, that Casey didn't have time to read and ruminate about what he'd written on the pages he so often held up. Every second counted, and dead airtime was forbidden. If he showed her a message, she would read it into the mike without even thinking.

And that's exactly what he was counting on.

Jake hid this message under the stack of Valentine statistic printouts he'd been reading on the air. When she returned, Casey handed him a cup of cold water. "You look like the cat that swallowed the canary. What's up your sleeve?"

"It's the TV cameras," he fibbed. "Guess I'm gonna have to learn how to control my on-air grin, huh?"

Tilting her head, she studied his face. "No. Don't change a thing. I like your smile just the way it is."

The red light above the camera went on, and the TV show's producer held up the "all-quiet" sign. "In five, and four," he said aloud, then counted with his fingers, "three, and two," and lowering his arm, mouthed, "Go!"

Jake launched into the opening to the final segment as Casey got the theme song ready for the closing. He kept a careful eye on the clock, and with precisely two minutes to go, slid his message out from beneath the stack of printouts.

Casey, busy plugging tapes into the tape deck, saw him hold up the paper. Leaning into her mike, she hit the "on" button and, stuffing a diskette back into its box, said, "I love you, Jake McCafferty."

There was a moment of utter silence as what she'd said reverberated in her own ears. Half the East Coast had heard her admit what she'd been trying so hard to deny for nearly nine months. Casey's gaze locked on Jake's as she flipped off her mike and mouthed, "Are you crazy?"

He read her lips and smiled. "This show might have started without a hitch," he whispered, his hand over the mike, "but it isn't gonna end without one."

Then he leaned forward and said into the live microphone, "I love you, too, Casey Wallace."

Eyes wide and mouth agape, Casey gasped as Jake reached over and turned her microphone back on. He scooted his chair closer to hers and, without taking his eyes from hers, spoke into her mike. "Casey, will you marry me?"

She blinked once, twice, then hid behind her hands. It all made sense, suddenly. The way he'd been looking at her the past couple of days, the questions he'd asked before they went on the air. *He* loves *me!* she acknowledged. *Thank You, Lord,* she prayed, *for making all my dreams come true!*

When she came out of hiding, there were tears shimmering in her brown eyes. "Yes," she sighed, throwing her arms around his neck. "Yes, Jake. Of course I'll marry you."

"It's about time," came Buddy's voice from the back of the crowd.

Jake turned off both mikes. The applause from the crowd that had gathered to watch the show drowned out their final words:

"I *love* Valentine's Day," they said in unison.

Loree Lough

A full-time writer for over twelve years, Loree has produced more than 1,700 published articles, dozens of short stories that have appeared in various magazines, and two books for *The American Adventure* series for 8 to 12-year olds (Barbour Publishing). The author of fifteen inspirational romances, including the award-winning *Pocketful of Love* (Heartsong Presents), Loree also writes as Cara McCormack and Aleesha Carter. A prolific and talented writer, gifted teacher, and comedic conference speaker, Loree lives in Maryland with her husband, two daughters, and two constantly warring cats.

Castaways

Debra White Smith

Dedication

Dedicated to my "angel" friends, Christina Harrison Grimes and Francis Shaw. Thanks for all your love, prayers, and support. And thanks for believing in me!

Chapter 1

February 1

"I must be hallucinating." Bethany Townsley's heart drummed in dread. Gripping her best friend's slender arm, she stared across the crowded ski lodge. Stared at the tanned, blond, lean man who bestowed a winsome grin on a simpering clerk. Stared at what she hoped was Devin Carmichael's double. *Please don't be Devin,* her mind said. But her heart whispered otherwise, and his slight limp confirmed those whispers.

This must be some cruel coincidence. Or had her ex-fiancé somehow discovered she would be here this weekend? Within the last six weeks, Bethany had returned six of his letters unopened. In his desperation to contact her, could he have somehow learned of her Colorado vacation?

"Hmm?" Christina Harrison turned distracted brown eyes from the ski lodge brochure to gaze up at her friend.

"Look!" Bethany hissed as her throat tightened, her eyes stung, and she forced herself to focus on Christina. *You will not cry. This is a public place. People are watching.* "Standing at the desk." A hurried glance his way. "No, now he's walking in front of the fireplace. See that gorgeous Oriental woman standing by the couches? He's in front of her now. I think it's—"

"It's Devin Carmichael." Christina's astonished gape reflected Bethany's own surprise.

"Stop staring," she pleaded, her palms damp despite Colorado's winter chill. "He might see—"

Christina's stiff smile, directed over Bethany's shoulder, preceded the slight wiggle of her fingers. "It's too late. He's already seen us and is headed over here," she mumbled, her lips never moving.

"This must be a nightmare." Keeping her back to Devin, she felt her spine tingle, felt the humiliation, the horror, the hatred of his despicable jilt and exit from her life.

One year. One long year on her own. Or had it only been one day? One day since he'd adored her, since he'd held her, since he promised her happiness. "I can't marry you," he rasped over her answering machine the day before their wedding. Then, despite Bethany's desperate attempts to talk with him, he had avoided her.

Tucking a strand of straight brunette hair behind her ear, Christina licked her lips and studied Bethany. "Are you all right?"

"No, I'm not all right." A compulsive swallow, and Bethany glanced toward the ceiling's polished pine beams to conjure up every scrap of composure her aching soul could spare.

"Fancy meeting you two here."

That voice. Bethany closed her eyes. Even if she hadn't seen him, she would know his mellow tone in a blizzard.

Schooling her features into a bland mask, she turned to face his casual good looks, feigned a smile, and forced her quivering voice into its even, soprano tones. "I was just asking Christina if that was you or your double," she said as if they were old friends, not ex-fiancés.

You were wrong, Mom. I should have been an actress after all.

"It's me!" A soft chuckle. "Can you believe it? After all this time?" His searching, smoky eyes didn't match his light tone.

Awkward silence. A silence which drowned the typical, crowded-ski-lodge noises. A silence which seemed to suspend the six returned letters between them. Bethany had scrawled "Return to Sender" on each of them. The first three letters had ignited her fury. But by the sixth letter, Bethany realized her love for Devin had never died. In an attempt to survive, Bethany had buried her love. Buried it alive.

Now what? She shoved up her purple sweater's baggy sleeves and tried to think of something clever to say, but her mind preferred sarcasm. *So, how does it feel to abandon your future wife the day before the wedding? Ever feel any guilt? Ever wonder if I'd come after you with a bazooka?*

Her palms suddenly itched to slap that assured look right off his rugged face, to pull out all of his wavy, blond hair. Bethany's thin nostrils flared. She gritted her teeth. Who did he think he was, approaching her as if they were the best of buddies? After all those letters she had returned, couldn't he get the hint?

Chirstina cleared her throat.

"You've changed, Princess—hmm—Bethany," Devin said softly.

Princess. He called her the pet name she had once cherished.

"You've cut your hair. And your eyes—"

"I got colored contacts," she said flatly. "And I got tired of my hair long. . ." *Mainly because you liked it.* "So I had it cut." Bethany rubbed the nape of her exposed neck and wondered why she had explained anything to him. What business was it of his what she did with her appearance? The day before their wedding, he had left her, her green eyes, and her blond hair without a backward glance.

Almost gagging on the smell of his spicy aftershave, the same aftershave that had lingered on her coat weeks after his desertion, Bethany crammed her hands into her jeans pockets and tried to think of a dignified means of escape.

Run! Run! Run! a voice urged. She suppressed the desire to bolt like a scared doe.

"There you are," a familiar, midwestern voice called from behind Bethany.

Impulsively, she turned, glad to see the man who would have been her brother-in-law. Brett Carmichael, Devin's half brother, had been her self-proclaimed champion since the moment he met her.

"I figured this is where I'd find you. . ." Brett continued, gesturing toward Bethany and Christina as he approached, "standing around with the ladies."

He didn't recognize her. Was her appearance that

much altered?

Then his smiling, brown eyes shifted back to her. The surprise followed. *"Bethany!"*

"Hello, Brett."

In typical brotherly fashion, he wrapped his muscular arms around her for a swaying bear hug. "I can't believe it!"

"It's good to see you," she said against his gray parka, her voice sounding wooden even to her own ears. She *was* glad to see the tall, debonair stockbroker, but the shock of seeing Devin, too, dampened her joy.

He held her at arm's length. "So what have you been doing with yourself?"

"Oh, not much," she said vaguely, not wishing to give Devin the satisfaction of a specific answer.

"Not much," Christina snorted. "She's just doubled her business holdings *and* her income in the last year, that's all."

Brett turned to Christina, and this time his face registered what he had apparently missed before. Christina's pug nose and her abundance of freckles stopped her from being a raving beauty but not from being attractive. *Fresh*. That was the perfect word for Christina's looks and personality. She was like a breeze of fresh spring air.

Brett's expressive eyes begged for an introduction, and Bethany could never remember his being so arrested by a woman. Just before Devin and Bethany met, Brett's wife had been killed in a car wreck. The loss had nearly destroyed Brett. Bethany wasn't so sure the shadows had left his eyes, but at least he was showing an interest in another woman.

"This is my best friend, Christina Harrison," Bethany supplied, all the while feeling Devin's scrutiny. It was the oddest, most uncomfortable sensation. Almost as if he were trying to read her mind.

Please God, she prayed, more to herself than to a Being she had rarely considered of late, *let me leave before I explode.*

As Christina and Brett shook hands, Bethany removed the suite key from her jeans pocket. The sooner they got away from Devin, the sooner she could repack, and the sooner she could be back in Dallas with her warm, safe townhouse and her dress shops.

"Devin and I were just going to have some coffee." Brett waved his hand toward the lodge's glassed-in restaurant. "Would you two like to join us?"

"Sure," Christina answered.

"No! We were about to pack and head back to Dallas," Bethany said emphatically, her gaze sliding to Devin of its own volition.

Something fluttered in the depths of his eyes, something which looked like disappointment. "That's too bad," he said.

No, it couldn't have been disappointment. That was only Bethany's traitorous heart imagining things that didn't exist. Just as she had imagined his devotion, his adoration, his love.

Proud of her continual, feigned composure, not sure how much longer it would last, Bethany grabbed the sleeve of her petite friend's sweater and turned toward the nearby elevator's opening doors.

"Well, it was good to see you again, Brett. . .Devin," she called over her shoulder while Christina stumbled close behind. "Have a good vacation."

She rushed into the elevator, pulled Christina in, pushed the button for the third floor, and collapsed against the wall.

Chapter 2

The elevator doors hissed to a close. Speechless, Christina watched her dearest friend.

Bethany, staring vacantly ahead, gripped the wall rails until her knuckles were white; a white which matched her blanched cheeks and lips. Shock. Christina, a pediatric nurse practitioner, had seen such shock when tragedy struck the unsuspecting. She never imagined Bethany would be the unsuspecting.

A cloud of haunting, accusing guilt descended on Christina, sinking its cold fingers into her veins. As if she were listening to a recording, she relived her Saturday phone conversation with Devin.

Devin had called her to ask about Bethany. He had professed his undying love for the woman he had jilted and asked Christina if there were any way she could convince Bethany to read the letters he had been sending her. Christina hadn't even known about the letters. But that did explain Bethany's odd behavior of late, her distracted demeanor, her nail biting. Devin Carmichael was up to his old tricks.

In an attempt to assure Devin that Bethany was surviving without him, Christina had mentioned their vacation. Never had she suspected he would follow Bethany to Colorado. In her mind, Christina's comments about their trip repeated over and over again until they turned into a chorus of accusation. *Scatterbrain, motor mouth, chatterbox, airhead*—these names and more had been her elder brother's favorite tags for her. They had trailed Christina her whole life. She had always been too quick to speak, too slow to think.

If only I had kept my big mouth shut!

Devin was here because of her thoughtlessness. Bethany was in shock because of her thoughtlessness. Their vacation was over because of her thoughtlessness.

In the middle of all this, another thought struck her. What if Bethany were to learn Christina was to blame for Devin's presence? Visions of her decade-long friendship dissolving into disdain tormented her. Another onslaught of anxiety.

"I'm sorry," Christina muttered as the elevator glided to a halt. The words seemed to bounce off the walls in echoes of betrayal.

"What?" Blinking, Bethany turned her almond-shaped eyes to her best friend.

"I said, I'm sorry."

"You're always apologizing for things that aren't your fault," Bethany said, the color slowing returning to her cheeks.

If only you knew.

"Let's just get packed and get out of here," Bethany croaked. "This was a bad time for a vacation, anyway. I didn't need to leave the stores in the first place."

"Okay." An unexpected thread of disappointment twisted through Christina. Their long-anticipated vacation would never be. Neither would her acquaintance with Brett Carmichael.

Velvet brown. The color of his eyes could start an avalanche and had done exactly that in Christina's icy heart. She had never experienced the electricity which had almost blasted her through the ceiling when he touched her hand.

It was nothing, Christina tried to convince herself as Bethany opened their suite's oak door. Besides, she had vowed a year ago never to trust her taste in men. As Bethany had said, leaving now was probably for the best, before Christina once again made a fool of herself.

A depreciating chuckle. With Valentine's Day almost upon them, she and Bethany were both running from romance.

❧

Bethany, carrying her two pieces of designer luggage, trudged toward the ski lodge's massive receptionist's desk. Christina followed. Repacking had taken an hour. Bethany hadn't wanted to waste another minute waiting on a busboy. The sooner she put miles between her and Devin, the better.

Is it really for the better? a shadowed room in her heart whispered, the same room where she had imprisoned her love for the man who had cast her away like some rejected rubbish.

"Would you slow up?" a breathless Christina called. "Not everybody has your long legs!"

"Sorry." Smiling her apology, she stopped, turned, and awaited her friend, who swiftly closed the yards between them. "I forget."

"Don't give me that," Christina snorted, dropping her oversized luggage to massage her red palms. "You and your photographic memory! I don't buy this 'I forget' routine! I think it's a plot. I think all of you tall people are secretly planning to run us shorties to death. Then you can take over the world!"

"No, it's a plot of the fat people against the skinny people!"

"Oh, brother, we're on the fat kick again. You're not fat. A size twelve isn't considered—"

"Well, I might not be obese, but I'm not a size five like some people I know."

"That proves it! All these years I've suspected it. You resent me because of my shoe size!"

"Ha-ha-ha," Bethany said through a genuine grin.

No matter how gloomy the horizon, Christina somehow always managed to make Bethany smile. Even that awful week after the canceled wedding. That dreadful day she had taken off her engagement ring. The day Bethany had felt as if her soul had died. Even then, Christina had made her laugh until she cried.

"Steamboat Springs Inn," the nearby receptionist said into the phone while eyeing Bethany and Christina. "Okay. . . That's what we were afraid of. It's been coming down like crazy. . .two feet! Already?"

Bethany instinctively glanced toward the massive, glass doorway, to the parking lot, and beyond. The snow fell as if the skies were assaulting Werner Mountain.

"Oh no," she groaned, dropped her bags, and rubbed her aching temples. "Please tell me I'm hallucinating."

Earlier, she had noticed some snow flurries, but this looked like a blizzard.

"Wowee kazowee," Christina said. "I guess we'll be here a while."

"You're right," the overweight, blond receptionist said. "I just got a report from our other lodge that Rabbit Ears Pass has been closed. There's been a wreck due to the snow."

"Do you know how long it will be closed?" Bethany asked, dreading the answer. How could she keep from encountering Devin if they were trapped together?

"The last time this happened, it took them about twelve hours to reopen the pass."

A muffled groan. And Behtany was assulted by sorrow, loneliness, and an intense yearning she had presumed long dead.

❧

All afternoon, she tried to deny her emotions by feigning interest in an old movie. Christina had remained respectfully silent, and Bethany inwardly thanked her. What a great friend.

By dinner, Bethany's contradictory emotions had been replaced with ravenous hunger; a hunger she experienced only when deeply disturbed. With great disappointment, she listened to the cheery receptionist respond to her request for room service.

"I'm sorry," the receptionist said. "We're not offering room service this evening. The snowstorm has resulted in all our guests eating in the restaurant, and it's taking every available staff member to serve them.

We'd love to serve you downstairs, though."

"Okay, thanks," Bethany said into the receiver, her stomach growling anew. "No room service tonight," she said, flopping onto one of the queen-sized beds. "Now what?"

"Hmm?" Christina looked up blankly from perusing her devotional Bible.

The very Bible Bethany had given her two years ago. That was when Bethany considered herself a devout Christian, before she had deliberately turned her back on God. Bethany simply couldn't trust Him anymore. After Devin's treatment, she feared God would likewise betray her. Perhaps He already had. After all, He allowed Devin to break her heart. Something in the deepest valley of her soul contradicted this assumption and left her experiencing more than a little discomfort. But somehow, Bethany couldn't shake the idea.

She also couldn't shake the feeling that Christina prayed for her. Some days, Bethany felt as if a cloud of prayers hovered overhead. This knowledge left her feeling a combination of assurance and uneasiness.

Other than an occasional invitation to church, though, Christina had never mentioned the Lord to Bethany. And Bethany knew she never would. That was Christina's way, never pushy, just living out her faith, demonstrating Christ's love, for everyone to see. Sometimes it was almost enough to bring Bethany to her knees once again.

"What did you say?" Christina asked.

"Uh—I said, 'No room service.' The restaurant is so

crowded because of the snowstorm they need all employees down there."

"Well, I'm starved!" Christina closed her Bible and placed it on the oval oak table.

"Me too," Bethany said, more hungry than she ever remembered. Some people lost their appetite when upset. Bethany, however, grew ravenous. That was part of the reason she seemed destined to a lifetime in a size twelve—exactly three sizes larger than she would like to be.

"Why don't we just go down to the restaurant and eat?" Christina asked.

"You can. I think I'll skip supper." Bethany's stomach roared in response.

"Oh, come on, Bethany. Devin's probably already eaten and gone back to his room."

"Yeah, but he may be lurking by the fireplace, waiting for me to come down."

"Well, you can't hide from him your whole life. I don't think he'll bite you or anything."

"Thanks for being so sympathetic," Bethany said sarcastically, nervously pinching the folds of the plush burgundy bedspread.

Silence. "I'm sorry. I just hate to see you like this."

"Why don't you go on down and enjoy your meal and order whatever you have for me as a carryout. I'll eat when you get back."

"Okay," Christina said reluctantly and walked toward the clothes rack.

"The thing I keep wondering is whether Devin's

being here is a coincidence or if he somehow knew about my vacation," Bethany mused, rifling through her luggage for the retail magazine she had brought "just in case."

Christina seemed absorbed in her choice of outfit, and Bethany let the subject die. The whole thing was probably some horrid coincidence. If she didn't know any better, Bethany would think Cupid was playing some sick joke on her. She and Devin had planned their wedding for Valentine's Day last year. A year ago, their wedding had been two weeks away. The next two weeks were going to be hard enough for Bethany without having Devin trailing her. For no matter what he promised or did, Bethany could never trust him again. That was the reason she had returned all his letters. Yes, Bethany knew she still loved him. But a solid relationship must be built on trust as well as love. *Trust*. The one thing Cupid had yet to supply; the one thing Devin had yet to fulfill.

❧

Fifteen minutes later, Christina emerged from the rest room wearing a new red corduroy pantsuit. Christina had never been as attentive to her makeup as Bethany. But tonight she had taken extra care and was pleased with the effects of red lip gloss and smoky eye shadow. While Bethany wanted to avoid Devin and Brett, Christina couldn't deny the hope that she would encounter them—or rather, *him*. Regardless of her resolve to distrust her taste in men, Brett had haunted her thoughts all afternoon.

So had the horror that Bethany would somehow learn

of her telling Devin of their vacation. Only moments ago, when Bethany had mentioned the possibility of Devin's presence being a coincidence, Christina had stiffened in fear.

Presently, Bethany erupted in a chorus of wolf whistles, her eyes widened in admiration. "Don't you look gorgeous!"

"I wouldn't go that far—"

"I would. Who are you trying to impress?" Bethany sat up and tossed the magazine onto the nightstand.

Christina removed a pair of flashy gold-toned earrings from her jewelry pouch and paused before clipping them on. "Who says I'm trying to impress anyone?" She stooped to grab her bag and room key. "Are you *sure* you won't come with me?" A quick glance at her sporty silver and gold-toned Timex. "It's seven-thirty, I seriously doubt—" She stopped herself. Somehow, it seemed less than honest to tell Bethany she doubted they would see Devin and Brett while all the time she hoped they would.

"Most women find Brett attractive," Bethany said with a knowing smirk.

"And what's that supposed to mean?" A guilty flush warmed Christina's cheeks.

"You know what it means. We've known each other too long and too well for me not to see through—"

"Oh, stop it!"

"If it's any consolation, I think he's probably hoping he'll run into you again."

"Well, that doesn't mean he'll have Devin with him. Why don't you come to dinner with me? You really need to eat."

For the first time, Bethany seemed to consider going. A nervous pinch of her bottom lip. "I guess hunger will make you do crazy things, but I'm not sure I can wait until you get back to eat. I feel as if I could devour this bedspread as we speak." A mischievous grin. Bethany had a charming way of smiling which left one side of her mouth closed, and Christina was relieved to see that smile. Her friend had done nothing but frown and worry all afternoon.

"I'll wait while you get ready."

Chapter 3

Thirty-six. Devin had turned thirty-six last month. And what had his life amounted to? A joke. One huge joke.

"Come on," Brett said. "It can't be *that* bad."

"She looked at me as if I were Satan himself," he said, staring at the inky darkness which had cocooned the lodge in winter chill.

"Well, what did you expect?"

"I knew it." Devin turned narrowed eyes to his only sibling. "You're on her side. I always did think you liked her better than me." Then the twisted, teasing smile.

"Let's face it, she's got better legs than you." Brett adjusted his black wire-rimmed glasses. "I do have my limits, you know."

A soft chuckle. "I just wonder what *her* limits are. I wonder if I pushed her past them."

"Well, like I already told you once, big brother, Bethany Townsley is a classy lady, and I'm not going to sit here and pretend like you didn't do her dirty. We both know you did. If you can get her back into your life, then you should sell that newspaper of yours and go into miracles."

"Thanks for the encouragement."

"If it's any consolation, I think she could do a lot worse." Brett chomped down on his gourmet hamburger. "Mmm. Nothing beats a good burger. Aren't you going to eat yours?"

"Yeah." Devin toyed with a warm french fry. At least he could be thankful for the snow. The red Jeep in which Bethany and Christina had arrived still sat in the parking lot and attested to their being trapped like everybody else.

Intersecting her at a romantic spot had seemed the perfect opportunity to tell her his side of the story. He so wanted to explain why he left with nothing but a backpack. If she would only give him the chance, perhaps he could reignite the love they once shared.

Christ had made, was making, such a drastic difference in his life, in him. Devin had been a Christian since adolescence. But he had recently learned that Christ could be more than a friend. He could be a healer, something Devin had desperately needed; something Devin didn't even know he needed until the memories began.

The memories had started when he learned of his father's death, the morning before his wedding. They had invaded his mind like enemies from the past, but they had been his gateway to God's healing power.

If only Bethany would listen.

❧

Brett swallowed the last bite of his charbroiled burger and glanced toward a movement at the crowded restaurant's doorway. Bethany. She scanned the crowd as if she were looking for Devin and planning to take flight if she saw him. And beside her, Christina Harrison.

Christina, dressed in a pantsuit that should be outlawed. The color of strawberries, it did lethal things to the red highlights in her hair, and, even at this distance, made her brown eyes sparkle.

He swallowed against a throat, suddenly dry. When he had seen her, his initial reaction had been, *Why haven't I met you before now?* But after he walked away, Brett had remembered Stephanie. He rubbed his thumb against the thin, gold band on his left ring finger. Two years had elapsed since his wife's death. Was it such a crime that he was attracted to Christina? Brett toyed with the idea of removing the band but postponed what he knew was inevitable.

"Don't look now, but Bethany and Christina just walked in," Brett muttered. "And I think they're heading for the table next to ours." A quick glance across the crowded restaurant. "It's the only one in the nonsmoking section that's vacant."

"You're kidding," Devin hissed as if he had just won a million bucks. "Does she know we're here?"

Bethany followed Christina, who followed the erect hostess. All the while, Bethany scanned the restaurant like a shepherd, searching for the demoniacal wolf that had assaulted the sheep.

"No, but she's looking." A sudden surge of pity engulfed Brett. Poor Devin. The man didn't stand a chance with Bethany. He was playing a loser's game. "Oops. Now she's spotted us."

Horror. Not even Bethany's ever-present, meticulous makeup could hide the horror cloaking her face.

Brett's first impulse was to rush forward and comfort her, as any brother would. Instead he put the comfort in his smile.

Her immediate, tight-lipped grin did nothing to assure him on Devin's behalf.

"And here we are, ladies," the prim hostess said, placing menus on either side of the neighboring table. "The waitress will be with you shortly. Because everyone's snowed in, we're crowded, so we appreciate your patience."

❧

Bethany, her heart racing as if she had run a marathon, pretended she didn't see Devin. Picking up the menu, she buried her nose in it, then peered around the edge at Christina.

"I cannot believe this," she whispered.

"Me, either," Christina mouthed back then shrugged helplessly.

The aroma of steaks and burgers and baked potatoes only heightened the nausea which, at the sight of Devin, had amazingly depleted her ravenous hunger. Even now, Bethany felt him watching her. Biting her lip, she suppressed the urge to turn and tell him she could live without his scrutiny, while all the time her traitorous mind replayed the last time he had held her. She hadn't felt complete since.

"Er. . .nice snowstorm, isn't it?" Devin said, his usually smooth voice sounding strained.

Concentrating on the outlandish price of a T-bone, Bethany kept the laminated menu between her and him and occasionally glanced toward Christina. This was definitely not working.

"Yes," Christina said merrily. "We hardly ever see a good snowstorm in Dallas. Except—"

Bethany compulsively kicked Christina's shin and mouthed, "Shut up."

In response, Christina glared back and finished her statement. "Last winter before Valentine's Day the weather surprised us, didn't it?"

"I remember that," Brett said. "I was planning to fly from San Francisco for the wedding, but. . ." His words trailed off as he apparently realized his mistake.

Brett had been coming from San Francisco for *Bethany and Devin's* wedding. "Excuse me," Bethany spoke in a clipped voice, laid down the menu, and glared into the fathomless depths of Devin's dark eyes. "But I've just decided to skip dinner."

Grabbing her bag, she stood, only to look eye to eye with Devin, now standing. Then a faint gasp as his lean fingers encircled her wrist. Or was this a caress?

"Please don't go because of me," Devin said, his eyes bottomless pools of regret. "Look, we're almost through. We were about to leave."

Bethany glanced toward Brett who had just received a thick slab of cheesecake.

"Let go of me," she ground out through gritted teeth as tingles inched up her wrist and arm. "And don't you ever touch me again!" She wrenched her wrist from his hold. Trying to ignore the surrounding patrons' prying gazes, Bethany raced toward the door which opened into the massive lobby.

"Bethany. . .wait! Bethany!" he called over the

collective, curious murmur.

She heard his footsteps close behind, felt him pursuing her as if she were somehow attainable. There was no way he could ever understand how deeply he had hurt her. There was no way she would ever trust him again.

☙

"Mind if I join you?" Brett asked as Christina watched first Bethany, then Devin disappear into the lobby.

She turned to stare wide-eyed into his soft brown eyes.

"She's not a very happy camper, is she?" Brett asked.

"No. Do you think I should go after her?"

"I think you'd better leave well enough alone."

"If only I had done that in the first place. I wish—" Christina bit her lip, not knowing how much Brett knew, not wanting to involve any more people than were already involved. She and Devin were enough.

"You wish you had never told Devin about your vacation?"

"You know?"

A quick nod. "Yeah. Devin dragged me along for moral support. I'm beginning to think he made a terrible mistake."

"I think I'm the one who made the mistake."

"Well. . ." A jaunty smile, and he adjusted his black wire-rimmed glasses. "Maybe not. Which brings me to my original question. Mind if I move to your table?"

You can move to my neighborhood, honey. "No, of

course not. I think there's room for you *and* your cheesecake."

"Oh good, I wouldn't have come without my cheesecake. Dessert and I—we go way back." Standing, he took the two steps which separated their tables and folded his tall frame into Bethany's vacated seat then arranged his dessert and coffee.

"That looks sinful," Christina said, eyeing the confection. "I think I'll order two."

He snickered, and the corners of his eyes crinkled into faint lines.

Tucking a strand of hair behind her ear, Christina momentarily forgot where she was as that same electricity from earlier zoomed through her midsection.

Brett was as dark as Devin was fair. His hair, sprinkled with premature silver at the temples, reminded her of shiny, black satin. The faint white scar at the corner of his tilted mouth gave him the look of a polite pirate. And his broad shoulders, clad in a teal designer sweater, were so like. . .*Keith's*.

That thought jolted Christina back to reality. His next words completed the transition.

"You sound like my little girl, Angie. She lives for dessert."

"Your little girl?" she croaked, gripping her water glass as if it were her only connection with sanity.

"Yeah. She's six, going on twenty. My wife and I had her young. The first year of our marriage. We were only twenty-four. Here, I've got Angie's picture." He flopped open his eelskin billfold to reveal an angelic blond-haired, blue-eyed child.

That's when Christina noticed his thin, gold wedding band, and her heart wilted. How had she missed the ring earlier? It must be fate. The only men she seemed to be attracted to were married. At least this guy wasn't trying to hide his family, as Keith had. Earlier, Bethany had hinted at Christina's attraction for him. Why hadn't Bethany told her he was married?

"And here's a picture of her in last year's Easter play at church. She's the angel on the right."

"She fits the role."

"Yes, in looks and disposition. She's a wonderful child. Never gives me a bit of trouble. And that's a miracle in itself, especially since—" He pressed his full lips together and stared at the picture as if it had somehow ordered his silence.

This brief conversation had supported what she had already assumed about herself. Christina, ever the gullible, had no business talking to any man. The innate feminine warning system which Bethany relied on seemed absent with Christina. She had gotten lucky with Keith. The police had arrived before he regained consciousness. Next time, she might not be so lucky.

"I'm sure you and your wife are very proud of her." Not knowing what else to say, Christina searched for any means of escape.

"I'm not married," he said and tore his lonely gaze from the photos.

Yeah. And I'm Wonder Woman. I'm not falling for that one again, buddy. "Then why are you wearing a wedding band?" she demanded, suddenly irate with the whole male gender. Who did these guys think they were? Running around, handing out smooth lines as if they thought women were stupid enough to believe them.

He glanced toward the worn gold band and rubbed it with his thumb. "I've been wearing it as a reminder," he reflected. Then the polite pirate removed the ring and slipped it into his jeans pocket. "My wife was killed in a car wreck a couple of years ago." A sad smile drooped across his face.

"Oh?" Christina fought mixed emotions. Elation, that Brett said he was single. Compassion, that his wife had died. But should she believe him? His being a widower would explain why Bethany hadn't told Christina he was married. Bethany would probably have warned her if he really were married. Desperately, Christina wanted to believe him.

Chapter 4

"Bethany, wait!" Devin called for the fourth time.

Frantically, she raced into the elevator and pushed the third-floor button. "Come on, come on," Bethany muttered, her palms drenched in cold sweat. But the door seemed determined to stay open until Devin entered. He was mere feet away. As she prepared to dash for the stairs, the door finally started closing. Relief melted her anxiety.

Then Devin managed to squeeze into the elevator.

The door's sigh seemed the groan of death itself—emotional death. Bethany pressed herself against the farthest wall as she stared in dread distaste at the man who had ripped out her heart, mutilated it, and hid it only God knew where. Bethany had been numb since his jilting. Numb, until that fourth letter.

"Bethany, please, just listen to me."

"Listen to you? Why should I? If I remember correctly, I was the one who wrote you and called you a year ago and tried to get you to listen to me. If you wanted to talk, you should have talked then." She glanced toward the floor indicator light while, as if in slow motion, it lit up the number 2.

Hurry, hurry, hurry, she urged, feeling as if she were caged.

"I still love—" he blurted then stopped, his face stricken.

He hadn't meant to say it. She could see it in his eyes. The surprise, the consternation, the resignation. Silence —intense, thick, silence—filled the elevator like a suffocating pall; a pall which snatched Bethany's every breath.

"I still love you," he rasped again, his eyes those of a lamb going to slaughter.

The elevator's humming halt preceded the door's automatic opening, and Bethany stared at him, aghast.

He still loves you! He loves you! He never stopped loving you!

Reality's icy grip strangled her elation. The sarcastic laugh followed. "You're lying. If you loved me, you would have never jilted me. You never loved me."

Then, the stinging tears; the ocean of tears she had harbored all afternoon; the tears she had guarded like a jealous lover, afraid to relinquish hold. And she ran. She ran as if her very soul would perish were she to stop.

Castaway. Castaway. You're nothing but an excess ornament he could rid himself of when he tired of you.

Bethany sightlessly fumbled with the suite's lock then stumbled into the room.

"Bethany, listen—listen to me. There's a lot going on here. I don't believe it was a coincidence that you sat right next to us tonight. Don't you think it's a little strange that we were down there at the same time?"

Releasing a sob, slow and mournful, she closed the door on his torrent of words. As a new sob erupted,

Bethany felt as if she must wash away his touch, his words, his presence. With fumbling fingers, she took off her denim coat dress, navy boots, and underwear, then stepped into the nearby shower.

The water, hot and stinging, mixed with her tears and seemed to wash her life down the drain. Her body shook with the strength of each sob as she hugged herself, turned her face into the corner, and leaned against the cool, burgundy tile.

Then a weeping wail for the child she had dreamed of bearing by now. A little boy. She and Devin had both wanted a boy first.

She massaged her abdomen as if to somehow expel the maternal urges which would never be fulfilled. Without Devin, without their marriage, she would never know the completeness only motherhood could bring.

Bethany didn't know how long she stayed in the shower, but the sound of the suite's door closing jarred her from her agony. Christina. Christina must be back from the restaurant. Bethany should compose herself. Christina had never seen her so distraught. *No one* had ever seen her so distraught.

Turning her face into the hot spray, Bethany massaged her swelling eyes and knew she couldn't hide the remnants of her mourning. And suddenly, she didn't care if Christina knew she had been crying. Bethany had every right to cry. Her life had been wrecked, and the person responsible was back.

Devin said he still loved her. Was this another of his lies?

"Bethany? Are you in here?" Christina asked. "Are you okay?"

"I'm going to live, if that's what you mean."

"I *know* that. I ordered you a hamburger and fries. And, um, unless you need to talk, I'll just leave it on the table by the window and go back to finish my meal. I left Brett in the restaurant; we're not through eating. I just thought I'd bring this up to you since you were so hungry."

Bethany's stomach growled anew. "That's sounds great," she called, turning off the water. Secretly, she was glad that Christina would leave her on her own for a while. Bethany still needed some solitude to sort through all her feelings. "Go and enjoy your meal," she urged. Bethany grabbed a plush towel.

"Uh. . .I did have one quick question, Bethany."

"Yeah?"

"Brett says his wife was killed?"

Bethany couldn't hide the smile. Poor Christina. That experience with Keith had completely reversed her trusting spirit. She had gone from doubting no one to doubting everyone. "Brett really is single, Christina, and one of the greatest guys I've ever met. You can believe everything he tells you."

"Thanks," her friend breathed.

❧

Snowflakes snuggled against the tinted window and seemed to smother Devin's heart in icy finality. After two hours of aimlessly wandering about the lodge, he had discovered this quiet corner off the east wing. He wasn't even sure what floor he was on, but the nook was just perfect for a man seeking solitude. Not that he necessarily wanted to *avoid* Brett. But there were moments in life when a person needed to be alone.

Brett understood. He had always understood. The two had been through a lot together—and apart. Perhaps that was why they were more than brothers. They were best friends.

Two plaid upholstered chairs sat beside a trio of floor-to-ceiling windows. Devin sat in one chair and rested his feet on the other. Like throbbing reminders of his past, Devin's left ankle and knee ached, but that was expected in this weather. During the last year, he had repeatedly thanked God for Brett's father, Devin's stepfather, the man who had adopted and raised Devin. Willis Carmichael hadn't been abusive. Devin couldn't say the same for his biological father. But for once, Devin chose to ignore his past in preference for his present ache. His heartache.

Naively, he had allowed himself to hope he could somehow get through to Bethany. With faith, he had prayed that God would arrange a means of contact with her. In triumph, he had believed God was answering his prayers when she sat right next to him at dinner.

Now Devin had blown it. His plan had been to calmly befriend her, then slowly rebuild her trust. But there was nothing calm in the way he had chased her from the restaurant, through the lobby, onto the elevator, and to her room. Subtlety had never been his greatest asset. Add to that the trait of focusing on and going for what he wanted, and Devin should have known blurting out his love was inevitable.

With an embarrassed groan, he rubbed his eyes and wished he could edit the whole day, like one of the articles in his newspaper. Yesterday's mail should have told him how Bethany would react to his presence. As he figured, she had returned his most recent letter, unopened. If, after six letters, she still wouldn't listen to him, why did he ever think she would heed him in person?

At this point, Devin knew only One who could make any sense of this mess. "Lord," he mumbled, still watching the snow, "You've taken me through some miraculous healing, and I'm so grateful that You've replaced my anger with Your love. So here I am again, asking for another miracle. Couldn't You please, please soften Bethany's heart? Help her to see I really mean what I say. I believe she's the woman for me. I believe You put us together in the first place. If You could only. . ."

As his mind began to wander, he trailed off to stare, mesmerized, at the snowflakes, falling from a seemingly infinite paradise of ice. That's what Bethany's heart seemed to be, a paradise of ice; a place Devin desperately wished to be, but just as desperately feared. With an exhausted yawn, he propped his head against the chair and didn't resist his heavy lids as they descended over his eyes.

❧

Bethany stood transfixed. The man was Devin. She would know his disheveled hair in a crowd of thousands. Its various shades of blond created the look of sun streaks the year round. And there he sat, sound asleep, his feet in the seat of one chair, his head on the back of another.

Christina and Bethany had spent the last half hour discussing all she had withheld from her friend concerning Devin, his letters, and Bethany's feelings of betrayal. Christina had been an angel of support to whom Bethany poured out her soul and her tears.

While Christina showered, Bethany had gone in search of ice. They planned to continue their conversation over some colas. And one of the topics would concern Christina's dinner with Brett. Bethany hoped that Christina and Brett would fall in love. Each deserved a good mate.

In her musings, Bethany had taken a wrong turn and ended up on the other end of the hallway. Funny that she could fight her way through the Dallas traffic without ever getting lost. But put her in a big hotel, and she got lost every time. This time, her detour had led her to Devin.

She shivered against a chill, a shiver which seeped into her soul. Strange that she should keep running into Devin like this. First, his being at the same hotel was a wild coincidence. Next, the snow had trapped them together. Then, she sat by him at dinner. Now, she had stumbled onto him once more. Was he right when he suggested their chance meetings weren't coincidences? Despite their stormy relationship, both of them had felt that God had originally put them together. Was He doing it again?

Another chill.

Bethany could no longer fathom such nonsense. She had decided a year ago that God had somehow forgotten about her or was ignoring her or simply didn't care for her. So why would He take the time to throw her and Devin back in each other's paths?

Pinching her bottom lip, she caught her breath as Devin shifted in the chair. Once he settled, his arms were crossed, as if he were cold.

Something inside Bethany twisted in response to the boyish turn of his lips. She couldn't deny that she had never stopped loving him. That was the greatest heartbreak of all because, despite her feelings, she could never allow him, or any other man, close to her again. It was too risky. If only she *could* stop loving him.

He shifted again, and this time Bethany detected a shiver. Impulsively, she set her ice bucket on the floor, then removed her sea green bathrobe. Her matching pajamas really looked more like a slinky pantsuit, so she didn't mind being seen in them. Without analyzing her motive or her actions, Bethany silently hurried to cover Devin in her bathrobe. The robe and pajamas had been a specially ordered and expensive set. She didn't know if she could reorder just the robe, but somehow that didn't matter.

Catching her breath, she hovered for mere moments to cherish a stolen glimpse of the man with whom she had once planned to spend her life. His sand-colored lashes fanned against cheeks, tanned because of his love of the outdoors. His prominent chin held the dark stubble of the last twenty-four hours. And his thick brows, marred by a scar Bethany knew was from childhood, made him look like a thinker.

Fleetingly, she wondered if he were dreaming of her. If his declaration of love were true, then he probably was. Bethany reached to stroke his forehead, but stopped. Her eyes stung. How had life ever become so complicated?

His spicy scent trailing her, she reluctantly turned to pick up her ice bucket and continue on her journey, confident that Devin would never know who covered him.

Within ten minutes, Bethany found the ice machine and arrived at her room. Only when she automatically reached for her plastic card key in the pocket of her absent robe, did she realize her mistake. The key was in the robe. Her eyes widened. Her hand trembled. Her mind spun with all the implications.

If Devin awoke before she retrieved that key, he would know who left the robe. But if she tried to get the key, she might wake him. And if he awoke with her hovering over him. . .

Still, Bethany felt she had no choice. She simply could not risk his learning she had covered him. That would further complicate an already volatile situation.

Chapter 5

With resolve, Bethany silently set the ice bucket outside her door and turned back the way she had come. In seconds she retraced her steps and once again watched the sleeping Devin. Her heart palpitated in dread and anticipation. If she were completely honest with herself, Bethany would admit that Devin pulled her like a magnet. Regardless of the warnings of her common sense, she still thrilled in his presence. Ironically, she also feared waking him. That would force her to explain more than she understood herself.

Holding her breath, Bethany tiptoed across the few feet separating them. Biting her bottom lip, she reached into the robe's pocket and wrapped her fingers around the plastic card. Sighing, she dashed a last glance at Devin.

As if her glance alerted him, Devin grunted in surprise, sprang upward, and tackled Bethany.

The nearby ottoman broke her fall as she crashed first against its cushion and then to the floor. A swoosh of air escaped her lips, and her lungs felt as if they had released their last breath.

Devin, eyes blazing in sleepy rage, roughly pinned her wrists to the floor and straddled her torso. "I won't let you hit me again! I won't! I won't," he cried in the voice of a small boy. "I'm tired of you always hurting me!" His face contorted in agony.

Immediately, Bethany knew he was dreaming and hadn't awakened. "Devin! Devin! It's me. Bethany!" she said urgently, afraid of what he might do to her if he didn't regain consciousness. Who was hitting him in his dreams?

He blinked. The rage in his eyes disappeared. His face relaxed. Silently, motionlessly, he stared at her for what felt like an eternity.

And Bethany returned the stare. His hands still pinned her wrists to the floor. He still straddled her. But the anger turned to wonder. When his gaze trailed to her mouth, Bethany couldn't deny the jolt in her midsection.

"What are you doing here?" Devin rasped.

"I—I—would you mind letting me up?" she said, not sure exactly how to explain her presence.

"Sorry." A sheepish smile. And he released her. "You surprised me, that's all. I'm not used to waking up with somebody hovering over me."

Slowly, Bethany sat up and gingerly tested her joints.

"Are you okay?" Devin asked, concern lacing his words.

"I think." She began standing on quivering legs.

Devin, taking her arm, tried to help her up.

Instinctively, Bethany jerked away and gained her footing on her own.

"You know I'd never hurt you, Bethany," he said with regret.

"I know." And she meant it. Even though their relationship had been marred by Devin's temper, Bethany had never once thought he would become physically violent.

"I just didn't know it was you. I thought you were—"

Curiosity drove her to anxiously await his next words. Who had been hitting him in his dream? Was there something about Devin that Bethany didn't know?

"I was having a nightmare," he finished, his eyes evasive.

"Oh." Bethany experienced an anticlimactic disappointment but brushed it aside. Her hands shaking, she gripped the plastic card key, and stepped toward the hallway.

"You never answered my question," he said, stepping in front of her. "What are you doing here?" Deep in his smoky eyes a shadow of hope danced like a fairy at midnight.

She couldn't tell him why she was here. That would reveal more than she ever intended him to know. Her mind frantically grasped for any means of escape. Earlier, Bethany had run from him. Somehow, she didn't think that would work this time. He had already tackled her. She envisioned him picking her up and hauling her back to this very spot until she answered his question. Once he set his mind to something, Bethany had never known Devin to give up easily.

"Did you think I was going to harm you?" she asked, trying to parry his question.

His eyes momentarily clouded. "Like I've already said. I was in the middle of a bad dream. You startled me."

"Oh. Well, um, Christina will be wondering what happened to me." Her right hip began to ache as Bethany edged for the hallway.

"Please don't go, Bethany."

His plea stopped her as if she had run into a brick wall. In the elevator, Devin had said he still loved her. Could he be sincere? Bethany didn't dare look into his eyes again. Already, her anger of the afternoon was ebbing. Another glimpse into his turbulent eyes might instigate her saying something she had no business saying.

She felt her resolve melting like ice on a scorching southern day. This was the man who had written her six letters. *Six.* What had he been so desperately trying to tell her? Deliberately, she studied the plastic card, all the while feeling his scrutiny; a scrutiny which rendered her immobile.

"Would you at least consider having a cup of coffee with me? We could go down to the restaurant now, and—"

"I'm in my pajamas." She dared glimpse his way. "I don't think—"

"That looks like a pantsuit."

"I know." She glanced toward the sea green robe which lay crumpled behind Devin.

His gaze followed hers. "I guess this is yours then?" Devin bent to retrieve the robe.

"Yeah."

"How did it get on the floor?"

"Uh—" Her cheeks warmed, and the truth spilled out. "I stumbled upon you sleeping." A shrug. "You looked cold, so I put my robe on you. I forgot the key in

215

the pocket. I was getting it when you woke up."

Once again, that shadow of hope danced through his eyes in fairylike glee. "Thanks for caring," he rasped. "At dinner, I didn't think you'd pour water on me if I was on fire." He produced a strained smile.

"I've been through a lot, Devin." *Or rather, you've put me through a lot.* "You can't expect to just plop back into my life and have everything the way it was. Life doesn't work that way." A bitter thread tainted her words. And Bethany reminded herself that regardless of her attraction for Devin she could not trust him.

The shadow of hope left his eyes. "Would you at least give me the opportunity to explain everything, Bethany?"

"I've already told you once today that you had plenty of opportunity to explain a year ago." The bitter thread turned to a challenging edge. Her back rigid, she dared him to defy her.

"I know that." Wearily, he rubbed his eyes.

Bethany once again wanted to stroke aside the hair falling on his forehead. Something in his demeanor cut through her negative emotions, and Bethany felt as if she were on a pendulum, swinging from anger, to compassion, to anger, to love.

Yes, she still loved him. She had already admitted that to herself. Even now, she would trade ten years of her life for two minutes in his arms. If only. . .but no, Bethany would rather grow into an old spinster than ever relive what Devin Carmichael had put her through. She had read that being jilted right before a wedding was like a death. Bethany wondered if it were worse than death.

"I just thought perhaps you'd listen," Devin continued. A heavy sigh. "I guess I was wrong." Silently, he looked at his loafers.

"If I do listen to you, it won't change anything," she blurted, wondering where the words had come from.

His head snapped up. "I'm not asking for that. I just want to tell you why I did what I did. And to—to ask your forgiveness. Even if I no longer have your love, Bethany, I need your forgiveness."

"I'm not sure I can forgive you," she whispered, a tear seeping onto her lashes. *You have my love, Devin, and you always will. That should be enough for you.* Their gaze lengthened, and Bethany felt as if she were spinning in a whirlwind of emotions. Her heart begged for his touch while her head scoffed her weakness. A tear spilled onto her cheek. Devin reached to brush it away. She recoiled from his touch.

"Sorry." He crammed his hand into his jeans pocket.

"I'll listen to your explanation," she said, fumbling with the plastic key. "But that's all."

"At least that's a start."

"It's not a start," she insisted. "It's the end. The very end."

"You can't deny that you care for me."

"No, I *can't*. I never *stopped* caring for you, Devin. But I can't pretend that I'll ever trust you, and you need to understand that. No matter what you tell me—"

"Okay. Okay." He held up his hands in resignation. "I understand where I stand." Yet that fairy danced through his eyes once more.

Bethany, gritting her teeth, felt as if she had somehow been manipulated. She had just agreed to doing what she had vowed not to do only hours before.

"Oh, there you are," Christina's voice preceded her person by mere seconds. "I got worried about you. I found the ice at the door, and—" As Christina neared, she halted, her attention riveted on Devin. "Oops. I didn't notice you."

"It's okay. We were through talking anyway," Bethany said with more purpose than she felt. For her traitorous heart still longed to feel Devin's arms around her.

"Bethany." He took two halting steps forward. "Would you please go with me tomorrow—just for a drive. After breakfast. The roads will be cleared by then. We could go into the mountains, get away from the distractions, and I could tell you. . ." He glanced at Christina, who awkwardly stood by.

Devin Carmichael, if you think I'm going anywhere with you alone, you're crazy. But she heard herself say, "Okay. Just this once."

❧

Suppressing a shout, Devin watched Bethany walk up the hall with Christina at her side. *Thank you, Lord!* Inside, he cheered at the miracle God had rendered. Bethany still wasn't welcoming him with open arms, but at least she hadn't run from him this time. And on top of that, she covered him with her robe! She also admitted she still cared for him. This was more than Devin had dared hope for. But he had prayed for a miracle. Looked as if God was answering his prayer. Like a kid on Christmas morning, Devin dashed for his room, whipped open the door, and interrupted Brett's reading in bed.

"She's going to go out with me in the morning!"

Nonplussed, Brett stared at him. "What?"

"Bethany. She agreed to take a drive with me tomorrow after breakfast."

"You're kidding!" Brett laid his espionage novel on the rumpled burgundy comforter and sat up from his reclining position. "What happened? The last I saw of you two, she was running from you." Mischief in his eyes, he held up his hand. "Don't tell me. Let me guess. You caught up with her, knocked her down, and sat on her until she agreed to go out with you."

Devin relived the moment he had tackled Bethany. At the time, he had been trapped in a nightmare about his early childhood. When he had half awakened to someone looming over him, Devin had thought Bethany was his father. "Actually, that may be closer to the truth than you know." He chuckled dryly.

"Oh?" Brett adjusted his black glasses.

In minutes, Devin related the story.

"So you're going to tell her about the abuse?" Brett asked.

"I've *got* to. It's the only way I can even start repairing our relationship."

"And what about the money? Are you going to tell her about that too?"

"No." Devin took off his sweater and jeans and rummaged through his suitcase for the sweatpants which doubled as pajamas. "If we get back together, I want her to want me for me, not for an unexpected inheritance."

"Oh, come on, man. Bethany Townsley wouldn't go after someone for his money."

"In my mind, I know that. But another side of me needs to know she wants me, whether I'm broke or—or broken." Devin paused and stared blankly into his suitcase. Broken. That was what he had been. A broken little boy walking around in a man's body. His father's physical abuse had left Devin with enough suppressed anger for three men. But the fury had still leaked out. That was the reason his and Bethany's relationship had been so stormy. Regardless of his temper, though, Bethany had still loved him with an abandonment most men only dream of. And Devin had thrown that love in her face. Would she see that God had begun a miracle in him? Or would she be blinded by their past? *O Lord, open her eyes.*

"Are you going to answer me?" Brett asked.

Picking up his gray sweatpants, Devin turned to his brother. "What?"

"I was asking you about Christina Harrison, but you must have been on Mars. You didn't answer."

"Sorry. I was thinking." He stepped into the sweats and flopped onto his bed.

Brett swung his feet to the floor and leaned toward Devin. "What do you know about Christina?"

"Why?" Devin smirked.

"You *know* why."

"Well, she's known Bethany longer than I have.

They're like sisters." Devin, remaining obstinately silent, stared at the ceiling.

"*And.*"

"And?" He faked a bland expression.

"You always did enjoy tormenting me." Brett grabbed a pillow, stood, and whacked Devin in the face.

"Help! Attack!" Devin scrambled from the bed as Brett threatened another blow.

"Talk or you're dead meat!" Brett growled, a fond smile curving his lips. "Don't forget, I'm six years younger than you, and I can take you down fast."

"I'll talk! I'll talk!"

A mutual chuckle.

"She's a nurse practitioner at a pediatrician's office in Dallas."

"I know that. Tell me something I don't know." Brett raised the pillow and took a threatening step toward his brother.

Devin backed into the corner. "Well, what do you want to know?"

"Has she ever been married?"

"Not that I know of. Why? Do you already want to marry her? You always did work faster with women than I do. Maybe I need to take a few tips from you."

Rolling his eyes, Brett tossed the pillow back to his bed. "Do you know how dedicated of a Christian she is?"

"The last I knew, she practically camped out at church."

Brett, removing his glasses, chewed the earpiece

and walked toward the rest room.

"Is that all the information you need, sergeant?"

But it was Brett's turn to retreat into his thoughts.

Chapter 6

"Hi!" Christina turned from her musings at the lobby's window to smile up at Brett, dressed in a blue sweater and jeans. "Good morning." His dark hair, still damp at the temples, shone in the morning light, which streamed through the floor-to-ceiling windows. Christina shook herself, sure she would awaken and Brett would be a dream. A dream from heaven.

"What's so interesting out there?" He pointed toward the snowy peaks laden in skiers.

"Well, um. . ." Did Christina dare admit she had been spying on Devin and Bethany as they got in Devin's truck?

Brett grinned a lazy, indulgent, lopsided grin that left Christina's heart fluttering. "If it's any consolation, I was watching them, too."

She quirked one brow and feigned shock. "Don't tell me you would stoop to such nosiness!"

"You bet I would. After what I've been through with Devin, he owes me. He didn't touch his pancakes and sausage at breakfast, and he talked nonstop while I tried to eat. I figured I had earned a free spying session."

Christina tucked a strand of straight brunette hair behind her ear. "You know, I was just as perturbed but for the opposite reasons. I ordered breakfast in, and Bethany ate mine and hers. She always eats when she's disturbed. And instead of talking nonstop, she hardly said a word. I was forced to talk to myself if I wanted a conversation."

"Do you think they'll get back together?"

"I don't know. Bethany barely spoke to him when they met in the lobby. She seems pretty set on giving him his say and then going back to Dallas today."

"Today?" Brett's eyes posed a silent question.

She bit her lip and glanced at the cranberry-colored carpet. If Brett asked her to stay, she would finish her vacation as planned and let Bethany go back to Dallas on her own. But he would have to ask. She wouldn't push herself on him. Christina sensed she was his first romantic interest since his wife's death. If the Lord was for it, Christina wouldn't mind being his last romantic interest. She was so tired of being single, tired of the dating scene, tired of men lying to her. Brett's candid eyes and open honesty seemed an answer to prayer.

"I know Devin loves her," Brett muttered.

She watched Devin's four-wheel-drive truck pull from the parking lot and speed out of sight. "Yeah. And the sad part is, she loves him too, but—"

"But." With an understanding shrug of his shoulders, Brett looped Christina's hand through the crook of his arm.

This time, she made a point of investigating his left ring finger. A flash of excitement. The golden band was still missing.

"Now. Enough about those two. No sense in wasting our time together talking about *them.*" His jaunty grin once again reminded her of a polite pirate.

"Exactly what did you have planned?"

"Well, we are at a ski lodge, aren't we?"

"Yes," Christina said as he turned her toward the crowded reception area.

"Do you know how to ski?"

"No. Do you?"

"Yeah." He adjusted his glasses. "And while I'm not a professional by any means, the faster I go, the better I like it. Want me to teach you how?"

"I hadn't really planned to learn. That was going to be Bethany's goal," she said hastily, picturing Brett zooming down a slope while she toppled head over heels behind him. "I have to support myself, you know. I can't afford a broken leg or arm or neck."

"I won't let you break any bones. I promise. Come on." He tugged her toward the elevators. "Let's go get our coats. I brought my ski gear with me. We can rent some for you."

"Brett, I really would rather spend a nice, quiet day touring downtown, or—or—what about ice-skating? I know how to do that."

"How boring." He stopped and exposed her to a flir-tatious wink. "I had hoped to catch you if you fall. If you know how to ice-skate then you probably won't *ever* fall."

A rush of pleasure warmed Christina's heart. "Okay. If you promise to catch me."

"Oh, I'll promise to catch you. . .if you'll promise to fall."

"I think I might have already fallen," she said spontaneously. Immediately embarrassed, Christina wanted to clamp her hand over her mouth. Would she ever learn to curb her tongue?

"I think I might have fallen too." His eyes growing serious, Brett stroked her cheek. "Are *you* going to catch *me?*" he whispered.

A nod. And Christina thought she would drown in the tide sweeping her soul.

᨞

"If it's okay with you, I thought we'd head toward Oak Creek. It's a small town about twenty minutes south of here. It will be less crowded, I hope. We could stop at a restaurant there and get coffee if you like."

"That's fine," Bethany said coldly, determined not to encourage Devin. He hadn't made life easy for her the last year, and she was obstinately determined not to make this easy for him. Half the night, she had lambasted herself for agreeing to go with him. He had caught her in a weak moment. But as Bethany leaned against the truck door and took in the new smell of the rented vehicle, a tendril of guilt curled through her chest. She stared at him from the corner of her eye.

Devin gripped the black steering wheel as if it were his last chance at life. The fine lines around his mouth seemed deeper than they had been last year. The dark circles under his eyes attested to a sleepless night. He seemed oblivious to her scrutiny, and Bethany wondered if he were going to wait until they were facing each other in a restaurant before he spilled his "story." Despite herself,

Bethany's curiosity was piqued.

Before he had broken their engagement, Bethany had thought she knew all about Devin. Perhaps she had been wrong. The dream she awoke him from last night had not been a pleasant one. Did it reflect a facet of him she had yet to learn?

A stubborn strand of hair fell onto Devin's forehead. Just as she had done the night before, Bethany suppressed the urge to lovingly brush it back. His lips tilting upward, he glanced at her from the corners of his eyes.

She guiltily focused on the bank of snow and rolling mountains lining the road. Bethany bit her bottom lip, irritated that Devin had caught her looking at him.

"Did you get a good night's sleep?" he asked.

"No." Bethany didn't expound.

"Neither did I."

Serves you right, she wanted to add, but refrained. A tense silence settled between them, and Bethany refused to look at him again. She also refused to analyze her behavior. For if she got to the bottom of her actions, she might see that all Devin Carmichael would have to do was halfway try to put his arm around her and she would turn into putty. Why, after all the misery he had caused, was Bethany still so drawn to him?

Once again, she lambasted herself for agreeing to come with Devin. No matter what he said or how she felt, she still couldn't set herself up for more heartache. Desperately, she tried to pound that truth into her heart.

Bethany, snuggling into the warmth of her parka,

focused on erecting a wall around herself. In her mind, she visualized an invisible fortress behind which she would hide, never letting Devin penetrate the barrier.

In what seemed like seconds, Devin slowed and pulled into the parking lot of a quaint mom-and-pop restaurant. Immediately, Bethany got out, not daring to give him time to open her door. Like a boxer about to enter a championship match, she took a cleansing breath of the icy, mountainous air. She scanned the horizon and breathed a prayer. *Lord, I haven't said much to you lately. But if you'll get me out of this with my dignity, I promise I'll try to pick up where I left off.* The surrounding mountains seemed to echo her prayer and drape it over the layers of snow covering the trees and roofs.

A resigned sigh. She crunched through the snow and toward the restaurant's rustic wooden door. Not once did she glance toward Devin, who followed closely.

"Bethany?" he said, touching her shoulder.

She turned and stared at the top of his cream-colored sweater under his parka's open neck. Bethany refused to look into his eyes. Their smoky depths had a way of throwing her into a tailspin. No, she *must* keep her composure.

"If you'd rather not talk, we can just get in the truck and go back. As badly as I need you to listen to me, I don't want you to feel that I'm forcing myself on you." His voice, kind and considerate, overflowed with empathy.

Her commitment to avoid eye contact ended. She looked into eyes overflowing with love, with pain, with

228

uncertainty. A hard swallow. Did he know she really wanted to throw herself into his arms and pretend they had never parted?

"I promised you I would listen," she rasped, not recognizing her own voice. "And I will."

A frigid gust of wind whipped around the restaurant and lifted his streaked blond hair in its frosty fingers. He smiled in self-derision. "I would really rather not talk with you if you're going to look like I'm cramming cod liver oil down your throat." His right eyebrow quirked. "Come on, I can't be *that* bad."

Bethany bit her lip against a smile.

The plea in his eyes melted her reslove as the truth haunted her. *You will always love Devin Carmichael.*

Run, a frantic voice urged. *Run while you still have your dignity. You can call Christina to come pick you up. You can pack and catch the next plane to Dallas. Don't let him worm his way back into your good graces. YOU CANNOT TRUST DEVIN CARMICHAEL!*

Mutely, Devin took her arm and steered her toward the doorway. Bethany, like a complying lamb, didn't resist his prompting. She walked into a foyer decorated in knotty pine and lush greenery. A sprinkling of cheap Valentine decorations seemed to mock her. In a daze Bethany listened while Devin ordered a table for two in a secluded corner. She followed the bony waitress and plopped into the padded chair before her trembling legs collapsed beneath her. Bethany mechanically removed her parka and straightened her tweed jacket. As if she were a mouse being hypnotized by a cobra, she stared at Devin while he ordered gourmet coffee and her favorite cheese Danishes.

None of this was going as Bethany had planned. During her sleepless night, she had purposed to coldly listen to Devin, curtly tell him to stay out of her life, regardless, and request that he drive her back to the hotel. She had adhered to her calculated plan until that dreaded moment when he had teased her. The secret to maintaining her composure lay in not letting him get past her boundries.

With the waitress's courteous departure, Devin turned his complete focus on Bethany. "I guess this is the part where I begin, huh?" He rubbed the nape of his neck.

Bethany, toying with the forest green napkin, remained silent.

With new resolve, he began. "First, I just want to say that I meant what I said in the elevator yesterday. I love you, Bethany, and I never stopped loving you."

Why did that admission make her want to cry again? Bethany focused on the cinnamon candle flickering between them and blinked against the stinging tears. She would not give him the satisfaction of seeing her reaction. *She would not.*

"The morning before our wedding I received a disturbing phone call. It—it was about my biological father."

"Oh?" Bethany, her interest tempted, remembered Devin saying he had only trace memories of his real father. His stepfather, Willis Carmichael, had adopted the five-year-old Devin shortly after marrying Devin's mother. A year later, Brett had been born, and they had been a happy family of four. "I didn't think you knew if your biological father was even alive."

"I didn't." Devin swallowed. "But I found out he had been living in Mexico. I also found out he had been very much alive in me."

"What do you mean?"

"I mean, Bethany, that I never got over his abuse. That nightmare you woke me up from last night was about the abuse. My limp came from his abuse," he continued in an impassioned whisper. "And that horrid temper I badgered you with was the anger I had suppressed because of his abuse."

"What does this have to do with our wedding?"

"Like I already said, I received a phone call early Friday morning from my dad's lawyer. He said my father had passed away that week and had already been buried, but—" Devin halted as if he wanted to hide something.

A warning arose in Bethany. What was he trying to hide?

"Anyway, I had been having some nightmares for about six weeks before our wedding. They were so disturbing I didn't mention them to anyone. In the dreams, I was a grown man in the body of a four-year-old and a blond-headed man with a monster face was beating me with a broomstick." Clenching his fists, Devin hunched forward as if he were taking a blow at that very moment.

Bethany stilled herself against wrapping her hand around his tight fist. She shouldn't let anything he said dissolve her purpose to remain distant. Or should she?

231

So far, this story was more poignant than anything she had expected.

"Hearing news of my father somehow threw me into a series of flashbacks, and I relived that nightmare, Bethany. I relived it, and I was *awake*. The monster in that dream was my *father*. And I felt as if I were four again. I was so devastated that I could hardly put a sentence together, much less get married. I barely remember leaving some crazy message on your machine before I called my stepdad and mother. They came over. I don't remember much of anything else for about twenty-four hours. They say they found me hiding behind the couch and wailing like a little boy."

"Oh Devin, I'm so sorry." New tears. But this time the tears were for Devin. Bethany, forgetting her former resolve, reached across the table to clasp his hand. Although his face was impassive, Bethany knew Devin's pain wasn't spent. Last night's bad dream attested to that.

"Within a week, I had gotten a moderate grip on myself and had several long talks with my pastor and my mother. She told me things about my early childhood she had never told me before—I think because they were as painful for her as they were for me. To make a long story short, my father abused us both. Finally, my mom had the guts to get out of the marriage and secretly move from California to Texas. She says my father swore he would kill her, but he either didn't hunt for her or couldn't find her. We never heard from him again."

"Until the morning before our wedding."

The skinny waitress interrupted with their order,

and Bethany reflected over Devin's story. If he were telling the truth, she might remotely consider possibly rebuilding a relationship with him. If he were telling the truth. Devin had broken his word once. Could this be another fabrication? But then there was the nightmare from which she had awakened him.

After the waitress left, Devin absently stirred creamer into his fragrant coffee. "Anyway, I soon realized that I hated my biological father and that I had hated him most of my life. The whole thing threw me into a bout of questioning all my relationships—including ours. In all honesty, Bethany, I wasn't sure at the time if I *really* loved you."

"Why didn't you just call me?" she asked in frustration.

"I couldn't. What was I supposed to tell you? I wasn't even sure who I was anymore, let alone how to maintain a relationship. I don't expect you to understand that part. I'm not sure I even do. Maybe I should have called you. I don't know. All I know is that I had to get away from everybody and everything. By the first of March, I sold everything I owned except my car and a few personal items, bought a backpack, and headed for Wyoming."

"Wyoming?"

"Yeah." He shrugged. "I didn't know anybody there and hoped I could experience some solitude. I checked into a remote hotel and did a lot of hiking and praying and. . ." Devin stared past her. "And crying."

"How—how long were you there?"

"Six months." He toyed with his spoon. "Don't let

anyone tell you God doesn't heal, Bethany. I'm a living example. Even though I'm still working through some of the pain, I believe I can claim a miraculous recovery." A slight smile. "Anyway, once I got over the brunt of it, I came back to Fort Worth in August. When I got back, I opened my own newspaper with the money—" Once again he stopped in midsentence. Devin stared at the untouched Danishes as if he wanted to bite off his tongue.

"I might as well tell you," he blurted out. "My biological father left me a fortune. I was his only living relative, and he had kept up with me even though I never knew it. Believe it or not, he eventually found the Lord and wanted to somehow make amends for the abuse. That's why the lawyer contacted me in the first place. My dad left me a long letter, and then the money."

"You didn't want to tell me."

"No."

"Afraid I might be a bit money hungry?" Bethany asked, a sarcastic twist to her words.

"I never said that."

"Why else wouldn't you want me to know?" She resisted the urge to pour her hot coffee in his lap and leave him sitting there. Devin Carmichael had his nerve. He dragged her to this remote town, told her a sob story, then insinuated she might take him back for his money alone. Did he have a shock coming!

"I just didn't want the money to color your perspective, Bethany. If you would ever consider marrying me, I wanted it to be for *me*. Just for me."

"Isn't that the reason I agreed to marry you in the first place?"

"Yes, but that was before. . ." His eyes pleaded for understanding.

"You should have been a used-car salesman," she ground out.

"What's that supposed to mean?"

"It's supposed to mean that I think you're more interested in yourself than anything else, and you have a fine way of covering it. You don't give one flip about how I feel, and you never did." She stood, her legs now shaking with fury. "I'm sorry about your father's abuse, Devin. But do you want to know what I was doing while you were off in Wyoming?" Her voice rose, and a couple from a nearby table didn't hide their interest. "I was mourning a loss of my own! Do you know what it feels like to be jilted the day before your wedding?"

Devin stood. "Bethany, I—"

"You have nothing more to say that I want to hear." Blindly, she pivoted and rushed from the restaurant.

Chapter 7

S tunned, Devin watched Bethany dodge the scrawny waitress and run into the foyer. He pulled a ten-dollar bill from his billfold and tossed it on the table. Feeling as if he had been dropped into a scene from one of Brett's espionage novels, Devin raced from the dining room, into the foyer, and onto the snow-lined parking lot. No Bethany. Urgently, he peered into the cab of his ebony rental truck. She glared back at him through the windshield. Relief. The kind that warms the stomach.

A light smattering of snow had begun to dot the truck's windows. Devin, opening the door, dubiously glanced toward the gray sky. Hopefully, today's precipitation wouldn't turn into anything like yesterday's blizzard.

Within seconds, he cranked the engine, steered onto the road, and sneaked a peak at Bethany. Stonily, she stared out the front window.

"I'm sorry," he mumbled to the road. "I didn't mean to make you angry. That was the farthest thing from my mind."

He felt her scrutiny but didn't dare glance from the road, now frosted in a light veil of snow. More silence. More scrutiny. Then, a sniffle.

He dared look at her.

She dashed away the tears as fast as they spilled onto

her cheeks.

"Is this a bad sign?"

"I don't know," she choked out.

Impulsively, Devin slowed the vehicle and steered onto a narrow side road which had just been serviced by a snow plow. "Bethany. . ." Devin crammed the truck into park, removed his seat belt, and slid toward her.

Without a word, she met him halfway, and Devin's arms encircled her. How many times in the last months had he dreamed of holding her? Too many to count. But in his dreams, her hair hadn't smelled half as sweet. Her face had not seemed half as soft. Her lips, not half as delightful. Their kiss deepened. The kiss of two reunited souls.

"Ah, Bethany," he groaned against her lips. "If you could just give me another chance. I've prayed and prayed that you would at least consider. Please say you will."

Another kiss. A kiss which made the first one pale in comparison. And Devin, feeling as if he were drowning in passion, forced himself to pull away and gain control of his ragged breathing. Beseechingly, he looked into the depths of her eyes, now masked in blue contacts.

"I'll con–consider it. But. . ." She shook her head. "I can't promise."

Devin suppressed a shout. "At least it's a start," he said, amazed at his steady voice. Last night, she had told him today would be the end. The very end. Instead, today might be a new beginning.

"Look," Bethany said, a note of alarm tainting her voice. "The snow is getting really heavy."

He peered out the window, stunned at the snow-storm's growing intensity. "We need to go back to the hotel," Devin insisted, angry with himself for getting caught in such an onslaught. But he had been too busy with other thoughts. "I didn't check the forecast. Did you?"

"No. I hope we don't get a replay of yesterday."

"Me too. We've only got about fifteen miles to go. Maybe we'll get there before the snow gets any worse."

❦

As Devin began the northward trek, Bethany stared blankly at the great, fat snowflakes which assaulted the windshield. In her mind, she was reliving that kiss. The kiss which had catapulted her into star-studded orbit. Never had she planned for this outing to culminate so.

Everything had changed. Everything. Somehow, Devin had gotten past her defenses. But could she trust him? *Maybe*.

Then, another scene implanted itself in Bethany's mind. Last year. February fourteenth, 7:00 P.M. She should have been draped in white satin. Should have been walking down a church aisle on her angular father's arm. Should have been taking Devin's outreached hand. Instead, Bethany had been sobbing into her pillow.

Could she trust him? *No way!* a voice urged. *If he jilted you once, he could jilt you again.* But a conflicting thought barged in. *Devin will marry you this time. Trust him.*

O Lord, what do I do? I've blamed You for all of this. Now. . .I don't know. Maybe our wedding last year wasn't Your timing. Maybe Devin needed to deal with

his childhood before we could have a successful mar-
riage. I'm so confused, Lord. I've been so wrapped up
in my own pain, that I haven't been able to see anything
else. Please help me know what to do.

As if she were seeing the snow for the first time, Bethany started watching the amount accumulating on the roads. Those great, fat flakes had turned into a dense, blustering downfall. Until yesterday, Bethany, a native Texan, had never witnessed blizzard-type conditions. Now, she had witnessed them twice. Occasionally a car crept by in the other lane. A glance in the side window revealed an all-terrain vehicle not far behind them.

Bethany looked at Devin. Mouth drawn in frown. Brows knitted in concentration. White knuckles against the black steering wheel.

The digital dash clock announced that thirty minutes had elapsed since that sizzling kiss. Had Bethany been deliberating that long? Seeing the Steamboat Springs city limit sign stopped her from asking Devin how much farther they had to go.

"I've never been comfortable driving in this kind of weather," Devin said, his voice a bit tight.

"Me, either." Bethany didn't tell him that she had been more worried about their relationship than arriving safely.

"At least the snow seems to be slowing some. The way it was coming down, I was afraid we would be stuck on the side of the road together." Silence. "But would that have been so bad?"

Refusing to answer, she stared at the row of quaint,

old-timey stores which lined the main street. Her heart insisted she would be thrilled to be snowed in with Devin, especially if they were on their honeymoon. Then, the recurring doubts assailed her again.

Within minutes they were parking at the Steamboat Springs Inn. Woodenly, Bethany opened the door and slid from the truck. No sooner had her boots descended into the fresh snow than Devin was there.

"I'm sorry for rushing you." He grasped her hands. "I promise I'll give you as much space as you need, Bethany."

As she stared up into his earnest face, the diminishing snowfall dusted his fair hair and eyelashes. Then, that same stubborn strand of hair fell across his forehead. This time, Bethany gave into the urge to brush it back, and Devin closed his eyes.

Despite the questions, the doubts, the deliberating, Bethany felt herself gravitating toward trying to rebuild their relationship. She would be risking a lot, but what worthy venture came without risks?

"You're right. I can't be rushed. If. . ." she left the obvious unsaid. "I will need space."

That shadow of hope from the night before danced through his eyes in fairylike glee.

Bethany bit her lip. "Please don't be hasty to assume the best. I would hate to hurt you." She marveled at her enormous change in feelings. A few days ago, she would have welcomed hurting him as badly as he had hurt her.

Despite Devin's impassive face, more fairylike glee twirled through his eyes. "I promise I'll jump to no unfounded conclusions."

Another bite of her lip and Bethany turned for the inn, wondering how much of her feelings she had unwittingly revealed to him. Devin, as if she were once again his, took her arm and steadied her while they traipsed through the snow.

In seconds, they entered the inn, teaming with guests. Then, Christina and Brett materialized.

"I'm so glad to see you." Christina almost knocked Bethany off her feet with a bear hug. "We were really worried you guys were going to slide off the road or get stuck in the snow. We've been waiting in the lobby for about forty-five minutes."

Bethany, grappling for her footing, laughed at her friend's spontaneity.

"Hey! Didn't you have any faith in my driving skills?" Devin chided.

"I've driven with you, remember?" Brett teased.

"The receptionist kept saying there was no severe weather forecasted for today and that the snow would probably pass," Christina rushed on, her brown eyes flashing with relief. "But all I could think was, *I'll never forgive myself for telling Devin that Bethany was coming here. They would have never been at the same inn and never gone for this ride if it hadn't been for my big mouth.*" As if her words didn't register until after she had spoken them, Christina's eyes rounded in horror.

A horror Bethany felt herself. "You *told* Devin I'd be here?" she blurted out.

Helplessly, Christina nodded. "Accidentally."

Her head spinning with the implications, Bethany turned to Devin. "You *knew* I was going to be here when you came?"

"What does that matter?" Devin tried to reach for her hand.

Bethany jerked away.

"*Bethany*. What—"

"You *lied* to me, that's what." Like a great coiling cobra, fury slithered through her stomach. Bethany now possessed the answer to the question which had tormented her since last night. No. She could not trust Devin Carmichael. Now, or ever.

"What are you talking about?" Devin demanded.

Forgetting Christian and Brett and the crowded ski lodge, Bethany's voice rose in accusation. "You followed me here, but you acted like you were surprised when you saw me yesterday."

"What was I supposed to do?"

"You were *supposed* to be honest, Devin. Totally honest. You were supposed to tell me you knew I'd be here, not act like it was some huge coincidence or—or like you thought *God* had put us in the same spot to try to get us back together."

"I never said that. All I said was that I thought it wasn't a coincidence that we sat by each other last night."

"But you implied—"

"Well, what exactly was I supposed to do?" he asked again. "You *ran* from me!"

"You've had plenty of opportunity to tell me the whole story today. But you chose not to. This only proves one thing to me. You cannot be honest."

"No," he snapped, a red flush inching up his face. "It proves you can't be reasonable."

She flinched as if he had struck her. "Now that we understand each other, I'm going to do what I should have done yesterday and go back to Dallas."

"Bethany," Christina said. "Give him a break! Can't you see, the man is trying to—"

"How could you?" Bethany turned on the person she had thought was her dearest friend, her strongest ally. "How could you tell him I'd be here? You knew he was the last person I needed to see."

"Apparently not," Christina retorted. "Not the way the two of you looked a few minutes ago when you walked in here!"

"We've all been under a lot of pressure," Brett soothed. "Christina and I have been worried about you guys out in the snowstorm, and you two. . ." He pointed to Devin and Bethany. "Well, we've just been under a lot of pressure. Why don't we all go back to our rooms and relax. I'm sure once we've calmed down, this won't be as big a deal as—"

"This has nothing to do with calming down," Bethany snapped, feeling as if Brett were patronizing her. "It has to do with *trust*." Noticing a group of people boarding the elevator, Bethany rushed toward them. For the fourth time in twenty-four hours, she was running from Devin Carmichael. Or was she running from her own feelings?

Chapter 8

Christina looked from Devin to Brett and back to Devin. "I'm sorry I told her you knew she was going to be here," she croaked.

"There's no reason for you to apologize," Devin said, a painful twist to his lips. "She would have found out sooner or later. Somehow, I think she was looking for an excuse to leave." Sighing, he rubbed his forehead. Then, like a weary warrior, Devin passed his hand over his face. "I'm going up to my room to pack." He strode toward the massive stairway.

"Well, that's that." Brett removed his black-rimmed glasses to place the earpiece in his mouth. He draped a consoling arm around Christina's shoulders.

"Now I think I feel more sorry for Devin than Bethany. Since you told me about Devin's childhood, I can understand his canceling the wedding. Why can't Bethany?"

"Don't ask me to try to figure out women." He quirked one brow. "I've been skiing with one all morning who never once fell my way—and after such a welcome invitation from an ardent admirer."

Christina playfully punched his midsection, a flush of pleasure warming her cheeks. During Brett's ski lesson, she had purposed not to "accidentally" fall his way. The temptation had been great. But so had her hesitation.

She would rather keep an interested Brett at arm's length than overpower him with her spontaneity; a spontaneity that had already gotten her into more trouble than she cared to get out of.

"Well, I guess I'll go see if I can talk with Bethany." Regretfully, Christina stepped out of the circle of Brett's arm.

A disappointed fog dampened the velvet softness of his eyes. "If Bethany goes back to Dallas today, that means you will too. Right?"

She remembered her vow not to seem overly eager with Brett. She remembered it, then dismissed it. "Not necessarily. Our reservations were for a week. We've only been here one night. If you'll stay, I'll stay."

A huge smile. "I'd give my life savings for a chance like that. I was beginning to think you—never mind." He replaced the glasses. "Want to join me for dinner tonight? I noticed a great steak house not far from here."

"I'd love to."

Gallantly, he bent and pulled her fingers to his lips, his eyes never leaving hers. "Perhaps the lady will fall tonight."

Christina swallowed. "Perhaps."

Brett, straightening to his six foot height, stroked her cheek. "If we weren't surrounded by people, Christina, I would try to take you in my arms. Would you stop me?"

Christina, her pulse racing, thought of the last time a man had tried to take her in his arms. Keith. They had been in her apartment. Alone. She had just learned of his wife and children. Soon, she also learned he wasn't the Christian gentleman he had purported to be.

The emergency phone call had saved her from being a victim. The phone call and the brass candlestick. Just as Keith had ripped her blouse, Christina had whacked him over the head with the candlestick. He hadn't gained consciousness until the police arrived.

Bethany had said Brett really could be trusted. Christina, purposing to forget the Keith incident, smiled at Brett. Like the gentleman that he was, Brett had asked permission to kiss her.

Would she stop him?

"No," she whispered.

"No? Is that a 'yes' no or a 'no' no?" he teased.

"What do you think?"

❧

Bethany, sniffling against the tears of fury, blindly crammed her belongings back into her suitcase. If she were in Dallas *now* it wouldn't be soon enough. She had been crazy to even remotely consider rebuilding a relationship with Devin Carmichael. He had implicitly lied to her about his very presence at this inn. From the second he hinted Bethany might be interested in him for money alone, she should have known she couldn't trust him. But what had she done? Practically swooned when he kissed her. With an embarrassed groan, she threw the last pair of jeans in the designer suitcase and zipped it.

Momentarily, Bethany wondered how God fit into all this. Earlier, she had begun to think she had unfairly blamed Him for all her pain. Perhaps that was a correct

246

assumption. But right now, the only clear thought which she possessed was how to get away from Devin Carmichael and back to her townhouse.

As Bethany reached for the doorknob, Christina opened the suite's door and stepped into the room. Silence. The two stared at each other. More silence. Bethany, groping for words, felt awkward with Christina for the first time in their decade-long relationship.

"Devin called me last week." Christina shut the door and leaned against it. "And I accidentally told him you would be here."

"Why didn't you tell me before we left Dallas?"

"Because I didn't think he would follow you here. I never even gave his phone call another thought."

"Why did he call you in the first place?"

"He just told me about the letters you had been returning and wanted to know if I knew of any way I could get you to listen to him."

"Well, looks like you complied." Bethany, feeling betrayed and manipulated, couldn't keep the bitterness from her words.

"I've already told you, I never dreamed he would be here. After we ran into him yesterday, I almost passed out." Her brow crinkled in a worried frown.

"You should have told me then, Christina."

"It really doesn't make that much difference. Can't you see? Whether Devin is here by accident or because he followed you, it doesn't change the way things stand."

"Which is?"

"He loves you, Bethany. Brett told me why Devin

247

called off the wedding, and I can't say that I blame him."

"Whose side are you on?"

"There are no sides to this."

"Oh yes, there are. Devin implied that he didn't know I was going to be here. He *lied* to me."

"The man was desperate to see you. A lot of women would be flattered."

"I don't want flattery. I want honesty."

"You need to grow up." Christina's nostrils flared. "You're acting like an immature child, Bethany. I think it's time for you to stop worrying about your own hurt feelings and start seeing the situation as a whole. You aren't the only person involved here."

The words, like an angry swarm of bees, stung Bethany's mind, her heart, her spirit. "I'm going back home. Are you coming with me?" she bit out.

"No. I'm staying here. I want my vacation."

"I guess Brett is staying too?"

"Yes, Brett is staying."

Bethany, feeling more alone than ever, grabbed her purse, her luggage, and the last scrap of her hurt pride, and stomped from the suite. She half expected Christina to follow and try to make amends. Christina, forever tenderhearted, hated to be at odds with anyone. But this time Christina didn't follow. This time, Bethany was completely alone.

One week later Bethany had still heard nothing from Christina. The loneliest week of her life. Not only were her thoughts haunted by Devin, they were also haunted by Christina. By her final words.

In her dress shop's black and white office, Bethany opened the daily newspaper which had become her tormentor. *The Metroplex Times,* Devin's publication. Last week, Bethany, driven by a need she didn't want to comprehend, had searched the newsstands until she found Devin's newspaper. After careful study, she soon learned *The Metroplex Times* was a secular paper with a conservative Christian slant. Every day Devin had an editorial. Sometimes those editorials were hilarious. Sometimes they tackled serious social or political issues.

Today, Bethany didn't care what he'd written, she just wanted to see his face. Hastily, she scanned the front page of the editorial section. Devin's infectious grin jumped out at her. As if he had walked into the room, her heart rate increased. Bethany had relived their kiss every night for the last week. Even if her usually demanding businesses kept her occupied during the day, her dreams belonged to Devin.

Not wanting to further torment herself, Bethany dropped the paper. But that dreadful scene she had caused in the hotel lobby tortured her mind. At the time, Devin's dishonesty had seemed insurmountable. Now, Bethany couldn't conjure her negative feelings, no matter how hard she tried.

Yesterday, she had attended church for the first time in months. Yesterday, she had knelt at the altar during family prayer time. Yesterday, she had asked God to cleanse her from the unforgiveness she knew she had harbored. Toward Devin. Toward Christina.

Poor Christina. Bethany now saw that Christina had gotten caught in the middle. Bethany also saw that she owed her friend a heartfelt apology. Christina had been right. Bethany had acted like a selfish, immature child.

Would Devin ever forgive her? Or would he reject her as he had a year ago?

Sighing, Bethany pushed her chair away from the black lacquer desk. Grabbing her purple sweater, she donned it and restlessly walked to the store front. The floor-to-ceiling windows looked out onto the almost empty parking lot. Today had been unusually slow for the whole shopping center. An unexpected cold front had plummeted temperatures to the teens and threatened Dallas with an ice storm. Earlier, Bethany had been thankful for the slow day because her two employees had the day off. Yet the day was barely half over, and Bethany wished for some company.

She eyed the red, heart-shaped pillows which lined the display cases and adjusted a few of them. The four mannequins were all dressed in red. A suit. A sequined gown. A sweater dress. And a pantsuit. Two of the four mannequins held a bouquet of scarlet silk roses. A pink sign Bethany had painstakingly painted in red said, "Be Unforgettable This Valentine's Day in Something Special from SOMETHING SPECIAL." And her own Valentine's display seemed to mock her. The name of her dress shop itself even mocked her. Something Special. The last week her life had been anything but special. Bethany felt as if she had been dragging a boulder wherever she went.

"Oh Lord," she prayed, propping her forehead

against the front door. "Direct me in where I go from here. I know I've blown it in my relationship with You the last year. Help me to make the right choices now."

A light tap against the glass door jolted Bethany from her reverie. Stunned, she stared at Christina's smiling face, wondering if her prayer had materialized her friend.

"Are you going to let me in?" Christina said, her voice muffled by the glass between them. "It's freezing out here."

"Sure." Bethany stepped out of the way.

Immediately, Christina breezed through the doorway to clutch Bethany in a tight hug. "I missed you so much this week. How are you?" She backed away to peer into Bethany's face.

The frigid air which Christina brought with her seemed to sweep away the clouds from Bethany's day. "I'm so sorry about last week," Bethany blurted, not attempting to answer Christina's question.

She rolled her eyes. "I'm the one who should apologize. I should have never said what I did to you. I can't believe you're still speaking to me." Other than her sun-reddened pug nose, Christina looked as she had last week. Everything, except her eyes. They sparkled with a mysterious excitement.

"I can't believe *you're* still speaking to *me*," Bethany said. Mutual laughter. And Bethany felt as if that boulder around her ankle disappeared. "You'll be glad to know I went to church yesterday, and well, I guess I've seen for the first time that God has got a lot of work to do on me."

251

"You're not the only one," Christina said ruefully. "But I'm glad you're back at church and back in touch with the Lord. You have no idea how much I've prayed for you." Her voice broke.

"Oh, yes I do," Bethany said, her own voice unsteady. "I felt your prayers even when I didn't *want* to feel them. Thanks for not giving up on me."

"Thank *God* for not giving up on all of us. You might be the one praying me back into focus next time."

"Somehow, I doubt that," Bethany said. "You're a much stronger Christian than I'll ever be."

"No," Christina insisted. "None of us is strong. If there is any strength, it's God's."

"I guess you're right," Bethany said thoughtfully.

"Well, there's a first time for everything."

A mutual chuckle.

"Come on back to my office. I've got some hot chocolate. We'll celebrate."

Within minutes the two had settled themselves on the ebony love seat in Bethany's office and sipped mugs full of steaming cocoa.

"There's something different about you, isn't there?" Christina asked. "Have you cut your hair again, or. . . No! It's your eyes. They're green again."

"Yes." A shrug. "I went back to my clear contacts."

"Oh, really?" Christina said, a calculating twist to her mouth.

"Yeah. I don't know, I got tired of the blue ones. They just weren't me." During their brief stay in Steamboat Springs, Bethany had told Christina she had switched to blue contacts and cut her hair in an attempt to rid her-self of Devin. In the last week, that need had vanished.

"Have you heard from Devin?" Christina asked cautiously.

"No." Bethany glanced toward her desk where his newspaper lay open to the editorial page. "Not unless you could count reading his paper."

"I thought he would have called you by now."

"Why? Has he called you?"

"No. I haven't seen or heard from him since I last saw you." Christina's brow wrinkled in a worried frown. "Bethany, I hope I'm not being too pushy, but I know you love him."

"I never stopped loving him."

"Look, why don't you just call him?"

Bethany, in the middle of a sip from her mug, choked against the sweet liquid.

"Sorry," Christina said dryly.

"I just wish it was that easy." A cough. And Bethany stood to deposit the mug on her desk and fold the paper. She carefully placed it in the brass trash can as if it were a family heirloom. With a final cough, she sat on the corner of her desk and stared blankly at the oriental fans and black framed mirror which hung over the love seat.

"Is it your pride, or what?"

"Or what," Bethany said flatly. How could she ever explain to Christina that she feared Devin might reject her? She had thought of calling him a dozen times. But after the way she had acted, would his offer of love still stand? Her last words to Devin had made him angry, very angry. Was his anger great enough to cause him to reject her again? What if Bethany called him and he hung up? Christina, ever the trusting spirit, would probably tell Bethany she was worrying too much. But then Christina hadn't been jilted. And regardless of Bethany's totally forgiving Devin, she was still human. She was still unsure of him.

"So where's your engagement ring?" Bethany asked, skillfully changing the subject. "I can't believe Brett let you get away without one."

"We've only known each other a week!"

"Don't tell me the thought hasn't crossed your mind."

"Who, me?" Christina fluttered her lashes as if she were a 1920s coquette.

The two dissolved into laughter.

"We've decided to spend the next several months getting to know each other better," Christina said. "He wants me to get an apartment in San Francisco."

"What?" Bethany shrieked.

"Well. . .how else would we get to know each other? It's a whole lot easier for me to move to San Francisco than for him to drag his little girl to Dallas."

"You sound like you've already decided to move."

A shrug. "What would you do?"

Bethany relived the first months of her and Devin's relationship. At the time he had been a well-known reporter for *The Dallas Morning News* and a die-hard bachelor. They had met in the paper's lobby quite by accident. Bethany had been there to purchase some extra copies of the issue which advertised the grand opening of her first dress shop. Devin had been leaving for the day when they passed each other. Each had caught the other turning for a second look. Devin had immediately introduced himself and asked her out. Bethany had been swept away. Within six months, they were engaged.

"If I were you, I would probably move to San Francisco." Bethany smiled in self-derision. "Guys like Brett Carmichael don't come along every day. Or every decade for that matter. I'll miss you."

In a flash, Bethany contemplated the last week's solitude. Without Christina's bright smile, without Devin's love, last week's lonely existence would be typical of her life.

"Hey! I just thought of something. It would be really great if you and I turned out to be sisters-in-law!"

Feeling as if the boulder were back around her ankle, Bethany stood. "Want to see the new shipment of summer suits I got in today?" She pointed to Christina's jeans and sweater. "You could change and model for me."

Bethany simply didn't want to discuss Devin any further, even with her best friend. In one week, Valentine's Day would be upon them; a day which should have been Bethany's first anniversary. The whole situation evoked nothing but pain.

Chapter 9

The next day, Devin aimlessly tapped a pencil against the computer keyboard, wracking his brain for something—anything to write for tomorrow's editorial column. Twice, he had started with a reminiscent Valentine's theme but had scrapped each attempt. Thoughts of February fourteenth brought thoughts of Bethany. Yet when Devin tried to address a more serious subject, like the recent increase in drive-by shootings, his mind wandered to Valentine's Day. Then to Bethany. And Devin started all over again.

The rhythmical sounds of the printing press pumping out the advertisement pages of *The Metroplex Times* seemed to taunt him. Absently, he stared from his cluttered, glassed-in office to see his dedicated editorial staff efficiently carrying out their duties. This was a dream come true. Two years ago, Devin never imagined he would have the funds to start his own newspaper, let alone launch it into the competitive market. So far, the venture had been a huge success. *The Metroplex Times* was well on its way to competing with some of the most influential newspapers in the state.

And the whole experience seemed flat. The truth—without Bethany at his side, Devin's accomplishments were nothing but empty endeavors.

He desperately wanted to call her, wanted to hear

her voice. But Devin didn't think he could endure more rejection. Just when he thought he had broken through her defenses, Bethany had erected them once more and left him in the cold.

"Dear Lord, what is it going to take?" he muttered. "I believe she's the woman for me, but—"

The telephone cut through his prayer. With a growl, Devin swiveled from the computer and reached for his desk phone. He had instructed his secretary not to put any calls through. "Hello," he bit into the receiver.

"Devin, this is Christina."

"Oh, hi," he said, glad to hear her voice despite his wish for solitude. Christina, although a bit absentminded, had always been one of his favorite people. Devin would not be surprised if one day she were his sister-in-law.

"I'm sorry to bother you. I had to convince your secretary this was an absolute emergency."

"What happened?" Devin sat up straight. "Bethany? Is she hurt? Is she all right?"

"Yes, yes, just calm down. The emergency isn't physical. More emotional, I guess." She hesitated. "I hope I'm not being too nosy, but I felt like I should call you. I couldn't get over the feeling. I've prayed about it, and it's getting stronger."

"Oh?"

"Yes. Have you talked with Bethany since last week?"

"No."

"Well, I thought you might like to know she's reading your column *every day.*"

"Really? That's the *last* thing I thought she would do."

Shocked, Devin stared at the framed photo which sat on his desk's only uncluttered corner. The picture was of Bethany. Outdoors. Her smile as bright as the sunshine.

"I was in her shop yesterday and today. Both times she had the latest issue of your paper."

"Really?"

"Really."

Silence.

"Well?" Christina prompted.

"Well," Devin said blankly, his joy overriding any new thoughts.

"*Well,*" Christina said again, "am I going to have to spell it out for you?"

"What?" Perhaps Bethany wasn't as far removed from him as he had presumed.

"Call her," Christina insisted. "She loves you, and I'm convinced—"

"No, I'm not going to call her." Devin turned back to his computer, now sure of what he would write.

Christina huffed. "All I've got to say is, you and Bethany Townsley are about the most stubborn two people I have ever met in my life. If you ever get together, then you *deserve* each other."

"Okay," he mumbled absently. "Thanks, Christina." And Devin hung up, vaguely aware that he hadn't replied correctly. But his mind was racing with the words which his fingers itched to type.

❧

The next morning, 10:30. Bethany picked up the February 11 issue of *The Metroplex Times* from the corner of her desk where her salesclerk had laid it. She had requested that the manager, Tanya, buy it at the nearby newsstand that morning.

"I'm taking a break now, you two," she called to her trusted employees.

"Okay," Tanya called back. "Take your time."

Without Tanya, Bethany didn't know how she could run two businesses. If Bethany ever opened a third shop, Tanya would be indispensable. And without anything else to do with her time, Bethany probably *would* open another shop. There was certainly no prospect of a husband or family to interfere.

Simultaneously dreading and anticipating Devin's smile, Bethany plopped into her black leather chair and perused the opinion page. Reading his daily column had become an addiction which Bethany already wished she could shake. Each day that she went without Devin, she depended more and more on that column. Bethany felt as if it gave her a tiny peek of what was going on in his life.

Wondering whether today's column would be humorous or serious, Bethany began reading.

Valentine's Day should have been a very special day for me. It should have been my first wedding anniversary with the woman I still love, Bethany Townsley. But since I called off the

*wedding, Bethany and I never got married. I
won't bore my readers with the details, but I
will explain that Bethany Townsley is the most
spectacular woman that ever lived. Recently, I
was fortunate enough to convince her to talk
with me. I did some explaining, but I'm afraid I
one again botched things.*

*Bethany, if you are out there, and you are
by chance readng this, I want you to know
what I said still stands. I love you as much as
a man can love a woman.*

*It's three days until Valentine's Day. I've
already talked to my minister. He will gladly
marry us this Valentine's Day if you will only
agree. We won't have the fancy wedding we
were planning last year, but we will have each
other. And this time next year, we will celebrate our first anniversary, as we should be
doing now.*

All I need is one word from you.
I love you, Princess.

Devin

Stunned, Bethany began reading the article again.
Had Devin actually used his column to communicate
with her, or had she hallucinated the whole thing? A
quick rereading affirmed that she had not hallucinated.
Devin had proposed.

Her eyes stung.

Her heart raced.

Her mind reeled.

Yesterday, she had feared that Devin might reject her should she call him. Bethany impulsively reached for the phone. Then she stilled. No. A phone call was too predictable. She had a plan that would be much better.

❧

Devin nervously glanced at the wall clock above his computer: 11:30. He had paced his office all morning, ignoring the mound of paperwork on his desk. Had Bethany read his column yet? If so, was she going to respond or ignore it?

Restlessly, Devin crammed his hands into the pockets of his worn jeans and stared out of his glassed-in office onto the editorial staff. They all *seemed* busy enough, but occasionally one of them exposed Devin to a concerned, curious expression.

They were a great group of people. Devin had prayed that God would draw together a Christian staff. He had. After six months of working together, they were more of a family than colleagues. Their concern for Devin reflected that family closeness.

A light tap on the door preceded Iris Reece, Devin's motherly secretary. "I just wanted to update you on the calls." She glanced at her notepad. "We're up to 151 calls since opening this morning." Her faded blue eyes danced. "Everyone wants to know if Bethany has accepted yet. It seems you're the talk of the town."

Devin tried to smile but felt as if he grimaced instead. "I really will be if Bethany doesn't respond." *Or*

261

if she rejects me. The thought had tormented Devin all night. This was his last attempt to win Bethany back. If she turned him down this time, Devin figured his chances were nonexistent.

"Don't worry, dear." Iris's grin looked like Mrs. Santa's. "I can't imagine any woman turning down a proposal like that one." Her telephone began ringing once more, and she rushed toward her desk.

But you don't know how badly I hurt her. Even though Devin knew he had done the right thing when he called off their wedding, he still regretted having to break Bethany's heart in the process. *O Lord, if you could only heal her as you've healed me.*

Deciding to take an early lunch, Devin ignored the staff's sympathetic smiles, gritted his teeth, and walked toward the newspaper's lobby. Past the advertising office. Past the circulation desk. Past the massive plants by the glass doors. Into the foyer. And right in Bethany's Townsley's path.

Bethany, her green eyes widened in surprise.

Bethany, her cheeks flushed from winter's chill.

Bethany, holding a dozen red roses.

"Devin," she gasped.

"Bethany."

For what felt like an eternity, they stared at each other as a message passed between them. A message of hope. A message of recommitment. A message of love.

"Happy Valentine's Day." An unsure smile. And she extended the flowers toward him.

"Christina said you were reading my column. You

read it today?" Devin wanted to make doubly sure his assumptions were correct.

She nodded, the smile growing more confident.

With an uncontrollable shout, Devin grabbed the roses, then picked up Bethany. He spun around, feeling as if they were the only people in the universe.

But a bright light reminded Devin that they weren't alone. Bethany and he looked into the continual flash of a camera.

"Hey, Eric, have some respect," Devin chided.

"Kiss her!" the photographer urged. "This will make great front-page news tomorrow. The way the phone's been ringing, half the metroplex wants a good ending to this story. Let's give it to them."

"Okay. If you insist." Devin looked back at Bethany, now beaming up at him. "Do you mind?"

"Not at all," she said against his lips.

Debra White Smith
Debra lives in east Texas with her husband Daniel and son Brett. She has authored numerous articles and books, including *The Neighbor* (Heartsong Presents). Debra believes she has received a calling from God to give a large portion of her writing profits to adoption charities and does so cheerfully. She enjoys gardening, cooking, swimming, and fishing in her spare time.

Masquerade

Kathleen Yapp

Dedication

To the congregation of the First Church of the Nazarene in Gainesville, Georgia. They demonstrate daily in their love of God and support of each other what it means to be followers of Christ.

Chapter 1

T he minute I saw my sister I knew something was wrong. *She's in trouble again,* was my first thought, and I was right.

I had just flown into Philadelphia from London, where I'd been working four years, and she was there at the airport to meet me. I had been looking forward to a relaxing week of visiting with my parents and sister. But after a warm hug and a forced smile, Monica pulled me to a far corner of the waiting room, almost pushed me down on a black vinyl seat, and announced, "Rayna, if you don't help me, I'm going to jail."

Tears gushed down her cheeks and my heart lurched, fearful of what she'd gotten herself into this time.

Growing up, she'd often come to me for help. Now, at twenty-four, just five years younger than I, she was still leaning on me.

"What's happened, Monica?" I asked her.

In a torrent of words, hardly pausing to take a breath, she told me all of her story, starting with a confession: "I stole a family heirloom from Andrew Goodwyn Rhett. He had promised to marry me but broke our engagement when he fell in love with someone else. In a moment of spite, I snatched a diamond and pearl brooch set in silver from a standing jewelry case in his mansion in Charleston, South Carolina."

"Oh, Monica," I interrupted. "How could you have done that?"

"I know it was wrong, and I'm sorry I did it now, but at the time I didn't care. We were together in the second-floor library—it's where Andrew keeps family memorabilia and treasures. 'I don't love you anymore, Monica,' he told me—with no feeling at all! 'I've found someone else.' I was so angry with him, Rayna, so humiliated that he was casually tossing me aside, that when he left me alone to take a business call in his office down the hall, I snatched the brooch from the mahogany cabinet and raced downstairs and out into the night. I never saw him again."

"How were you able to take it?" I asked. "Wasn't the cabinet locked?"

"It's never locked. Andrew likes to touch his possessions, not lock them away. Besides, he enjoys showing off his wealth to people," she said bitterly. "He is sure no one would dare steal from him and incur his vengeance. He's a man of great influence in Charleston."

"What does he do for a living?"

"He's in shipping. Exports American goods all over the world. His family has had the business since the 1700s. They were some of the original owners of the wharves at Charleston Harbor that are now his offices."

"He's wealthy then."

"Very, though some of his activities are. . .suspect, I would say," Monica confided. "He wears dark clothes when he goes out late at night, heaven only knows where."

"How do you know that?" I asked, though I was sure I knew how: they had been sleeping together.

Monica just shrugged and said, "That's too personal a question to ask, Rayna, even for a sister."

I jumped to my feet, disgusted with her. "I have to get my luggage." I walked out to the corridor hurried toward the baggage claim area. Monica ran along-side me.

"He's a heartless, unforgiving man, Rayna, who hoards his fortune and thinks every woman wants only to get her hands on it. If he knows I took the brooch, it's only a matter of time before he sends the police for me."

I stopped and stared at her. "If he knows? Do you mean you're not sure?"

She shook her head and sniffled. "I've been home four days and haven't heard from him. But, then, he probably doesn't know yet where I've gone." Her nose was running and I dug out a handkerchief for her from my shoulder bag.

"No matter what this man did to you, Monica, I just don't understand how you could have stolen from him." But I did know. She had always been impulsive and reckless, always thought with her heart not her head, and had often admired expensive jewelry she could not afford to buy. She also had never given her heart to the Lord, even though our parents are devoted Christians and she'd attended, all her life, a Bible-preaching church.

We continued through the airport and arrived at the baggage area. The carousel for my flight was going around and I spotted my two suitcases and retrieved them. As I turned to go, Monica clutched my arm.

"It was a stupid thing to do, Rayna," she admitted, "but I need to make it right." Her vibrant green eyes, her best feature, filled again with tears—and fear. She looked like a cornered animal desperate for a way of escape.

I took her in my arms. Her body, shorter than mine and too thin, I thought, shuddered against my own, and I felt a sympathy for her. I had been the victim of a broken engagement, too, when I was nineteen. I thought I would never get over it. Broken promises are a cruel thing. Almost unforgivable.

"Can't you just take it back to him?" I suggested, leaning back, holding her at arm's length. "Surely he'd understand it was your feelings for him that led you to do such a rash thing."

She shook her head. "Not Andrew Goodwyn Rhett. He'd show me no mercy. He'd call the police in a second."

A cold chill raced through my body. "How exactly do you think I can help you?"

Her bushy eyebrows, tinged with the same streaks of red as appeared in her short and curly hair, raised in expectancy. She grasped both my hands. "You can get into Andrew's house and put the brooch back into the jewelry cabinet—"

"Are you crazy? How could I do that? I don't know the man."

"You'll think of something, Rayna. You've always been able to get people to cooperate."

"I've never persuaded a man to take back his stolen property and not prosecute the thief," I quipped.

"Then you'll think of another way."

"I'm no good at breaking and entering either." This conversation was getting ridiculous. "Wait a minute—I get it. You're suggesting I deceive this man in some way to get inside his house!" I said.

"Well, he deceived *me,*" Monica declared. "He promised I'd have that very brooch on the day we married. It's been in his family since 1845 when it was given to his great-great-grandmother on the day of her wedding. It was a gift from a close family friend, Jefferson Davis, the president of the Confederacy."

I sighed and stared straight ahead. This story was getting worse by the minute. "Monica, you stole something priceless."

"Yes," she admitted in a voice I could barely hear.

"And now you're asking me to do something that's repulsive to me—deceiving someone—in order to right a wrong you're responsible for."

"But who's going to be hurt by it? Andrew will get his brooch back and I won't have to go to jail. Isn't that worth bending your conscience a little?"

"That isn't how a committed Christian lives her life, Monica."

"Just this once. Please?"

As a glimmer of hope shone in Monica's eyes, my resolve weakened.

"I know you have other plans for your vacation, Rayna," she said apologetically.

"That's right. I only have three weeks to spend some time here with the folks, tour a few states in the South to get a feel for it for my new job, then get to Atlanta, find an apartment, and be moved in before I have to start work."

"As head of Global Travel," Monica added, perking up slightly. "That was a big promotion, wasn't it?"

"Yes, it was," I answered.

"Will you miss London? The excitement? Did you ever see the Queen?" Her mood lightened as we started for the entrance to the airport.

"As a matter of fact I did. But, Monica, we have more important things to talk about than British royalty. If—and that is a huge IF—I agree to help you, how could I get inside Andrew's house to return the brooch? He'd recognize me as your sister. You know people have always said we look alike."

"He doesn't know I have a sister."

"Our names—"

"I used my former married name. I haven't gone back to using my maiden name yet. It's such a hassle."

Now there was a story. A whirlwind romance, a lavish wedding that had cost my parents far too much, and then, six months later, divorce.

Thinking of all Monica had been through, I began to shake my head from side to side. I wanted no part in this predicament. It was time for a decision. We reached the airport entrance and the sliding glass doors slid open. An icy blast of February Philadelphia wind whipped across my face.

"Monica," I said firmly, "I will not help you."

Chapter 2

Monica's look turned cold and her thin hands made tiny fists. "If you don't help me, whatever happens to me will be on your conscience."

Frustration welled up inside me. "Don't threaten me, Monica. This is a serious thing you're asking me to do. My conscience tells me to stay far away from it."

The traffic stopped and we crossed the street to the parking garage.

"I'm sorry, Rayna," Monica whimpered. "It's just that if you don't help me, what will I do?"

I stopped pulling my two suitcases on their wheels and took her hands in mine. "I'll think of something," I promised her, and I stroked her tangled, curly hair. Then I began to pray.

❧

In the second week of February, when I should have been driving through the Great Smoky Mountains, I was, instead, sitting in my car on East Battery, in the Downtown Historic District of Charleston, staring at The Jeremiah Rhett House. It was the ancestral home of Andrew Goodwyn Rhett, the man who had broken my sister's heart. I had agreed to do what I could to save Monica from a punishment she deserved.

What kind of man lives inside that three-story Greek

Revival mansion? I wondered. It had an impressive portico of Corinthian columns, a second-floor iron balcony, and a third-floor piazza from which the view of the Charleston Harbor just across the street must surely be incredible.

According to a brochure I'd picked up at the visitor's center, the house of Carolina gray brick was built in 1825 by one of Charleston's most successful merchants. It was set close to the street on a lush, green lawn, but was surrounded by a six-foot, black, wrought-iron fence. The east side of the house bordered the street; the entrance faced south, toward the harbor. An elaborate wrought-iron gate separated the public sidewalk from the private one leading into the property. It was closed and, I suspected, locked.

Through the fence, on the grounds, I saw swaying, fan-leaved, palmetto trees. Precisely clipped ornamental shrubs clustered around the front of the house, and green-leafed azalea bushes, not yet in bloom, bordered the walk that led to an impressive oak front door.

The thought of meeting Andrew Rhett face-to-face made my heart race, and I was nearly perspiring, though the temperature was only in the midfifties at nine o'clock in the morning.

I took a sip of the hot, black coffee from the foam cup I'd brought from the bed-and-breakfast inn where I was staying. I was still not sure exactly how I was going to get into the formidable—and beautiful—home.

I had prayed about what to do, but was not surprised that I had received no clear answer to my prayer. How could I ask the good Lord to guide me in an act of deception, even if my reason seemed worthy?

Because Monica had been so sincerely repentant of her rash act, I had agreed to do what I could to help her. And, too, I did see her reasoning that Andrew Rhett would have his precious brooch back and she would have learned a valuable lesson about controlling her feelings. What good would come of sending her to jail?

The ornate, wooden door of the house opened, interrupting my musings, and a tall, well-built man crossed the wide portico and descended the few stone stairs to the sidewalk, then strode toward the gate. He wore finely creased burgundy slacks, a long-sleeved white shirt, and a burgundy sweater draped over his shoulders, its arms looped casually across his chest. His long, deliberate strides, full of energy and purpose, made me wonder if he'd seen me and was coming to ask what I wanted, staring at his house for. . .how long had it been? A half hour?

He was almost to the iron gate when the front door opened and a slim woman with white hair stepped out. "Mr. Rhett," she called to him, "you forgot your briefcase."

He stopped, and turned back, but not before I saw a cheerful smile break the serious expression he had previously worn. His casually chiseled features gave him an earnest, good-looking appeal, and his full head of dark brown hair, as well as the neatly trimmed moustache that hovered over his mouth, let me see how easily my sister could have been attracted to him.

"Thanks, Mrs. Dorris," he called out, and walked

briskly back to the door where he took from her hands what he'd forgotten. "What would I do without you?" he asked. He displayed no bad temper for having forgotten the case.

As he resumed his walk toward the gate, there was no doubt in my mind I was looking at Andrew Goodwyn Rhett. He fit the description Monica had given me, right down to the confident swing of his arms and commanding set of his shoulders. He was a big man, a powerful-looking man, and handsome to a degree I had not expected. Monica had not mentioned he was so handsome.

I watched him open the gate, walk through, close it behind him, and turn left on the outer sidewalk, heading for the center of town. I hoped he had not seen me there, the lone car parked across the street. But he paused, turned, and looked straight at me.

I was so nonplussed by his gaze that I jerked away from the side window to look instead through the windshield. Gulping my coffee, I spilled a few drops on the legs of my hunter green wool slacks in the process. From the corner of my eye, I saw him standing there still, looking at me, then he walked on, and I breathed easier.

How well could he have seen me inside the car? Or was he even looking at me? Behind me, in the harbor, a luxurious, long, white yacht slowly passed. Perhaps that's what caught his eye. *Yes,* I assured myself. *That must have been it.* I looked down the street. I could no longer see him.

Until that moment, I had not given up the idea of just appearing at this man's front door and explaining, with simple facts, what had happened and hope he was a man of fairness. His kindness toward the woman at the door had encouraged me.

Now, though, another plan came to mind. I picked up the brochure on The Jeremy Rhett House and studied it. In glorious detail, it gave the history of the mansion and what hours it was open to the public. Today it was closed.

I had two choices. One was to wait for the next day's tour, attach myself to a group of visitors, and hope for a chance to slip away, find the room with the jewelry cabinet, and return the magnificent diamond brooch. How long would it take me to do the deed? Ten minutes? Five? Or, I reasoned, I could go up to the door immediately—providing the iron gate wasn't locked—introduce myself to whomever answered my knock, and, as the head of a worldwide travel agency, ask for a private tour.

I felt safer doing the latter because I knew that Andrew Rhett was gone and he would not be the one facing me across the threshold.

I was scared to death to implement either plan, but I had to do something. I opened the car door and stepped out.

Chapter 3

T he first obstacle, the gate, proved no problem. It swung open at a touch. Gingerly I made my way along the brick walk, bordered close to the house by dark green holly bushes, up the stone steps and across the portico to the front door. I rang the bell, but there was no answer. I rang it again. My hand shook as I did so. Again, no one came.

Disappointed and yet relieved, I turned and made my way back down the walk, but before turning left to leave the property, I looked to my right, to the other end of the brick walk. There, a tall, solid, wooden wall spanned the path. It had an intricately carved gate, also solid, on its left side. Above and beyond that wooden wall and gate I saw something that captured my curiosity: the twisted, winding limbs of a live oak tree, stretching like the arms of a benevolent parent over what I suspected was a considerable garden. It looked like something from the story of Jack and the Beanstalk, so far did the tree's branches, covered even in winter by deep green leaves, spread and provide shade for the hidden landscape below it.

I had never seen such a gargantuan tree, nor what draped its spectacular limbs in mournful, slender, silvery gray stems—Spanish moss.

From the quick study I'd made of the area before

coming, I'd learned of this Spanish moss. Though it is not really Spanish, it is so named because it was found in so many regions of the New World that were first explored by the Spanish. Nor is it moss; it's actually a photosynthetic plant that produces its own food, gets its water from the moisture in the air, and doesn't hurt the trees it enshrines. I longed to see it up close.

On impulse I ran to the end of the walk but was disappointed: I was unable to see into the garden because of the wall. Only the tops of several japonica camellia bushes, decked with bright-red winter blossoms, indicated the glory that must be on the other side.

But then I saw three mammoth rocks, a planned focal point at the left side of the gate. One was haphazardly lying on top of the other, and the highest was one large enough for me to stand on. I decided to use them for a ladder and to get a quick peek into the hidden garden. I carefully climbed from one to the other, testing each to be sure it would not give way, while grasping what part of the wooden wall I could to keep my balance.

Even standing on tiptoe, I could barely see over the top, and I was stretching as far as I could, clutching the top of the gate, when the sleeve of my sweater caught, just above the elbow, on a protruding nail.

"Oh, no," I groaned. I tugged at the sleeve, but it wouldn't give. My position was so awkward I could not use my other hand to free the material from the nail for I needed it to hang on. With one leg flailing in the air, to give me more height, I tried desperately to raise myself high enough to free the long sleeve from the rusty nail upon which it was caught.

"Trespassers are prosecuted here," a commanding male voice informed me.

With my back to the speaker, I had no idea who had caught me, standing on three rocks, peering into Andrew Rhett's garden.

"I am not trespassing," I assured the person, although I knew it looked as though I were. "I–I," I stammered. "I have never seen such a tree, and was naturally. . . curious."

"Curious."

"Yes. I've heard the gardens of Charleston are beautiful and I couldn't help wanting to peek at one."

"Peek? Half your body is over the wall."

"It most certainly is not." I whirled around to confront my accuser and, too late, forgetting my predicament, shredded the sleeve of my sweater and felt the rusty nail pierce my skin, tearing it open.

"Ooohh," I cried. A sharp stab of pain shot through my arm. I lost my footing on the rock and started to fall.

"Steady." I heard a rush of feet along the brick walk and felt a strong pair of arms scoop me into them before I hit the ground. As if I were weightless, the man held me, and I clung to muscled arms and wide shoulders and gulped in breaths of relief at having been rescued from what would surely have been a nasty fall.

"You're all right now," he said, his tone gentler than that he'd used to accuse me of trespassing and to hint at my fate for doing so.

"Thank you so much."

I leaned back in his arms to look at his face and stifled a gasp.

He was Andrew Rhett.

Why had he come back? I'd seen him leave only minutes before. My heart pounded with anxiety. He'd caught me in a suspicious situation and thought I was a trespasser. This was not at all the way I should be meeting him.

Being in his arms, my face only inches from his, I was struck by the power of his dark, compelling eyes, heavily fringed with pronounced lashes. His eyes assessed me silently until I began to think he could actually read my thoughts through my own eyes staring back at him.

He was probably a little older than I, and had that sophisticated way of an educated, confident man. His lightly tanned face, with its square jaw and straight nose, was clean shaven, except for a dark moustache, and his dark hair lay casually over a broad forehead. His skin emitted a woodsy scent.

Having felt the well-developed muscles beneath the fabric of his shirt, I was not surprised he was able to hold me as though I weighed little, although I was, regrettably, at least seven pounds (maybe eight) above what I would like to have weighed.

"You can put me down now," I said. "I'm quite all right except for feeling exceptionally foolish."

When he settled me carefully onto my feet, I continued, "I really meant no harm—"

"You're bleeding," he interrupted, and his fingers

gently lifted my right arm. I saw the bright red stain widening around the shredded fabric of my lightweight sweater just above my elbow.

"Oh," I moaned. There was enough blood present to make my stomach roll. I am hopelessly undone by the sight of blood—especially my own. My knees buckled, but his arm swiftly encircled my waist and held me safely against him.

"Easy now," he said. "You need to have that taken care of."

With one arm around my waist and a hand supporting my elbow, he led me down the walkway toward the street. I assumed he was going to take me to my car, help me inside, and give me directions to the nearest hospital. I felt lightheaded at having seen my own blood, and nausea crept into my throat. I'm afraid I clung to him tighter than I would have wanted.

"Have you had a tetanus shot lately?" he asked.

"Yes, just a few months ago."

"Good. Then we need to clean the wound and protect it. Let's hope you won't need stitches."

We? Did he mean he was going to do it himself? "I don't want to trouble you," I said.

"Would you expect me to leave a damsel in distress?" His words were spoken lightly, and I glanced up, into his eyes, and found a sincere concern in them that astonished me.

Quickly I looked down, away from the kindness I had seen so plainly in his expression. I was puzzled. How could he be a kind man, given what he had done to my sister—cutting her out of his life with no warning?

I braved a look at my arm. The circle of blood had expanded. I bit my tongue to keep from whimpering like a baby, but he had seen it, too, and quickly took a white handkerchief from the pocket of his slacks and held it tightly over the wound to stanch the flow.

Just seeing the crimson seep into the whiteness of the cloth made me dizzy. I was angry with myself for my weakness. *I'm a nineties woman,* I reminded myself. *Nineteen nineties, not eighteen nineties. Get a hold on yourself, girl!* Although I had never fainted in my life, I felt dangerously close to doing so now and my feet were getting tangled up in themselves. His arm tightened protectively around me and the nearness of him sent goosebumps racing to every nerve ending from my head to my feet. The subtle scent of his cologne tickled my nostrils.

"Who are you and where are you taking me?" I asked, pretending I did not know who he was.

"I'm Andrew Rhett. That was my garden you were . . .drawn to, and this is my house. I'm sorry for the long walk to the front door, but the drawing room by the side door is being painted."

"Quite all right," I said, and stumbled at the first of the stone steps. By now, I felt the total fool for having been so helpless. I gently brushed his arms away from me. "I'm sure I can manage by myself," I said with mock courage. In spite of my resolve, my legs felt like limp spaghetti. As Andrew Rhett looked on with concerned skepticism, I took over the task of holding the bloody handkerchief to my arm, then straightened my shoulders and gave him an I-can-do-this smile.

We walked between two Corinthian columns that stretched to the second story of the house, and across the expansive portico dotted with white wicker furniture softened by thick white cushions. He pulled a key from his trouser pocket, unlocked the door, and ushered me into an elegant hallway that was typical, in Charleston, of those found in a *double house*—two rooms wide and two rooms deep on each floor with a center hallway and stairwell.

"How lovely," I exclaimed, momentarily distracted from my predicament. I stopped to admire the grandeur of it all. The parquetry floor, made of three kinds of wood, was covered in the center by a magnificent Oriental rug. On the center of that rug stood a marble-topped table upon which sat a huge array of fresh red and white roses in what looked to be an ancient Chinese porcelain vase.

"For Valentine's Day," Andrew explained of the flowers when I looked back at him.

"They're beautiful."

I turned to face an impressive oil painting from the last century on the left wall. It was of a serious-minded man dressed in black. A matching picture, on the opposite wall, was of an equally dour middle-aged woman.

"Charles and Varina Rhett," Andrew Rhett said, in answer to my silent question. "My great-grandparents. He was once mayor of Charleston."

At the end of the hallway, a magnificent polished mahogany stairway rose one landing, then separated at

284

a wood paneled wall and branched off, one flight of stairs going to the right, the other to the left, on to the second floor. In that moment, the realization hit me: *I'm in. I'm inside The Jeremiah Rhett House.*

In my elation at having accomplished the first step toward getting the brooch back where it belonged, I quite forgot the throbbing ache in my arm. *Monica said the jewelry case was on the second floor.*

I began to walk toward the stairway, but Andrew Rhett stopped me.

Chapter 4

"**N**o time to gawk, miss," Andrew said. "We have to treat your arm."

He quickly ushered me toward the back of the house, past two rooms on the left where several women were dusting and vacuuming. I caught but a glimpse of a silver tea service sitting on a mahogany sideboard and a harp positioned by a fireplace.

"The house is not open to the public today," he explained and, at the end of the hallway, led me into a large and cheerful kitchen. Though equipped with modern conveniences, it was an old structure, but it was clear to me that it had been added on after the original house was built in 1825. A pecan pie was baking in the oven, its unmistakable scent wafting through the blue and white tiled room, reminding me of how hungry I was. Regrettably, my eagerness to get to the house had influenced me to skip breakfast.

The woman who had given Andrew Rhett his briefcase at the door was there, putting an armload of towels of assorted sizes and colors onto a shelf in a tall cabinet. She wore a lemon-colored suit and it hung over a slender figure, though her hair, glistening white with soft waves, belied her age.

When she saw us, she exclaimed, "Oh, Mr. Rhett, what happened?"

"A minor accident, Mrs. Dorris. The young lady cut her arm."

"Shall I take care of it, sir?" She moved quickly toward me and frowned when she saw the bloody handkerchief I still held over the wound.

"No, thank you," Andrew said. "I'll handle it myself. You may finish whatever you were doing."

He gestured for me to be seated at a square table that could easily have served twelve people, then went to the cabinet and grabbed one of the towels and placed it on the table under my arm. "Please relax," he said. "You'll be as good as new in no time." The sincerity in his voice assured me he would do his best to make that happen.

I liked his smile, and the one pronounced dimple in his right cheek.

Mrs. Dorris left the room after checking the pie in the oven, and Andrew threw his bloody handkerchief into a nearby wastebasket. "Mrs. Dorris sees to the house and staff," he said. "She's done so for over thirty years."

With a light touch, he eased the sleeve of my sweater over the wound, to give him access.

I took a quick look at it, jagged and raw, then thrust my head higher. The sick feeling returned to my stomach. I winced.

"Does it hurt?" he asked.

"A little. I'm afraid I'm a big baby who can't stand the sight of blood, especially my own," I answered.

He moved to a light oak cabinet above the blue and white tiled counter and took down a first aid kit. "I know an NFL football player who faints at the sight of blood," he said.

"Really?"

"Yes, ma'am."

I appreciated his attempt to minimize my aversion, and watched him take from the first aid kit a bottle of saline solution, some cotton, and a tube of antiseptic ointment. He washed his hands at the sink, then returned and sat across from me and examined the wound.

"Mmmm," he said.

"Mmmm, what? Is it bad? Will I need stitches?"

Slowly his eyes traveled upward from the wound to my face, to my eyes, and then, it seemed, inside my very soul. I caught my breath, hypnotized by his gaze.

"You'll live," he said.

Something happened between us, something unexpected. Sensations danced up and down my arms, from the wound, I knew, but also in response to the closeness of this dashing man. And then I thought of Monica. How could I be attracted to this man, nearly swoon over the masculine scent of his cologne, let the flow of his melodic Charleston accent charm me? I felt a traitor to my sister.

"You won't need stitches," he assured me with a smile that swept into my heart and held me captive.

With long, broad fingers, the kind that could easily hold and control a football or basketball, he gently applied the antiseptic ointment, then covered the wound with gauze and wrapped it securely with cling tape. He even sponged my sweater with cold water on a small cloth and got out much of the blood.

"Are you a doctor?" I asked, impressed with the ease with which he attended me. From what Monica had told me, Andrew Rhett was a businessman, but I was beginning to doubt what I had held as true before the touch of this charming man.

"I'm not a doctor," he answered, "but I've had experience with wounds such as this."

I wanted to ask him how, but then he leaned toward me, his head almost touching my own, the hair on our heads almost mingling. "There now," he said, examining carefully his handiwork. "How does that feel?"

"Fine," I said in a funny, little voice that sounded like a stranger's. "Thank you for your kind attention. Are all Southerners so protecting of one they believe to have criminal intent?"

The right corner of his mouth raised and his eyes narrowed. "I don't know. Do you have criminal intent?"

"Don't be silly. Do I look dangerous?"

He studied me a long moment and there was a twinkle in his eye. "I would say. . .yes, you are very dangerous, Miss. . ."

"Cameron. Rayna Cameron." Suddenly I remembered Monica and feared he would make the connection between us. Then, with relief, I remembered that Andrew Rhett had known my sister by her married name, Damien.

"Miss Rayna Cameron, I have the impression you are not easily known."

My heart began to race. More reaction from the wound? No, it was from a stab of Christian conscience that I was pushing into the background by being here, in this house, deceiving this man, even though Monica had convinced me it was necessary to do so.

I thought of Jacob in the Old Testament and how he and his mother, Rebekah, had thought it necessary to deceive old, blind Isaac. Mother and son were convinced their cause was just. Yet, because of that deception, Jacob had had to flee to another country, and he never saw his mother or father alive again, and for twenty years he lived in fear his brother, Esau, would find him and seek vengeance on him.

What problems will I have if I go through with my family deception? I asked myself.

"Actually, I'm easy to get to know," I told him, straightening myself in my chair, wondering if the same could be said of him. I had only known him for a few minutes, but in that time he had defied the description of a scoundrel Monica had painted of him. But how could I know the real heart of this man which beat beneath that polished surface?

I needed to remember my purpose for being there. I had a duty to perform, for my little sister, in the name of family honor. My resolve stiffened. I wanted to come right out and confront Andrew Goodwyn Rhett with what he'd done, how much he'd hurt someone I loved. But my tongue lay silent.

And so, the masquerade began.

He rose from the table and went to the refrigerator, extracting from it a large pitcher of iced tea, and from the freezer, two tall, frosty glasses.

"May I offer you some tea, Miss Cameron?"

"Yes, thank you."

He poured the tea into both glasses and handed me one. "We Southerners love our sweetened tea," he said. "It's an addiction."

Ice particles clung to the tips of my fingers and I was happy to relinquish the glass onto a coaster he placed in front of me. "Your accent tells me you're not from the South," he said. His eyes, dark, intelligent pools of brown, held friendly interest.

"That's right," I answered. "Till just recently I was living in England. London, to be exact."

His eyebrows raised. "Are you English born?" He took a long, slow sip from his tea, and watched me.

"No." I was about to say I was from Pennsylvania, when I stopped, not knowing whether or not Monica had told him our parents lived there and that's where we'd both grown up. "I've been working in England for four years."

"Doing what?"

"Gaining experience at the British office of Global Travel. We're a worldwide travel agency."

"Yes, I've heard of the company."

He stretched his long legs out in front of him, crossing his feet at his ankles. He seemed in no hurry to leave, at nine-thirty in the morning. *Maybe, as a member of the idle rich and a breaker of women's hearts, he doesn't have that much to do,* I mused. He probably had other people running his business.

"We're international," I went on, knowing, despite my confusing feelings for him, I had to find a way into his confidence.

"But you don't have an office here in Charleston."

"No. There is one in Atlanta, though." I drank some tea before I began to establish the reason why I would want to tour his house. "Actually, that's where I'm now based, or I will be as soon as I finish a short vacation. I've been transferred from London."

"Really."

He seemed impressed, and I relaxed a little, knowing everything I had told him so far about me was the absolute truth.

"So, you're vacationing in Charleston?" he asked.

"For a few days. I've never visited here before. Isn't it sometimes called the city of churches?"

"Yes, or the 'Holy City,' because we have around two hundred churches."

"Some of which are very old, are they not?"

"You're probably thinking of St. Michael's Episcopal Church. It's the oldest church edifice in the city, built in 1761."

"I must see that."

"And the First Baptist Church is the oldest Baptist church in the South, founded in 1682."

"My, my, Mr. Rhett, you should be in the travel business, too," I teased. It was hard not to like this man!

He laughed, then said, "Please call me Andrew. Are you just interested in old churches, Miss Cameron—"

"Rayna, please. Yes, I'm interested in their history, but I'm also looking for a place to worship this Sunday."

"You're a churchgoer?"

"More than that, Andrew. My faith is all-important

to me."

"I'm glad to hear that."

His eyes smiled at me, and so did that dimple in his right cheek.

"What do you want to see other than the churches?" he asked me.

"Everything and anything that might be of interest to my future clients. Fort Sumter, of course, because the first shot of the Civil War was fired upon it. I understand you can take a boat out to the site."

"True. How much time do you have in which to learn everything there is to know about the entire great South?"

I laughed. "Two weeks, and only a few days here in Charleston."

He groaned. "Well then," he said, sitting up and leaning toward me. "Since you have so little time, what you need is a knowledgeable person who can show you around the city and explain our history and the southern ways that still prevail here."

I stared back at him. "Are you offering to be my tour guide and teacher?"

"Why not? No one knows Charleston better than I— or has deeper roots in its history."

"Are you someone important, Andrew?"

"I'm not without influence."

His words echoed what Monica had said, which suddenly made me feel uneasy. Once more my thoughts returned to my little sister. Would I be able to keep this man from using his "influence" against her?

Chapter 5

"**I**'m sure you're a busy man, Andrew. I don't want to waste your time. There are many tours of the city. I thought I'd start with one from a horse-drawn carriage, then just walk around some."

"Good idea, except you won't know what you're seeing on those quaint, cobblestone streets, down those narrow, crooked alleys, peering into secret gardens."

I laughed and held up my hands in protest. "No more peering into gardens for me, thank you very much."

"If you're anxious to get started," he said, "why not begin here, in my house. Important history took place within these walls."

"Such as?" I queried.

"Robert E. Lee stayed a while to escape a fire that threatened his hotel. General P.G.T. Beauregard stood on our third-floor piazza and watched the bombardment of Fort Sumter. The President of the Confederacy, Jefferson Davis, visited here in 1863. How's that?"

"Pretty impressive."

"However, perhaps the most important of all events to take place in The Jeremiah Rhett House is the tradition that says one of our butlers, William Deas, at the turn of the century, invented she-crab soup, one of the most popular of our Charleston dishes."

I laughed. "I think I just might hire you as my tour

guide. And let's start here, if you're absolutely sure I'm not keeping you from important business."

"Business can always wait for a beautiful woman."

It was his roguish smile that made me understand how easily he could have captured Monica's heart.

I stood up quickly, and so did he. I was anxious to see the house, particularly the second floor where the jewelry cabinet was. We walked together out of the kitchen, and, in the hallway, I turned toward the stairs, but didn't want to appear too eager to ascend. That's when I noticed, in the center of the staircase, at the landing, a portrait of one of the most important men in the South's history: Jefferson Davis.

"That painting is magnificent," I said, easing my way up the first few stairs. Andrew stayed beside me. "And you say President Davis stayed in this house?"

"Yes. Once." His tone indicated some reverence.

"You sound as though you admire him."

"I do, for some of the stands he took; others, I abhor. He was a man who loved his country and believed fiercely in the sovereignty of each state. The Civil War was fought for other reasons, you know, besides slavery. Less than ten percent of all Southerners owned slaves, and thousands of black men valiantly fought and died for the South. There were places in the Northern Army where black soldiers were treated like slaves."

I saw passion in his eyes. "Are you still fighting the war, sir?"

He sighed and gave me an apologetic smile. "No. I

just wanted you to know that the Confederate stance was about more than slavery."

"Granted," I said. I walked up three more steps. I was on the landing when Andrew came and stood beside me. His shoulder brushed against mine. "He's a handsome man, your Mr. Davis," I said. "His eyes are kind."

Andrew turned to me in surprise. "You see beyond the obvious, Rayna. Most people see a monster who led nine million people against the North's twenty-two million, a defender of and apologist for the South until the day he died."

"Are you related?"

"No, but he was a friend of my great-great-grandmother." He folded his arms across his chest and looked at me. "What about your family, Rayna? Were any of them involved in the Civil War?"

I turned my back to the painting and looked down into the hallway. Intricate woodwork graced the walls, especially at the ceiling. A handsome brass and crystal chandelier hung over the table and the flowers. I pulled my attention away from them, though, and said, "My great-great-grandfather, Simon Cameron, was secretary of war under President Lincoln."

Andrew gasped. "Are you serious?"

"That's hardly something a girl would make up on the spur of the moment, in the house of a Southerner, under the very nose of Jefferson Davis," I quipped, glancing back at him.

He chuckled. "No, I suppose not. Well, we're quite a pair, Rayna Cameron." He stepped closer to me. "Do you think we can spend time together without starting the war all over again?"

I cocked my head to one side and gave him a saucy grin. "I'll behave myself if you will."

He laughed outright, then, and the rich, glorious sound of it rang through the hallway and landing and sent a shiver down my spine. He was so. . .so very appealing, but I reminded myself that he was a man of two sides: one that helped strangers in trouble and had a quick sense of humor, and another that hurt people without thought of their feelings.

In spite of myself, I liked more and more the one even while I despised the other.

"What a spectacular view from here," I said, standing on the top step. "I can imagine sweeping down these stairs in a long blue gown—"

"Ivory."

I turned to him. "Ivory?"

"Yes. With your long auburn hair, Rayna, cascading over bare shoulders. . ." He stopped, and swallowed. "Ivory."

He didn't move toward me. He didn't touch me. But his eyes caressed my hair and my heart skidded to a stop. His lips opened just enough so I could hear the heavier breathing that matched my own.

I spun to my right, to break the spell, and looked up the staircase, along the top of which ran the hallway that led to the library—and the jewelry case.

"Is there something to see on the second floor? This is such a large house." I started up the stairs. "You must have—"

His hand came down gently on my left arm, stopping my progress. "Only the first floor is open to the public."

"But what's on the second and third floors? Is there nothing of interest there?" I tugged to go forward; his grip tightened.

"There's only my living quarters and spare bedrooms."

And a library full of personal treasures, I wanted to say.

"On the first floor there are eight rooms with antiques and period furnishings from the late 1700s to the 1940s. Your clients would enjoy seeing them, I believe."

"As would I," I said with a smile.

I turned back, and we walked together down the stairs to the center of the hallway. I was disappointed he had thwarted my attempt to go upstairs but acted as though it didn't matter.

We crossed the threshold into the first room he wanted me to see and were greeted by two gorgeous Persian cats sauntering toward us. One was the blackest of blacks; the other the purest white of snow.

"There you are, ladies," Andrew exclaimed. I looked quickly at his face when I heard the jubilation in his voice. His firm mouth had broadened into the most genuine smile. He leaned over and effortlessly scooped the two felines into his arms and buried his face in the fur of each.

"Oh, they're lovely," I said. "I have always adored

cats." I stepped closer and cautiously put my hands out to pet them. They both accepted my advance while looking me steadily in the eye. The black one reached up a paw, attracted to the dangle of my gold earrings.

"Ladies," Andrew said, "may I present Miss Rayna Cameron. She's a northern spy, come to discover our southern secrets."

My hands froze in the fur of the cats. Had he discovered my true intent already? I glanced at him from the corner of my eye. "So you have secrets I may discover," I said boldly.

His grin became teasing. "You're welcome to try."

He turned his attention again to his cats. "Ladies, Rayna is interested in looking over your house. What do you say to that?"

His subtle southern accent drifted over the animals like feather down and I found myself, again, captivated by him. The genuine caring in his eyes showed him to be a man of considerable feelings—at least for animals. Clearly he was not the total monster I had imagined. Was this how Monica had begun to care for him, too?

"How do you do," I addressed the cats, scratching their ears. "And what are your names?"

"This is Ashley." He swept a broad hand down the black one's back. "And Cooper." He buried his face for a moment in the exquisite fur of the white cat.

"Those are strange names for cats," I said.

"They're named for the two rivers that meet at the Charleston Harbor to form the Atlantic Ocean."

I smiled. *Charlestonians certainly have a sense of*

pride, I thought.

"They are descended from a long line of felines who have inhabited this house since the turn of the century," Andrew went on. "They allow me to live here with them and see to their needs. In return, they give me the pleasure of appreciating them and petting them now and then. And spoiling them," he added.

"Who could resist doing so?" I ran my hands through the inviting fur of Ashley.

"I take it you're not allergic to cats."

"Heavens, no, though my sister sure is." The words left my mouth before I could stop them, and I almost bit my tongue from frustration. I silently prayed he wouldn't ask any further about my sister.

"Did your sister suffer much when around cats?"

"Yes, severely." I answered honestly, but I wasn't about to go into details.

"I knew someone just recently who was allergic to cats," he said. He put the cats down on the floor where they stayed at his feet and covered his shoes with their bodies, folding their forepaws under their breasts in that way cats do when they're contented. "She particularly disliked Ashley and Cooper."

My breath caught in my throat. Surely he was talking about Monica. "I can understand why she would not want to be around an animal which could make her miserable," I said, "but did she actually dislike these gorgeous creatures?"

"The young lady disliked a great many things, I came to find out."

A cold look crept into his eyes—a look that told me he was speaking of someone he strongly disliked.

He looked at me with that unfeeling stare and casually asked, "You wouldn't happen to know a young woman named Monica who's allergic to cats—and was raised in Pennsylvania—would you?"

Chapter 6

I managed a silly, high-pitched laugh which I was sure sounded as false to him as it did to me. Still, I had to play the masquerade. "I knew a Monica in Liverpool who wouldn't touch a cat of any kind," I said. "I don't think she ever lived in Pennsylvania, though." *Though I do know the Monica you're speaking of,* I thought.

"Speaking of England," I hurried on, desperate to change the subject. "Do you have any Victorian cranberry glass? I collect it."

"I do indeed. Follow me."

He led me into an adjoining room to an American Empire cherry wood table upon which sat a magnificent cranberry epergne, filled with more red and white roses, their stems cut short to fit the delicate glass holders.

"It's exquisite, Andrew," I gushed.

"I have more cranberry throughout the house."

"I want to see it all."

He smiled and we continued our tour through four of the eight first-floor rooms. The drawing room was not one of them as it was being painted, but we passed it and I heard the loud talking of the men working there. Andrew patiently answered my questions and gave me time to examine anything that caught my eye from the house's treasure trove of period antiques, silver, china,

302

documents, furniture, and works of art.

The cats gamboled about our feet and accompanied us, and I was flattered by their immediate acceptance of me. Their master seemed to like me, too.

"Have you worked all your career in London?"he asked.

"No. My first year was in Stockholm, my next two in Paris."

"Paris?"

"It was glorious," I replied, reminded briefly of the simple pleasures of Sunday afternoon walks through the residential area of Ile Saint Louis, concerts in Notre Dame, shopping for fruits and vegetables in the open-air food markets, sipping coffee in chic sidewalk cafes along the Champs Elysees.

I turned and faced him. "What do you do for a living, Andrew?" Of course, I already knew; Monica had told me.

He picked up a gold dinner plate, one of a set of four sitting on a Chippendale walnut table and moved his fingers around its rim. "I'm a businessman."

When he didn't elaborate, I asked, "What kind of business?"

"I export American products overseas—omputer components to European capitals, manufacturing tools to former Eastern bloc countries, farm goods to developing countries. Wherever there's a need, that's where my ships go."

An odd thought crossed my mind. I asked, half in jest,, "Have you ever smuggled Bibles into countries where they're forbidden?" I was smiling, waiting for his clever retort, but when he gazed at me a long time and did not answer, I started. "Oh, my goodness. You do, don't you? You smuggle Bibles." My mouth dropped open in amazement. "Where? North Korea? Cuba?"

Without answering, he abruptly looked at his watch. "It's almost lunchtime. Are you hungry?"

And with that diversion, he gently closed the door on that very personal subject, but I had learned something startling about Andrew: he was a Christian, and an active one. Why hadn't Monica mentioned that?

"I'm famished," I replied. "I'm afraid I skipped breakfast."

"Okay, then, we'll start our Charleston city tour at a wonderful restaurant frequented by locals who know and appreciate true Lowcountry cuisine.

"What exactly is that?"

"You'll find out."

"I'm game," I said, "but I warn you, I'm not one of those girls who picks at her food. I have a healthy appetite, too healthy, I'm afraid."

He crossed the few feet that separated us and stood in front of me. "You're perfect just the way you are, Rayna. Don't change a thing. Don't lose a pound."

"Oh," I groaned, "please don't hold me to that."

His eyes sparkled with mischief. "How can I get you to promise?"

"I don't dare, because once I make a promise, I keep it." At some level I meant to challenge Andrew Rhett with this. After all, he'd broken his promise to marry my sister.

"You're a woman of true integrity, then," he replied. "Keeping a promise is not always easy to do."

I looked into his eyes to see if he were teasing me or perhaps making excuses for himself for what he'd done to Monica. It didn't seem he was doing either. He was serious, and so was I, now.

"I cannot abide a person who does not keep his word," I said.

"I feel the same."

If I had hoped he would betray his guilt in having broken his promise to my sister, I was disappointed, for his face held only pensive lines as he weighed my comment.

I was not willing to let the matter drop, though. "Keeping one's word is something my parents taught me from childhood. 'It may be all you have to give,' they often said, 'but it's a worthy gift.' "

He cocked his head and a curious smile emerged on his lips. "Your parents are wise people. Are they still alive?"

"Yes. I love them dearly."

"And where do they live?"

I gave him an innocent look and, to avoid telling the whole truth, said simply, "Up North."

He laughed then, and nodded his head. He gently cupped my elbow and directed me to the front door of the house. Vacuum cleaners still whirred in the various rooms. Housekeepers scurried about carrying cleaning paraphernalia.

Mrs. Dorris handed Andrew a handwritten message

before we left. He read it.

"I'll call her when I get back," he told her.

"Very good, sir."

❧

Andrew Rhett took me to a seafood warehouse restaurant on South Market Street. It was a boisterous and busy place with brick walls and sturdy wooden floors, old-fashioned chandeliers, hanging plants in baskets, energetic young servers wearing white T-shirts and dark shorts, and a four-page paper menu that included a snippet of history about how shrimping got started in Charleston in the twenties.

We sat in a booth and, for an appetizer, I tasted my first bowl of that most popular Charleston delicacy, she-crab soup, which was supposedly invented by Andrew's ancestor's butler. "This is wonderful," I murmured. "What's in it?"

"It's a blend of blue crab meat and fresh roe."

"Fish eggs?"

"Yes."

"Mmmm," was my reaction. I dipped a soft roll into the creamy texture and savored the delicate seasonings.

At Andrew's suggestion, we shared a platter of shrimp, scallops, oysters, flounder, and deviled crab, served with creamy cabbage slaw, hush puppies, and cajun tartar sauce. "Is this Lowcountry cuisine?" I asked. I speared a small piece of shrimp and rewarded my taste buds.

"Yes," he answered. "It can be any creative presentation of seafood, choice beef, or pasta."

Several people stopped at our table during lunch

to chat with Andrew. I watched him carefully, appreciating the way he gave his full attention to whomever was speaking. His handshake was vigorous, his smile sincere. These folks were obviously his friends. I wondered who might be his enemies.

"Do your parents live in Charleston?" I asked him as we ate.

He shook his head. "No. My father died when I was twelve."

"Oh, I'm sorry. Had he been ill?"

He paused before saying, "No. He died from a 'self-inflicted gunshot wound,' the police report said."

I didn't know what to say to that, so I said nothing and self-consciously sipped on my iced tea.

Andrew stared at his black coffee. "My father inherited a thriving shipping company from his father," he finally continued, "but found that business was not his cup of tea. For. . .various reason, he lost the company, and our house, killed himself, and left my mother with a mountain of bills to pay."

"How did she manage?" I asked.

He sighed. "It wasn't easy, especially with two children to raise—my younger sister, Susan, and me." He smiled a little and his eyes softened. "She possessed great charm and grace, my mother—like Charleston. She knew everything about fine manners and the running of a great house like ours, but there wasn't much call for that in an era when not many women worked outside the home."

He stopped and shook his head. "I'm dominating

the conversation, and I'd much rather hear about you."

That, of course, was the last thing I wanted, so I said, "I'm happy to listen, Andrew. Tell me how you all survived."

He shrugged. "The long and the short of it is that we struggled for many years. My mother became a cleaner of other people's houses and I took every odd job I could find. I kept up my grades, got a scholarship to a good university, and, once I got my feet on the ground, bought back both the house and the business."

I tried to imagine the monumental effort that must have entailed, and couldn't. "A considerable feat," was my simple comment.

"I suppose. There were a few missteps along the way, but the Lord was with me and guided me."

His faith seemed strong, but was he one of those people who talked the talk but didn't walk the walk? Time would give me the answer, I supposed.

By the time we finished our lunch, a half hour later, I knew far more about Andrew Rhett than I had when we'd begun. I just hoped he did not want a similar rundown on my family.

He signalled the waiter for our check and we stood up to leave after it arrived. I had to ask one more question.

"Does your mother still live here in Charleston?"

Andrew didn't answer while we walked through the restaurant. He waved to several men and women who waved back with enthusiasm. Outside, though, he turned to me and said, "Thank you for asking about my mother. She died eight years after my father. She was a fine woman and deserved a better life."

"From what you told me, she certainly did. Was there no one to help you? No family? Friends?"

"Only some cousins on the West Coast, but they'd always been jealous of my father's wealth and position, so weren't about to help his family when we needed it."

"That's terrible." My sympathy was very real. I was a little frightened to note the intensity of my feelings for this man whom I'd known for such a short time.

"As for friends," he went on, "they distanced themselves from our misfortune, until the rumor started that my father had hidden a fortune somewhere. Then the deceptions began.

"People pretended to be our friends, promised to help us, but they only wanted to get their hands on that fortune. They tried to use us, Rayna, for their own gain." He frowned. "How could someone do that to a struggling widow with two young children?"

I could only shake my head in wonder.

"Do you know the one thing I despise more than any other in a person, Rayna?"

"No, what is it?"

"Deceit." His mouth tightened over his teeth and his jaw quivered. "I can forgive almost anything in a person, but not that. Lies and deceit turned my mother into an old woman at thirty-five and contributed to her death not many years later."

He stared at me, but it was actually through me. Still, I felt the white hot heat of conviction. I was a deceiver, and sooner or later, he was going to find this out.

Chapter 7

B efore leaving the Old City Market, circa 1841, we meandered by quaint shops, trendy restaurants, and down the aisles of the flea market. "They sell everything here: from produce to antiques to one-of-a-kind handmade items," Andrew said proudly.

As we continued our walk along East Bay Street, we passed Rainbow Row, fourteen pastel-colored private homes that had formerly been merchant houses built between 1740 and 1787.

"The wharves were in this area," Andrew explained, "so the clever merchants built their houses to front the water, using the first floors as stores, and the second for living. That gave them easy access to the many ships in the harbor that exported rice, cotton, and indigo from the Charleston area. . ."

I should have listened more closely to his history lesson. After all, I honestly wanted to learn as much about the South as I could, for my clients. Instead, I became preoccupied with ideas of how to get back into his house. As we neared it, I hoped he'd suggest we resume our prelunch tour, but he didn't.

"I want to show you The Battery and White Point Gardens at the southern tip of the city," he said.

He showed me, and he expounded on every bit of history that related to the area: every date, every battle, every general who fought there. I began to be irritated, a common fault of mine, I'm afraid, when I cannot get something accomplished on my own timetable.

I asked no questions, thinking that would hurry Andrew through his exposition and, hopefully, back to his house. No luck. There simply was no hurrying the man. He was enjoying himself immensely, so proud was he of his city, of what it had been through, how it had survived, and what it was today.

Finally, we crossed Murray Boulevard, climbed some cement steps, and walked along the elevated promenade, the rivers (or ocean) to our right. Andrew talked on. He gestured. His memory for details astounded me. I began to think I was going to be given a quiz at any moment.

"And, of course, this is Charleston's waterfront," he said. "Do you feel that crisp breeze?"

"I feel the breeze." It tossed my long, straight hair across my cheeks and into my mouth and made talking difficult.

"Do you smell the sea, Rayna?" he asked above the sound of the crashing waves.

I smelled the sea, and after a big lunch, it didn't smell good.

"Listen to those sea gulls," he said.

"I hear the gulls," I told him. Sleepily, I realized that my computer brain had been recording all this pertinent data but it was about to shut down.

And then he put his hand on the small of my back, and I came to life again. It was a light touch and I thought

I should tell him to take it away, but I couldn't. I liked it there. I liked walking beside him. I simply liked him, dimple-cheeked encyclopedia that he was. The masquerade was becoming more complicated.

"So, tell me, Rayna Cameron, from. . .the North," he said as we strolled slowly. "What do you think of my Charleston?"

Here it was, the test. My mind scrambled for an important date or bit of minutia that he'd recited for me. But before I could answer, a horse-drawn carriage passed us on the street below, the high-stepping hooves of the animal adding yet another distinctive sound to the ambience that made up this three-hundred-year-old city. The voice of the guide, dressed in his Confederate uniform and bright red sash, spoke above the hoofbeats. "And on our right, ladies and gentlemen, is the Jeremiah Rhett House, one of Charleston's most impressive mansions, first built in 1825 and owned, still today, by one of the descendants of old Jeremiah Rhett himself, a scoundrel and a pirate if ever there was one."

I turned to Andrew and tried to suppress a giggle, but was unsuccessful. "Did he mean Jeremiah Rhett was a scoundrel and a pirate, or the descendant who is the current owner?" I began to snicker and Andrew pretended disdain, until he burst out laughing with me.

We descended some stairs and were only a few feet from my rented car. I reached in my purse and pulled out the keys. "I've had an extraordinary time, Andrew," I told him, meaning every word of it. When I'd first pulled up to this parking place that morning, I certainly had not expected—"A ticket?"

I yanked the paper from under the windshield and almost screamed my dismay. I waved it at Andrew. "Why did I get a ticket? I don't see any sign that says I can't park here."

He calmly pointed down the street at a sign I hadn't seen. "I'm afraid parking is the one thing that warrants Charleston a bad name," he said. "Only residents with a special sticker on their windshields can park on most downtown streets, and then only in designated areas. Visitors usually go to the city parking garages. There are special signs—"

"I don't know anything about special signs. I just got into town last night."

"Did you go to the Visitor Center?"

"Yes, but I didn't talk with anyone; I just got some brochures."

Andrew leaned over to look at several lying on the passenger seat of my car. The one of The Jeremiah Rhett House lay face up.

"I see you have one on my house," he said.

"It was recommended to me." Suddenly I was nervous again.

"I thought you said you didn't talk with anyone at the Visitor Center."

"I. . .I didn't," I stammered. "The owner of the bed-and-breakfast where I'm staying suggested it."

"And who might that be?"

I stared at him. Was this an inquisition or just idle curiosity? Either way, I was prepared. "Nancy Dawson,"

I answered, congratulating myself for having remembered her name.

"Nancy," he murmured.

He smiled in a way that made me conclude he knew Nancy. Well. I waited for him to say more, but he didn't, which made me all the more curious. Then my mind focused. Could Nancy be *the one* for whom he'd given up Monica?

The sound of a beeper went off. Andrew pulled a small, black box from his belt and pressed a button that revealed the number of the caller on the tiny screen. "Excuse me," he said. From his shirt pocket he took a cellular phone, dialed a number, and listened intently, saying nothing, but grunting several times. "I'll be right there," he said, and abruptly ended the call and snapped the phone lid closed.

"Trouble?" I asked.

"I'm afraid so. I'm sorry, Rayna, but I need to leave you now. May I take you to dinner tonight? I have a place in mind I think you'll find unique."

I hesitated, not wanting him to think I was too anxious to see him, but finally, at another urging from him, acquiesced.

"I'll pick you up at 7:30."

"Fine. Do you need the address of the inn?"

He smiled. The dimple emerged. "I know where it is."

He walked briskly across the street and through the wrought-iron gate and into the house, the rooms of which I now knew something of. But not the library where the jewelry cabinet was.

❧

That evening he took me to an expensive Italian restaurant in the Historic District downtown. Afterward, we strolled down to Waterfront Park on Concord Street off East Bay where we walked out on the pier. We leaned on the railing and looked out over the water. Young couples strolled there, too, arms tightly wrapped around each other's waists. Older couples held hands and spoke softly as they passed.

"Are you anxious to start your new job?" Andrew asked.

"Oh, yes. I enjoy new places, new challenges." He stood a polite distance from me, but I felt his presence as strongly as if he were holding me in his arms.

"Do you know anyone in Atlanta?"

"I have a few acquaintances. They're going to help me find a place to live. Have you always lived in Charleston?" I asked him. I didn't dare talk about me. I might slip and make a mistake.

"Always, except when I went away to school. I've traveled all over the world, but nothing can keep me from coming home."

Coming home. Not since I'd been an adult had I had a sense of coming home, as I'd had as a child, living with my wonderful folks. My work with the travel company had taken me to exciting places in Europe. Now I was moving to a city still far from my parents and sister. Would I ever think of Atlanta as home? Would I feel about it the way Andrew felt about Charleston?

We returned to the land and sat in one of a half-dozen porch swings, each in its private, covered pavilion that faced the water. The sounds of the night assaulted our awareness and we sat in silence, staring out into the black but starry night. There was jazz music coming from a pub a block away, and people laughing several swings behind us. Somewhere, far away, a church bell rang the hour of ten.

"Why do you love Charleston so?" I asked Andrew.

He turned in the swing so he was facing me. The night air was invigorating but chilly, and even the light-weight coat I wore over my rayon-crepe dress did not keep my hands from being cold.

He reached for one of them and I let him hold it. The minutes passed.

"Why do I love Charleston," he said, as though he were beginning to recite a poem. "It's the combination of being in the present but belonging to the past. Everywhere one goes, there is history, and my family and I are part of it. We were among the original settlers who founded Charleston in 1670. We're part of that tenacity and spirit of a city that's survived pirates and rogues, terrible wars and brutal occupation, economic disaster, fires and earthquakes and hurricanes. The charm and mystique of Southern hospitality is not a myth, Rayna. It's a combination of culture, hard work, and good manners. It lives and thrives here in Charleston."

My eyes filled with tears at his heartfelt speech. The pride and love he felt for his city was what made him who he was—Andrew Goodwyn Rhett, from Charleston,

South Carolina.

"Shall we walk?" he suggested.

"Yes, let's," I replied.

We left the cement of the pavilions and made our way onto the grass. The harbor lay to our left, the twinkling lights of the Historic District to our right. There were fewer people now as the hour grew late. To those we passed who sat on benches engaged in quiet conversation, we nodded or spoke a soft greeting or said nothing.

We rounded a bend, quite alone here where the trees reached tall into the sky. Andrew stopped, put his hands gently on my shoulders and turned me to face him. I knew what he was thinking, for they were my thoughts, too. I wanted to be in his arms.

He drew me closer, bent his head, and kissed me. He did not hurry to end it, nor did I want him to.

Chapter 8

"I'm not a boy, Rayna," he said, after the kiss. "So I won't play boyish games. I'm attracted to you. I want to see you again. And again, and again."

I nodded my head, feeling the tingle on my mouth from where his own had moved over it. "I want that, too," I whispered.

The barest of smiles turned up the corners of his mouth and he reached out and touched my cheek in a way that stopped my breath. Then he took my hand and we started walking again. The light from the moon shone down on us and the sparkling lights of Charleston in the distance enfolded us in their charm and mystery. His hand was strong over mine and I felt safe with him, in the darkness. He was tall and solid, a man of strength.

My reverie halted when an ugly, gruff voice growled behind us, "Don't turn around. Give us your money or we'll hurt you. We have guns."

The threat cut like a knife through the darkness and I fearfully clutched Andrew's hand with both of mine.

"Now, man!" the attacker demanded.

Andrew slowly turned around, but he did not reach into his suit jacket for his wallet. He stopped my movement before I could see the faces of our accosters. "Don't look," he said to me calmly, but he faced the men with bravery.

I heard the quick intake of their breaths. "Sorry,

sorry, sir," both voices mumbled. The scramble of feet slipping on the night grass in hasty retreat made my mouth drop open. What had happened?

I started to turn, but Andrew grasped my shoulders and kept me looking the other direction. "Not yet," he said.

I waited until I thought I would scream from the frustration. Were the robbers gone, or lurking somewhere else to pounce on us?

Andrew relaxed his hold on my shoulders and started us walking back the way we had come. Our pace was brisk. I only wanted to get to our car and safety. Andrew said nothing, but I did. "Who were those men? Or were they boys? They sounded young. Why did they leave? You didn't say a word to them."

Andrew shrugged. "Try to forget it happened. They decided we weren't the ones they should rob."

"And they just left when you looked at them?"

He didn't reply, but I couldn't let it go. I stopped abruptly and stared up at him. "Andrew, what went on back there?"

"Don't worry about it."

"All right. I won't worry, but I do have a healthy curiosity as to why you were able to dispel two thugs without raising more than your eyebrows."

He grunted and nodded his head, understanding my position, I hoped. "I knew them," he said. "That's why they decided not to pursue their folly."

"You knew them? How?"

When he didn't answer right away, but looked, instead, over my left shoulder, I decided I was being not only ungrateful for his gallantry, but considerably rude for pushing a question he obviously did not want to answer.

"Forgive me," I said. "It's really not my business to question you like that." I slipped my arm through his. "Will you report them to the police?"

"No."

I was incredulous. "No?"

"I'll deal with it myself."

The evening ended not much later with a prolonged goodnight kiss at my bed-and-breakfast inn and an invitation from Andrew to meet him at his house the next day to go through more of it and to continue our tour of Charleston. Not even another hurricane, like the Hugo Andrew spoke of that had "slammed into Charleston on September 22, 1989 at 135 mph," could keep me from that appointment.

Now, it was not only the library I had to find, but also an explanation I sought for how Andrew had averted a potential robbery and mugging. Who was he that he had silent control over armed thugs?

My visit to Charleston had become something of a masquerade. Now I realized that Andrew Goodwyn Rhett, too, wore a mask. I resented how he'd treated Monica, but I was falling in love with him all the same. Despite what he had done to my sister, I found him irresistible.

I arrived at The Jeremiah Rhett House at 9:30 A.M., determined to get the brooch back into the jewelry case that day. I had it in a cloth bag in my purse. I only needed a few seconds.

"Miss Cameron," Mrs. Dorris greeted me at the front door and ushered me into the hallway. "How nice to see you again. I trust your arm is all right?"

I held up the injured appendage, the wound now hidden by a pale yellow silk knit turtleneck sweater and matching blazer. "Yes, it's fine, Mrs. Dorris. Thank you for asking."

"Good. Mr. Rhett is in the library. Let me take you to him."

The library? He was in the very place I wanted most to be! My heart speeded up and my hands clutched my purse.

But Mrs. Dorris led me to the end of the hallway, to the last door on the right, not up the stairs. Andrew sat behind an enormous oak desk of considerable age, inside a library, yes, but not the one where the jewelry case was located.

When I entered, he jumped to his feet and moved around the desk, reaching me in just a few long strides. He wore a collarless black shirt and trim black slacks. His black belt had a square gold buckle on it. He was the picture of a debonair man who had plenty of money to buy the finest clothes and the taste to do it in style.

"Rayna," he said, grasping both my hands, "you look gorgeous. Yellow suits you." I heard the door softly close behind me as Mrs. Dorris left and then I felt Andrew's mouth on my own. Abruptly I turned my head, breaking off the kiss. I turned my back to him.

"What's wrong?" he asked.

"I feel. . .uncomfortable being with you this morning. Last night I let you. . .I shouldn't have. . ."

He came around to stand in front of me. With both hands he cupped my face and lifted it so I had to look into his compelling brown eyes. "Rayna, you have nothing to feel awkward about. We shared a kiss. That's all."

"That's not all, and you know it. I gave you a part of my heart, and I had no right to."

He lowered his hands and his brow furrowed. "Why don't you have a right to?"

"It was disloyal of me to. . ." I struggled to explain the awkwardness of this situation, all the while thinking that the truth was about to be told. "You see, Andrew," I continued, "I have an obligation."

"An obligation," Andrew echoed. "You're seeing someone else, then?" His question revealed his disappointment.

"The fact is, Andrew, there is someone else." Indeed there was someone else: Monica! Once again I found myself telling only part of the truth, telling him only what I wanted him to know about me. And then, without my planning it or even deciding what I would say, the lie slipped out of my mouth. "I'm engaged to be married. The wedding is in four months."

It was as if I had rehearsed this lie a dozen times. Where the thought had come from, I had no idea, and I was angry at myself the moment I said it. But I knew I could not tell Andrew the true reason why I couldn't get involved with him, not when I knew the kind of man he really was, the kind of man my own sister had said he was. But still, *Oh, dear God, what's happening to me*? I prayed. *You know I hate what I'm doing. Please help me.*

Andrew reached out and took my left hand and lifted it. "I see no ring," he said.

"It. . .it only recently happened." I looked away from him to avoid his searching eyes. "We're going to pick out our rings as soon as I get to Atlanta."

"Childhood sweetheart?" he asked.

"No," I answered. How had I gotten myself into this mess? Now I was having to make up a fictional character as my fiancé! "He's a man I worked with in London. He's British. He was transferred to Atlanta a year ago."

"I see. So you'll be working together."

"Yes."

"And married, as well."

"Yes."

He watched me in silence and I knew my cheeks were turning pink from the deliberate lies I was telling. To break the mood I flashed him a quick smile and began walking along the bookshelves, pretending great interest in the mass of volumes that lined two entire walls.

"Do you love this man?" Andrew asked abruptly. He came up and stood behind me while I looked out a window at a small brick-enclosed garden containing a dozen camellia bushes. There were luscious red blossoms on all of them.

"Of course I love him, Andrew," I said, wishing he'd change the subject. "What a silly question."

"Tell me about him. What's his name?"

"His name?" My mind went blank. Though I had

known dozens of British men while working in England, at that moment the only name I could think of was the fifty-nine-year-old janitor who had cleaned our offices every night. "Matthew Etherington," I said and meandered away from the window and from Andrew, to the fireplace mantel where there was a family picture of him and, I assumed, his sister, Susan, and his mother.

"Do you call him Matthew?"

"No. I call him Matt." I was beginning to tire of all his questions.

"How long have you known him?"

I hurled around, angry now. My conscience was revolting against the challenge of creating an entire history for my fabricated romance and fiance. "I thought you asked me here today, Mr. Rhett, to see your home." I walked toward the door. "However, if that was not your intent. . ."

Andrew captured my arm when I passed him. "Rayna, I'm sorry," he said. "You're right. I did invite you here to see more of the house, not to pry into your private life."

"Good." I hoped the matter was settled. It wasn't. Although Andrew asked me no more questions, his attitude had turned decidedly chilly. I knew what he was thinking: how could I have kissed him with such abandon if I were in love with another man I would marry in four short months? Oh, well, what did it matter? I tried to remind myself that this trip to Charleston was not about making a good impression on Andrew Rhett.

❧

We were in the second room of our tour, the music room, and I was halfheartedly examining an eighteenth-century rosewood pianoforte, when Mrs. Dorris rushed in. "Mr. Rhett, you're needed in the drawing room. Those workmen are at it again. Paint is everywhere. They've gouged a hole in one of the walls—"

We could now hear sounds of the melee. It sounded fierce.

"Thank you, Mrs. Dorris," Andrew said. "I'll attend to it." He turned to me. "I'll be back in a moment."

He was so calm, so self-assured, I wondered if he'd heard Mrs. Dorris correctly.

After he left, I continued my examination of the music room, but only briefly, until the thought struck me with tremendous force that now was my chance. Andrew might be gone for some time. Maybe I could make it upstairs and down before he got back.

Clutching my purse under my arm, I decided against cautiously sneaking up the stairs to the second floor. That would waste precious time. I ran full out, dashing up the stairs, past the picture of Jefferson Davis, onto the second-floor landing, down the hallway to the third door on the left. It was closed. I stopped, gasping for air. *Dare I go in? What if the case isn't there? Andrew might have moved it after the brooch was stolen. What if Monica didn't remember correctly which room it was? It might be the second door, or the first.*

I reached out my hand and grasped the brass knob. I turned it to the right and, when it moved, I thrust it open and stepped inside.

Chapter 9

My hand quickly found the light switch and flipped it on. A small crystal chandelier bathed the intimate room with soft light. There was no window. I didn't bother shutting the door but turned to my left, remembering Monica's instructions.

There it was, just as she had described it, only in person, the jewelry cabinet was far more impressive. I hurried to it. Behind rounded, beveled glass doors there were four shelves. The top one stood just at my shoulder. Contained within were an assortment of small items: necklaces, rings, daguerreotypes, brooches, even a toy locomotive of painted tin and cast iron.

On the second shelf from the top there was one conspicuously empty spot, no doubt where the brooch Monica had stolen had lain. My hand unzipped my purse and delved into the odds and ends of personal belongings I always carried with me. My fingers came upon the small, brocade bag which held the brooch.

"Rayna?" It was Andrew, calling me from downstairs. "Rayna." He didn't know where I was.

I turned quickly to escape and my handbag bumped the jewelry case, the metal clasp making the glass sing. I gasped for fear I had broken it, but I hadn't. I scurried from the room, turning off the light, pausing but a fraction to close the door noiselessly. I zipped my purse and ran for the stairs. Down one, two, five steps. I was on the landing, my heart pounding so fiercely I was sure it was visible above the jacket I wore. I whirled to face the portrait of a man I had always condemned.

"Rayna!" Andrew sprinted up the stairs toward me, taking them two at a time. "I didn't see you here."

I smiled, not daring to speak and reveal that I was out of breath.

"Still admiring that portrait, I see."

"Yes." I pretended great interest in the painting and slowly took a deep breath, trying to keep Andrew from seeing it. Gradually, after I let it out, my heartbeat returned to almost normal. I knew it would not behave entirely, not as long as I was sneaking around in forbidden territory.

"Did you settle the fight?" I asked, still gazing at the painting.

"Yes. They're a couple of hotbloods. The threat of withholding their pay for the entire job was what finally convinced them to call it off."

"You weren't hurt, were you?" I spun around to be sure. My words sounded more anxious than I would have hoped, and a slow smile emerged on Andrew's lips.

"Would you have minded if I had been?"

I sighed. "Of course I would have. You'll remember how I am at the sight of blood."

"Yes, I do remember. Your knees go weak. You cling to me for support."

He stepped closer.

"Your face takes on a delicate glow and I can smell

your perfume." He leaned over me. "Just as I can now."

I closed my eyes, feeling myself drifting, momentarily immobilized by the vibrant, sensuous sound of his voice. I felt his mouth kiss the side of my neck. I swayed against him.

"Rayna."

He spoke my name as though it were a symphony. I felt his hand on my waist. In my mind I heard another sound, someone else calling my name, over and over. It was Monica, and I imagined her torrent of words falling on me for what I was allowing to happen—again.

I pushed away from the warmth of his hand. "Andrew, you're wicked. Why are you trying to tempt me?"

He stepped still closer to me. "You're not in love with him," he said.

I stared at him dreamily. "Who?"

"Matthew Etherington."

The mood was broken and I backed away from him. "We're not going to begin this conversation again, are we, because if we are, I'm going home." I started forward.

He held up his two hands, as though to prevent me from pushing him backwards down the stairs. "I've offended you, haven't I?"

"Horribly," I responded.

"What can I do to make amends?"

Before I could answer he rushed on, "Oh, I know. I have a small print of that portrait. Would you like it?"

My mouth opened in surprise. "Yes, I would. How generous of you. Oh, but I couldn't. . ."

"When is your birthday?"

"Tomorrow," I said.

He grunted. "You're kidding. Tomorrow? On Valentine's Day?"

"Yes," I replied, relieved at the change in subject. "As a matter of fact, my parents almost named me Valentine. Occasionally they do call me Val instead of Rayna."

Andrew's smile froze on his face, then slowly faded. "Val." He said the name as though he, too, might call me that. His eyes drifted slowly over my face, sending shivers of delight along my arms. "Well, Miss Val, the least I can do to make up for my boorish behavior is to give a small party tomorrow night in honor of your birthday. Will you come if I arrange it?"

I eyed him suspiciously. "Will there be more than two people at this party?"

He knew what I was thinking, but didn't smile the way he had before, in the library, and just moments before on the landing. "I won't push myself on you, Rayna. I have some friends from church who are always ready to get together. If you have no objection, I'll invite them and a few others. Then will you feel safe?"

"I'm not sure," I told him honestly.

"I'll have the print of Davis framed and ready for you, but you have to come and pick it up here, on this landing, beneath the original, so it will always remain a memory for you."

His eyes were almost dark now, and they bothered me a little. Was he so angry that I was committed to another man? Could I really matter to him, having known him for so short a time?

"What time tomorrow night?" I asked, thrusting my chin out in a brave gesture meant to convince myself more than Andrew that I was not afraid to see him again.

"Dinner will be at eight. I'll send a car for you."

"That won't be necessary."

"It's part of the apology."

I smiled and accepted. What other choice did I have? It might be my last chance to return the brooch. Now that I knew exactly which room the cabinet was in, and how long it took to get there from the main floor, there was every possibility I could pull off my mission.

"Tomorrow night should be interesting," I said. We walked down the landing together, shoulder to shoulder.

"I'm sure it will be," he agreed.

❧

The car arrived for me punctually at 7:30. It was a current year Lincoln Town Car. I got in and carefully arranged the long, flowing skirt of my dress over the ivory leather seats, the color of which matched that of my gown. It was not by accident I'd chosen an ivory gown since that was how Andrew envisioned me descending his stairs. I wanted to please him.

The chauffeur wore blue jeans and a brown corduroy jacket. He was a handsome black man with mammoth shoulders and a ready smile. His name was Glenn. Several years before, he had played professional football for the Kansas City Chiefs.

"But Andrew found me on the streets," he readily told me. "Saved my life."

"What do you mean, 'found you on the streets?'"

"I was an alcoholic. Andrew was patrolling the streets that night, and there I was, asleep under a bench in The Battery."

"Patrolling? Is Andrew a policeman?"

"Naw, he's just a guy who lives out his Christianity by finding those who need help. You know that passage in Matthew twenty-five that talks about feeding the hungry, giving drink to the thirsty, taking in a stranger, clothing the naked, visiting the sick and the prisoner?"

"Yes, I do know that. Jesus says to the righteous people before His throne on Judgment Day, 'Inasmuch as you did it to one of the least of these My brethren, you did it to Me.' "

"Well, I was 'one of the least of these,' and Andrew took me out of the gutter, cleaned me up, chewed me out like my old Chiefs coach used to do, put money in the bank for me, gave me a job, and made me pay the money back." He paused to chuckle, a happy, low sound that rumbled around in that mammoth chest of his. "Every last penny he made me pay back."

In those fourteen minutes or so it took to drive to The Jeremiah Rhett House, I learned that Andrew Rhett was an enigma. To Monica, he was the devil personified. To Glenn, he was a savior. He walked the streets every Saturday night looking for someone who needed "a chance for, or a shove into, a better life," Glenn explained. "He's the head of a group of church men and women known as Brethren Seekers. They're from different denominations and they'll give you any help you need. But they're tough. They tell you the truth about yourself, make you see what a mess you've made with your life. The help they give is on their terms: you work hard, you stay clean, you help others in return."

"And if you don't?"

"They offer you temptation."

"What?" I leaned toward the front seat.

"With me it was this car. Andrew knew I liked nice things. I'd had nice things when I was a football star. So he showed me this car. Let me drive it. Hired me to take care of it. He knew I'd want one of my own. He's showing me how to get it. And my self-respect back."

"I see."

But I didn't see. How could Andrew Rhett be a saint on the one hand and a sinner on the other? Who should I believe, a stranger or my own sister?

Chapter 10

"Here we are, Miss Cameron," Glenn announced when we finally reached the mansion.

I stepped out of the luxurious car and forced myself to make one resolve: *Tonight is for Monica. I will return the brooch, and sublimate my feelings for Andrew.*

My feelings for Andrew.

Glenn escorted me to the front door, where he handed me over to Mrs. Dorris (did the woman never sleep?). She showed me into the front parlor where the celebration was taking place.

I couldn't hold back an exclamation of surprise when I walked across the threshold and saw it was decorated in honor of my birthday, and Valentine's Day. An array of several dozen red and white balloons in one corner were tied to a chair with matching strings. Each balloon had my name printed on it.

The center of the small, intimate room had a table set for eight with a white cloth, elaborately folded white napkins, and a crystal vase in the center with a dozen long-stemmed red roses, some opened fully, others only partway or still as buds. White baby's breath floated beneath them and covered the top of the vase and English ivy trailed down to the tablecloth.

I was stunned to see we were using the gold dinner

service I had admired just the day before which had once been loaned to the City of Charleston for a banquet in honor of Lafayette. Lit candles were everywhere: on the dining table, on the marble mantelpiece, on the black baby grand piano that stood in one corner.

Andrew was not there, but six of his friends were, in formal dress: tuxedos with black tie on the four gentlemen, exquisite long gowns of velvet and crepe silk on the two women. I felt like a poor cousin in my off-the-rack chiffon, and not even the sequin and lace bodice, which had led me to buy it at Harrod's in London—for far more than I usually paid for such a dress—gave me the confidence to feel comfortable with these elegant friends of Andrew's.

Bea and Larry Sinclair introduced themselves first. "We're close friends of Andrew's from his church," Bea explained. I wondered if they were members of what Glenn had called the Brethren Seekers. Two other guests were Ron Fredericks and Stu Morrison. Both worked for Andrew at Rhett International and were in town for a conference scheduled to start in two days. Stu was English.

"I understand you worked in London for a time," he said. "I'm the head of Rhett's London division."

"And I'm based in Hong Kong," Ron added.

I appreciated Andrew's consideration in inviting Stu, for there would be many areas of conversation we could explore.

Then there was Andrew's brother-in-law, James, in town for a few days from Washington, D.C. where he worked for the State Department. "I'm delighted to meet you, Miss Cameron, if for no other reason than your birthday calls for a party." His words were slurred and his eyes held that glassy stare indicative of his already having had a few too many cocktails although, from looking around, there was no liquor anywhere, just various juices and sparkling ciders on a magnificent Charleston-made antique sideboard Andrew had shown me yesterday.

The last guest held the most interest for me. She was a famous television star, currently in a hit series that had been running on NBC for five years: it was Carina Carpenter. Blonde, svelte, and wasp thin, she wore a red sequined dress that would have cost me two month's salary.

"I'm a great fan of yours, Miss Carpenter," I said honestly. She was not only beautiful, but was a talented actress and singer as well.

"Thank you," she said. Her smile was charming and unaffected. She offered no explanation as to her relationship with Andrew, so I was left to my imagination, which had always been vivid. At that moment I decided to suspect her rather than Nancy, owner of my bed-and-breakfast inn, as the "other woman" responsible for Andrew's breakup with Monica.

"Andrew should be here in a few minutes," Bea Sinclair told me. "He was called away on business."

I immediately wondered if he were "on the streets." Glenn had mentioned that Saturday night was the usual time for the Brethren Seekers to go on the streets. Yet, Andrew had willingly scheduled this birthday celebration for me on a Saturday night.

Something serious must have happened to keep him from being host to my party. My mind slammed to a halt. Those two young men on the beach—the ones who'd threatened us—could possibly be the cause of his delay. Andrew had said he would take care of what happened himself. Was that where he was now?

"Would you like to freshen up?" Carina Carpenter asked.

I didn't need to, but, with Andrew away, what more perfect opportunity might I have to replace the brooch? "Thank you, I'd like that," I said.

"Let me show you to the powder room," she offered.

We walked out of the parlor and down the hallway toward the stairs. *She's certainly familiar with Andrew's house,* I thought.

"Have you been through the whole place?" she asked.

"Only here on the main floor. There is so much to see, so many valuable antiques and treasures in every room. Nothing's locked up." (I was thinking of the jewelry cabinet upstairs.) "Isn't Andrew afraid of being robbed?"

Carina shook her head. "Andrew's one great failing," she said, "is that he's too trusting. That's why he leaves his things around for all to see and enjoy. He doesn't want to believe anyone would steal from him."

"What would he do to someone who did?" I asked.

"Pray for them," she answered without hesitation.

I was shocked. Yes, I had learned he was a Christian, but, still, this did not sound like the vindictive Andrew

Monica had described.

Carina went on, "Anyone who's known Andrew more than a week knows this about him. He wears his vulnerability on his sleeve."

Why hadn't Monica seen this side of him? Did she really know him at all?

We reached the powder room. It was under the stairs that led to the second floor, in a perfect place for me to get on with what I'd come to do.

"I'll just be a moment," I said to Carina. "You don't need to wait. I can find my way back."

"All right. See you later."

I closed the door and leaned against it, listening to the staccato sound of her heels on the wooden floor as she walked away.

When I could no longer hear Carina's footsteps, I cautiously opened the door and peeked out. There was no one about. Taking off my own heels, I held them in my hand and dashed up the stairs and straight to Andrew's private library. The door was open. I hesitated at its threshold. *Why is it open?*

Hesitantly I entered, thinking another guest might be there. Or Mrs. Dorris. Or even Andrew, back without anyone knowing.

There was no one there. I was alone. I went to the jewelry cabinet, opened the door, reached into my purse, pulled out the pouch with the brooch in it, took it out, and placed it on the shelf in the open spot I had seen yesterday.

It was done. Monica wouldn't go to prison.

I took a deep breath and released it and was about to close the cabinet door when my eye caught a glimpse of red, no, cranberry, in the back of the top shelf. I moved to the side of the cabinet, to get a better look, and my curiosity was rewarded. There lay a most beautiful piece of Victorian cranberry glass, a master salt cellar sitting in a silver receptacle with engraved feet. I had never seen anything like it. The small antique holders of salt one usually found on a collector's table were typically crystal, not cranberry. I moved closer.

I couldn't resist the urge to touch it, hold it. Carefully, slowly, so as not to bump any of the other pieces displayed there, I reached into the cabinet and extracted it. I held it up, letting the light from the chandelier shine through it to see if there were bubbles from the glassblower or straw marks that would identify it as an authentic piece of glass. The telltale marks were there. It even had the ponte point on the bottom, where the glassblower had disconnected his tool.

"Have you come to take the rest of what Monica left behind?"

The bitter accusation from the doorway was like a gunshot that tore through me. I clutched the glass to my chest and whirled around.

There stood Andrew Rhett.

Chapter 11

"I kept hoping I was wrong," he said. "I didn't want to believe you were a thief like your sister."

I froze, speechless.

He stood in the doorway, his arms extended, the palms of his hands pushing on the frames, as though holding them in place. His hair was disheveled and he wore dark, nondescript jeans and a white T-shirt. He must have been on his way to his room to change clothes from whatever he'd been doing, when he saw the light in the library and discovered me.

"From the very first day, all you wanted was to get into my house, to steal more from me than Monica had already taken," he accused.

"Andrew, I can explain—"

He straightened and slowly walked toward me, his mouth a hard line, the muscles in his jaw iron firm. "Explain why you were trying to climb over my fence to get into my backyard?"

"I was only—"

"Explain why you were so interested in the portrait of Jefferson Davis that was just a landing away from the room that held the jewelry your sister found so fascinating?"

My throat went dry. "You know about the brooch?"

"Of course. From the very time she stole it."

With each step nearer, with each word harsher spoken, my hope dwindled that he would listen to reason and not punish Monica for what she'd done.

"It was an impulsive act," I said.

He grunted. "Are you excusing her?"

"Of course not, but you hurt her, Andrew."

"I hurt Monica? How?"

"By breaking off your engagement—"

"Our what?!"

Now it was my turn to be angry. "You promised her the brooch for the day of your marriage. When you casually tossed her over for someone else, she was heartbroken, then furious with you."

"And that gave her license to steal from me?"

"No, Andrew, certainly not."

"But that is what you're saying—that it's my fault she committed a crime."

"Can't you understand her anger and forgive her for acting so foolishly when the opportunity presented itself?"

"How can I forgive her when she sent you here to dupe me as well?"

"Don't be ridiculous. What do you think I am?"

"A thief and a deceiver, just like your sister," Andrew roared. "And you know what I think of deception." He was right in front of me and he reached out with both his hands and grasped the wrist of my hand that still held the cranberry salt cellar. "I suppose you were merely dusting this for me, rearranging it on the shelf?"

"I told you I collect cranberry glass. I've never seen a piece like this—"

"Stop it, Rayna. Stop the masquerade," he yelled. The sound of his own voice, bellowing through the small room, caught his attention and he fought to control his temper.

"I've known almost from the start you weren't what you pretended to be."

"What do you mean?" Had I been that dishonest? I hadn't told him about my sister, true, but not all of our brief friendship had been a sham.

"Three things tipped me off. First, that little saying your parents taught you about keeping your word, Monica quoted the same thing to me one day. It's a clever thought one remembers."

"And?" I was disgusted with myself for that slip, but then, I hadn't known Monica was even aware of the saying.

"And second, you told me your parents almost named you Valentine, and sometimes call you Val."

"Did Monica tell you that, too?"

"Not exactly. But she said she had a 'friend' born on Valentine's Day. 'Her parents sometimes call her Val,' she said."

I groaned.

"And, I know she's allergic to cats—she hated Ashley and Cooper. What a coincidence you have a sister who's also allergic." With his jaw tight, lips barely open, he ordered, "Get out of my house, Rayna Cameron." When I stood frozen, he raised his voice. "Get out before I call the police and have you arrested."

His tirade so stunned me, I couldn't think anymore of what to say to him to explain my predicament. All I

341

could think of was what Carina Carpenter had said Andrew would do if someone stole from him: "Pray for them," she'd said.

Pray for them! What a joke. He certainly wasn't praying for me now. He wasn't even giving me a chance to explain myself. He was convicting me with cruel judgment.

I slapped the cranberry glass into his hand. "Here's your precious cranberry," I shouted. "The brooch Monica took is in the case, where *I* put it." I stared up at him. "Do you see it?"

He turned and looked. Then his mouth fell open. Turning back to me he began, "Rayna. . ."

"I'm no thief, Andrew Goodwyn Rhett," I interrupted. "But I'll leave your house gladly."

I stormed out of the room. I had never been so angry. If he'd just listened to me, calmly, I would have explained everything to him. Then I would have listened to why he had used my sister so poorly. It should have been I forgiving him rather than the other way around.

I was in the hallway when he caught up with me.

"Why is the brooch back in the jewelry cabinet?" he demanded to know.

"Because I put it there." I kept walking. "That's why I came to Charleston."

"Right." Derision sent the words like a slap. "To return what Monica had stolen."

"Exactly."

I almost ran down the stairs to the landing. I did not look at the portrait of Jefferson Davis when I passed it. Andrew was at my shoulder. "You lied to me, Rayna.

You never told me you were Monica's sister."

"True. I didn't want you to know."

"Why?"

We descended the staircase, I in my ivory gown, the way Andrew had wanted to see me, only now I wanted no admiration from him. Only distance.

We were halfway along the center hallway. I was heading for the front door, my anger still hot against him. Carina, Stu, and Ron came out of the parlor and gazed at us with curiosity.

Andrew reached out and grabbed my shoulders and spun me around to face him. "Why didn't you tell me the truth?"

"Because Monica was afraid you'd send her to jail for stealing the brooch," I snapped. "But she wasn't sure you knew she'd done it, so I agreed to come and put it back."

He blinked. "You weren't here to steal more?"

"Take your hands off me," I ordered. From the corner of my eye I saw the guests leaving through the front door. I wanted to go with them, be anywhere than in the presence of this despicable man.

"You pretended to be someone you're not," he accused me.

"No, I did not. I *am* Rayna Cameron. I *do* work for Global Travel. I *did* work in London for four years. I *am* on my way to Atlanta. Now, let me go. I want to go back to my inn."

"You're not going anywhere, Rayna Cameron, till we get this settled."

I struggled to get away from him, but he kept his grip on both my arms and pulled me into the parlor.

"I'm going to scream for Mrs. Dorris," I threatened, "if you don't let me go."

We were in the center of the room now, and he threw my arms away in a gesture of disgust. "All right, go ahead and scream."

He glared at me.

I remained silent.

"Scream," he ordered.

I started to do just that, but was prevented from it when his mouth came down on mine, hard. His kiss so surprised me I didn't try to fight him off, but the kiss did not abate my anger.

He lifted his head and his voice broke when he said, "You stole my heart, Rayna, in just two days. I couldn't believe you would steal my possessions too."

"Oh, please," I said with mock sympathy. "Spare me your hurt feelings. You say you can't stand liars and deceivers, well, I can't abide a person who breaks his word. You broke a promise to my sister; she took her revenge, rashly. I came to right that wrong. End of story."

He backed away. "We have to talk about Monica," he said. He ran both his hands through his hair and threw himself down on a red velvet love seat. Happy birthday balloons bobbed nearby. He buried his face in his hands and leaned his elbows on his knees. It was then I noticed how tired he looked.

I remained in the center of the room, not sure what to do next. So, I waited and said nothing.

"I was never engaged to your sister," he said at last, but he said it into his hands, and I was sure I had not heard him right.

"What did you say?" I asked.

He looked up at me with a weary expression. "I said I was never engaged to Monica. I never promised to marry her or give her my great-great-grandmother's brooch on the day of our marriage."

"You most certainly did," I declared, incredulous. I took a step toward him. "That's why I came here, to keep Monica from going to jail for a headstrong mistake she made in retaliation for your ill-using her."

Andrew rose to his feet and slowly walked toward me. The look on his face was strange: half despair, half anger. I was frightened for what he might do to me. When he was close enough, I hit his chest with both hands. "Stay away from me," I ordered.

He stumbled back, and a grimace of pain shot across his face. His shoulders slumped. He swayed on his feet.

I frowned, wondering if he were suddenly ill. His face went pale and he fought to focus his eyes on me.

"Rayna, Monica and I never had a relationship of any kind other than employer/employee. She worked as a secretary in my shipping business here in Charleston. When I needed some cataloguing done of the antiques of the house for a new brochure we're going to put out. . ."

One of his legs collapsed, and he grasped a nearby chair to hold himself up. My eyes widened, but I would not reach out to help him. This had to be an act.

"She admired. . .the many pieces of. . .family jewelry I have," he went on.

He didn't finish the sentence, but sank onto the chair. Then I saw the blood, oozing onto his white T-shirt. His eyes closed. His breathing stopped.

345

Chapter 12

"A ndrew!" I gasped, running to him. "What happened to you?" Then I remembered he'd been out that night. I could only guess he'd been on the streets. "Tell me what's wrong? Should I call 911?"

He took a deep breath, grimaced, and shook his head. "No, I'm fine. There was a gang fight. I got cut with a knife. I dressed it once. Changed my T-shirt. . ."

"But I hit you right there. Opened it up. I'm so sorry, Andrew. What should I do to help?"

"Just get me into the kitchen. I need to stop the bleeding."

"No, *I'll* stop the bleeding," I declared. I helped him up and put his left arm over my shoulder. We made our way awkwardly to the kitchen. I went to where the towels were stored and took a thick white one and placed it over his chest. Then I got down the first aid kit and rather expertly, I thought, cleaned and dressed his wound which appeared not to be deep, but it did not want to stop bleeding.

"There," I pronounced, after some minutes. "You'll live."

He murmured his thanks and chuckled, probably remembering, as I was, that he'd said the very same words to me just two days earlier. I sat down in the chair nearest him, not knowing what to say next.

Then he smiled and held open his hand to me. With hesitation, I put mine into his and felt a tremendous thrill when his fingers closed around it. He slowly lifted it to his lips and kissed it. He pressed it to his cheek. Then his eyes focused on mine.

"Rayna, I work on the streets with some church folks to help people get back on their feet."

"I know. Glenn told me what you'd done for him."

"He's a great guy, and a perfect example of what can happen to someone who doesn't take personal responsibility for his own bad behavior. Nowadays it's the thing to do, to blame someone else—anyone else—for what goes wrong in our lives."

"But sometimes that blame is justified."

"True, but it can't be an excuse for us to ruin our lives. Monica could end up in serious trouble if she doesn't get over her craving for fine jewelry. She lied to you, Rayna. She used you royally."

I knew where he was going with this and I jumped to my feet. "Don't preach at me, Andrew. I don't deserve it."

"Yes, you do, because even if Monica had been telling the truth, and I had callously broken our engagement, that still would not have given her the right to break the law."

"I know that, and that's why I came here—oh, we've been over this before. Can't you understand why I agreed to help her?"

"No."

I stared at him. "It has to do with family honor. I

347

couldn't just let my sister go to jail."

"Yes, you could, because until we really understand that we're each totally responsible for our own actions—without blaming our parents, society, the poor education we received, our gender or race or economic status—until we accept that responsibility we can't grow and be successful in our lives."

I said nothing, but I did sit down in the chair.

"I'm preaching," he said.

"Yes," I agreed. "But what you say makes sense. I should have made Monica come to see you herself. I could even have come with her, to negotiate between the two of you. But I see now that I was wrong to deceive you in order to get her off the hook."

He smiled. "No more masquerade?"

"No more preaching?"

He laughed out loud and then put his hand on his chest from the pain that gesture had cost him.

"I'm sorry, Andrew, for trying to deceive you. It was wrong of me and I'm no better than Monica was in taking the brooch in the first place. Please forgive me."

"If you'll forgive me for judging you without hearing the truth first."

We smiled at each other and his eyes turned the softest brown.

"I don't want you to go to Atlanta," he said, reaching out for my hand again, which I gave him.

"I have a job waiting."

"And a fiancé."

I gulped and looked away from him. I had been a

very bad girl through this whole mess. "About Matthew Etherington," I began, "he. . .that is we. . ."

"You realize now that you don't love him because you're falling in love with me."

I gave him a saucy grin. "You're pretty sure of yourself, aren't you?"

"I have good reason to be."

"Why is that?"

"You overcame your squeamishness over blood to take care of me."

"Pshaw. I could hardly have let you bleed to death at my feet. You'd have made a big mess. That doesn't mean I'm falling in love with you. Besides, do you really think a person can fall in love in just two days?"

"It happened to me, Rayna." Now he was serious.

"Oh? What about the beautiful Carina Carpenter?"

"What about her?"

"Is there something between you?"

He paused. "I do love her," he said.

"But now you think you love me?"

"Wait a minute," he said. "I do love her, because she's my cousin and she led me to the Lord. And she taught me about tough love." He explained, "I got a little wild after college—didn't want to settle down to a career. To make a long story short, I became an addicted gambler—horses mostly—and got into trouble with a group of people in Atlantic City who would just as soon have broken my legs as let me walk away from a gambling debt.

"I went to see Carina in Los Angeles and begged her to help me. She refused, so I stole some money from her to pay those guys. She called the police and had them put me in jail for a week. Then she dropped the charges but made me pay her back every penny.

"It was that experience that inspired me to start the Brethren Seekers. Our philosophy of help is tough love and personal responsibility. It doesn't work with everyone, that's for sure, but for those who do profit by it, it's the beginning of their fight back to self-respect and dependability."

"Is it always so dangerous to work with these people?"

"No, and let's not talk about that anymore. What I want to know now is, how long can you stay in Charleston? I still haven't even begun to show you the town."

The thought of listening to his long, fact-filled lectures now thrilled my heart.

"And we can talk about how you're going to break your engagement to Etherington," he added.

"That shouldn't be a problem," I promised.

"So, when will you break the news?" he asked.

"Soon."

"There's a phone. Call him now."

I bit my lip. He had me against a wall. "You know he doesn't exist, don't you?"

An aggravating grin raised one corner of his mouth and exposed his dimple. "I suspected."

"You beast!" I moaned. "I'm beginning to think you can read my mind."

He nodded his head in agreement. "I know what you're thinking right now."

"You do?"

"Yes. You're wishing I'd stop preaching and do this instead."

He rose to his feet, pulled me up from the chair, put his arms around me, and kissed me for a very long time.

"So, that's what I was thinking?"

"Yes," he murmured, slowly tracing my lip with one finger, "and you want me to do it again."

And I did.

And he did.

Kathleen Yapp

An author of more than eight inspirational romances, including the award winning *A Match Made in Heaven*, and most recently, *Golden Dreams* (Heartsong Presents). Kathleen's story, *No Groom for the Wedding*, was part of the 1997 inspirational romance bestseller, *Summer Dreams* (Barbour Publishing, Inc.). She writes inspirational fiction because "the love between a Christian man and woman is like no other love in its depth, fulfillment, and excitement." Kathleen and her husband Ken have four grown children and seven grandchildren, and make their home in Gainesville, Georgia.